MY MOTHER'S QUESTION:

TRUTH AND CONSEQUENCES IN A FAMILY STORY

Also by Wallace Vickers Kaufman

Look Back and Cheer

Nurse Buster

Invasive Plants (co-author with Dr. Sylvan Kaufman)

Coming Out of the Woods: The Solitary Life of a Maverick Naturalist

No Turning Back: Dismantling the Fantasies of Environmental Thinking

Amazon

Finding Hidden Values In Your Home

The Beaches Are Moving (co-author with Dr. Orrin Pilkey)

My Mother's Question:

Truth and Consequences in a Family story

by

Wallace Vickers Kaufman

Library of Congress Cataloging in Publication Data:

Kaufman, Wallace Vickers. 1939 –

    My Mother's Question: non-fiction/ Wallace Vickers Kaufman

    ISBN 061549594X

    EAN-.9780615495941

Cover photos:

For information address:

Wallace Kaufman
34251 Mt. Tom Dr.
Harrisburg, OR 97446 USA

DEDICATION

For my cousins with thanks for their patience, honesty, insight, and encouragement.
They preserved the records and clear memories.

Catherine Pickering

Eleanor Millwater

Anne Claire Gallagher

Elise Hiller

ACKNOWLEDGEMENT AND THANKS

Catherine Pickering. Without the keen eye and intuition of Catherine Pickering this story might often have gone astray and the text would be embarrassingly full of typing and dictation errors and an occasional misspelling. Catherine is also responsible for initial research breakthroughs in opening hidden doors in English history.

Anne Claire Gallagher and Eleanor Millwater. Anne Claire and her younger sister Eleanor preserved vital pieces of family history both physical and remembered. Eleanor for many years patiently stored letters from my youth and many pictures from family history.

Myrna Sloam. As the Bryant Library Archivist in Roslyn Harbor Ms. Sloam has been diligent in collecting photographs and information about everything to do with the village including William Pickering and his family. She provided me with access to articles and photographs I had not seen, and she is a fine curator for a collection of William Pickering photographs.

Cumbria Family History Society, especially Mrs. Janet Thompson and her colleague Elaine, whose last name I never knew. They used their personal experience to mine local records and people for essential clues to the history of the Vickers and Pickering families or northern England.

Elise Hiller. Elise has the extraordinary ability to recall clear memory that stretches over 8 decades. When we first talked I met a good intellect and strong opinions. I thought I had better check the details wherever possible. She made no mistakes about facts that go as far back as her childhood. She is as careful and sensitive to fact and opinion as a professional journalist. Without her many details of Kaufman family history would be lost.

Andrew Mathis. When I first began to grope for clues to the origins of the Kaufman family, Andrew Mathis' careful research gave me a firm foundation to work from.

What's In This Book

WARNING AND DISCLAIMER 2

CHAPTER 1. WHY? 4

CHAPTER 2. THE FUTURE IN 1939 14

CHAPTER 3. MY FIRST INHERITANCE 21

CHAPTER 4: HAPPY SEEDS OF DISCONTENT 28

CHAPTER 5. MOVING ON: STABLE BOY TO STOREKEEPER 41

CHAPTER 6: FOR RICHER OR POORER 54

CHAPTER 7. WILLIAM OF ROSLYN 74

   The Pickering Store and The Family, An Album...................................81

CHAPTER 8. THE BEGINNING OF THE END 98

CHAPTER 9: THE NEW AMERICA 114

   THE CONKLINS AND PICKERINGS, An Album..............................118

CHAPTER 10. TED AND BILL GO "OVER THERE" 128

   World War I. An Album 161

CHAPTER 11. BUSTER BLACK SHEEP 163

CHAPTER 12. HOME FRONT 169

CHAPTER 13. BUSINESS TROUBLES 179

CHAPTER 14. VICTORY 192

   EPILOGUE: BILL'S ENGLISH FRIENDS 203

CHAPTER 15. CROSS BURNING, CLASS AND KLAN 206

CHAPTER 16. THE COLLECTOR 209

CHAPTER 17. THE BLACK SHEEP'S CHOICE 236

CHAPTER 18. LOCKED UP AND LIBERATED 251

   Emma and Artie: An Album...266

CHAPTER 19 HOW THE OTHER HALF LIVED: 268

CHAPTER 20. DEATH AND BIRTH 279

CHAPTER 21. OUR MOTHER'S KEEPERS 293

EPILOGUE: MY MOTHER'S QUESTION 297

Edwin "Ted" Pickering, 1893-1934. 299

William Hasell Pickering, 1895-1991 301

Thomas Vickers Pickering, 1896-1954 303

Dorothy Nolan, 1897-1972 305

John "Jack" Howard Pickering, 1898-1944 307

Wallace George "Buster" "Pick" Pickering, 1901-1990........................... 310

Arthur Charles Pickering, 1903-1952 312

Annie Pickering, 1906-2005 313

Emma Hazel Pickering, 1911-2001 315

Frances "Fannie" Kaufman, 1905-1968... 317

Miriam "Marion" Kaufman, 1907-1974 319

Cecelia Kaufman, 1909-1975... 320

Arthur Kaufman, 1911-1957 322

Harold Kaufman, 1913-1987.. 324

POSTCRIPT: ROSLYN AGAIN, AND GOOD-BYE 326

1

WARNING AND DISCLAIMER

Far out in any ocean wave trains arrive from many directions and bump into and pass through one another. The chaotic pattern they create compares to the random meeting of families and individuals in history. Now and then for both waves and families two currents combine energies, roll forward united. As they approach shore the wave begins to drag on the bottom, crests, breaks, dissipates and its substance recedes back into the ocean. This book tells the story of several families that united in the ocean of history and rolled on to the shores of the present. Many readers of this book arrived on the shores of our time. Other readers may recognize in this story how they came to be here.

The story begins in the 18th century in the wild border country by England's Scottish border with families named Vickers and Pickering whose members were tenant farmers, stone masons, miners, and ragpickers. On the other side it begins in mid 19th Century Bohemia and Austria with families name Hesky, Lauber, and Kaufman, all Jews.

The narrative in this book ends as the wave of my grandparents' generation begins to spread out and get lost in the growing ocean of humanity. They are now named Banner, Bougard, Bisbee, Brewer, and Botker; Clemente, Carpenter, Chu, and Crain; Duval and Draper: Hiller, Hazell, and Howard; Junge, Judge, and Jacobson; Michel, Mills, Morrell, Merchant, Mathis and Millwater; Gates and Gallagher; Sodaro, Stein, and Spillane; Ullman, and Ulz; White, Whitmill, and Wilcox. Plus the names born by my father and mother, uncles and aunts--Kaufman and Pickering. They live on every continent except Antartica.

That's the way it is with most families. So why tell this story? Because I know it, and because I have always tried to understand things by taking them apart. That process began at age two or three when I received the gift of a toy drum. This story, of course, will do no permanent damage to the families in it, but I have to warn readers, especially those with some genes from these families and pride in these families, that I found a number of gritty facts that others have tried to hide or avoid. I also recognize that at times the details may leave the reader with a too-full feeling. My explanation is that this book is also a warehouse of facts. What good are they or will they be? I don't know. I do know if they are not set down, most are likely to disappear.

I did write this story with one very specific purpose, but it was not mine. It was my mother's. To put it bluntly, she wanted to know why she tried to kill herself twice and why four of her six brothers succeeded in killing themselves. She started to write this history, but could not write more than disconnected notes. She made it quite clear that she wanted me to write it. At least I am pretty sure she did. I was a good Boy Scout, and I have followed the command, and her command, "Honor thy father and mother." Her loving bark at me and the world is the subject of the first chapter.

CHAPTER 1. WHY?

When my mother gave up living by herself at eighty–eight years old, age had transformed all of her except her mind and her eyes. Time had relentlessly removed a good eight inches from her backbone. Too much exposure to the sun had nurtured dozens of small melanomas that had been regularly frozen off leaving behind pink spots and translucent pearly dots. Smoking and weather had conspired with time to dry her face into deep wrinkles that frightened a five-year-old grandson almost to nightmares. Her face was the permanent soft tablet etched by the defeats of aging, but in that face, beneath that ever thinning white hair her eyes endured like hard, unmarked gems. She still possessed the eyes of the sturdy but shy six-year-old girl starting her newspaper route in in a Long Island village that she loved and because Roslyn Village held her like a comfortable cocoon of love. Her eyes were also still the eyes of a handsome young woman of 22 standing next to my father, embarrassed and proud that she was in love and had her man, a city boy, a sharp dresser with wavy black hair and a grin that said their conquest was mutual.

Whatever age had done to her body, the eyes projected her mind into the world. She was at the same time fiercely independent, puzzled, and burdened with old wounds of the mind and spirit. They went back as far as she could remember. The wounds to the spirit went back to her father whipping her brothers and setting her to work before she could read and write, assigning her to a tiny dark room lit by a dim red bulb where she had to stand and constantly stir a deep sink full of her father's freshly printed photographs. She, like her brothers and her mother, became one more tool of his ambition to rise in the world. But he was also the immigrant father who had won the respect and admiration of the outside world from the fabulously rich whose estates surrounded Roslyn Village to writers and artists to boat builders, store owners, carpenters, blacksmiths and casual laborers.

The lasting wounds to my mother's body and its ambitions went back to 1917 when she started to race across the street to show a friend her new Dolly Dimple paper dolls and fell in front of an oncoming milk wagon whose horse stepped on her knee, weakening it for the rest of her life. The ruined knee dealt a fatal blow to her hopes of figure skating, and frightened her out of any dance except a slow fox trot. Instinctively, she took to the water. She jumped, then dove from the bulkheads by the boatyard. Then she swam, and for the rest of her life

she was at home in any water deep enough to swim. The peak of her aquatic triumphs came in the 50 yard swim at Bar Beach long before I was born. The swimmer clawing through a roiled water had been cast on it before the race and was a man. I didn't consider that. For me that strong swimmer was my mother. And that hefty bronze octagon was a talisman throughout my childhood. For the first five years of my life, when we lived in New York's borough of Queens it said great good and great adventure awaited in Roslyn Village where my mother had grown up, where my kind grandmother told us nursery rhymes that were three hundred years old, where my mother's sister drove a car and where her several brothers, hard brown men, were always glad to see us. And that medal was proof that I had the blood of heroes and heroines.

The other side of my family could not compare. By the time I met my father's mother, she was an unhappy, sharp voiced, shriveled little woman with a hooked nose like a witch in a folk tale and she wore strange thick brown stockings. "Say something in German," my brothers and I commanded because German made us laugh. She taught us what she frequently wanted us to do, "Mach die tur zu." (Close the door.) The only visits to her that I remember were to featureless rooms without sunshine. In those early years of my life, I could not know that she had once been a lively little woman who enjoyed enduring happiness in marriage. She was the city part of life. We lived in the city. We hated it. Roslyn with our jolly grandmother and several laughing uncles and aunts and green lawns and trees was everything the city was not. When we moved to Roslyn just in time to begin kindergarten, we lost touch with our city cousins and our four uncles and aunts. What we lost I would not discover until I began writing this history.

In fact, I didn't begin writing it. My mother did.

At eighty-eight my mother had survived the deaths of two husbands, a broken shoulder, a broken arm, and the partial loss of a lung to cancer. She resolutely kept her own household and took her daily walk a block or two to the library, bank, thrift store, ice cream store, or church. Two or three times she forgot her limits or pushed on in hope of extending them, willing her bad knee, her collapsing spine, and her diminished lungs beyond the point of no return. She would stop and gather her strength. Occasionally she took a ride from a friend.

Then a few days before Thanksgiving in 1999, when she had shrunken to about the height of the six year old newspaper girl but three times the girth, she moved from her two room apartment in the North Carolina village of Pittsboro to an assisted living complex near one of my two older brothers, a Congregational minister, in the Berkshire hills of Massachusetts.

She left for Massachusetts a few days before Thanksgiving while I was working half way around the world in Kazakhstan teaching young journalists how to report facts plainly. When I returned to clean the apartment, I began with the cheap, little pine roll-top desk my mother had bought from one the dozens of mail order catalogs that arrived every week. To give it gravitas and dignity she had paid a local man more than its purchase price to convert the cheap white pine into walnut with generous coatings of stain. She considered it her safe and sanctorum. She kept in it her medical, insurance, social security notices, checkbooks, and bank statements. She knew that when I returned, I would check the desk first. I stepped into the room from the front door. Her presence had disappeared, leaving a cheap, generic apartment with white walls and brown carpets and birch cabinets in the kitchen nook. Her only presence was the desk to the left of the door. Facing me from exactly in the middle of the lowered roll-top was a rectangle of large glossy black letters cut from magazine pages and pasted to half a sheet of typing paper. The letters spelled the single word: "WHY?"

I first thought that she had made yet another blunt criticism. Why had I been away? Or why hadn't I arranged for her to be cared for there where she had lived for 15 years, the years in which he had turned from late middle age to painful, bone-porous, dwarfing old age, battled lung cancer, and had half of her face frozen off spot by cancerous spot? Or her motive could have been simpler, why did she have to move so late in life?

Whatever she had meant at the moment when she had clipped and taped the question to her desk, she would not have done it at all except for the many other unanswered questions in her life. The obsession with the question why is the obsession that plagues many people who struggle every day not to be sucked into the blackness of depression. Unlike the whirlwind that came to answer Job in the Old Testament, silence answered my mother as it answers most people who suffer from depression. But like Job, my mother endured. She believed God had given her a husband and three sons and more than a dozen grandchildren and several great grandchildren for a purpose. She could not say what that purpose was. Living for that purpose had been hard, and she could not say why it should have been so hard or even why it had become her duty and joy.

In her own search for the answer to why she had written and rewritten and written again the beginning of an autobiography. Several particular events and characterizations of her parents and her brothers and sisters appear over and over. She also had annotated lists of people and places in Roslyn Village. She was sure she would find the answer or at least revealing clues somewhere in the past.

The past that she herself had lived in Roslyn Village and the old house on East Broadway she remembered in bright and specific detail, from the closet hideaway and the outhouse at home to the contents of shelves in village stores. She was also sure that the dark past before her birth also held answers. Through the long passage of her life she had remembered and repeated several verbal talismans. One was her mother's description of the crowds of people and horse carriages around London's Picadilly Circus in the 1880s. Another was the name of the town where her mother had been a young serving woman when she met her future husband--Tunbridge Wells. And in that town stood what seemed to my mother's memory of her mother's memory, the most beautiful town center in the world, The Pantiles. One of the few long words I ever learned from her came from her one sentence description of her mother's description of The Pantiles: "Young couples used to *promenade* through the Pantiles in the evenings."

Picadilly, Tunbridge, Pantiles, promenade—the words to my ears were as good as music. For her the places were not magic places in themselves. They were the names of doors that she believed might open into rooms of bright truth, a time when her mother was young and happy.

She often wondered what had happened to her mother and to herself. At age 88 on the first page of the diary I gave her for her 70th birthday she had written, "I was advised by psychiatrists to continue therapy. I never did & so do not overcome my antisocial complex. . . . (My mother also antisocial)" Antisocial was another word for depression. Neither had been a happy hermit.

For my mother's 75th birthday my brothers and I gave her a trip to England where both of her parents had been born and where they had met to bring together the north and the south of England's working class and plant that proud grit and determination in America's immigrant garden. I was her guide on this first and only trip outside the United States. We met cousins and second cousins and listened to stories of great uncles and aunts. They were all solid workaday English, retired from entirely ordinary lives— ordinary for the working English. They had all had lived through Hitler's Blitz. A couple had seen parents march and be stoned in the streets of their own country as radical Salvation Army soldiers. One had parachuted behind Nazi lines in Holland, been rescued by the Dutch and taught to act like a Dutchman, riding on trolleys and stomping 'accidentally' on the toes of German officers.

My mother and I spent one afternoon in a green and tree studded cemetery near London, a chilly but bright day in April. Dwarfed inside her long quilted blue coat, with

a red knit cap pulled tight over her ears, she hobbled along row after row of gravestones looking for her mother's mother and father. She was looking for Hasell because that was the family name she inherited from her mother as her own middle name. But maybe the name had been Hassell or Hassel or even Hazell. If she had ever heard her maternal grandmother or grandfather's first or middle names, she had forgotten them long ago. She strongly suspected that in the Hasell story lay the

beginning of her mother's depression. Her mother had never spoken of her parents, only of the Aunt Mary Ann Hasell who had raised her. If history were a person, my mother would have harried it until it confessed the family secrets.

After passing up and down many rows of monuments and markers, my mother went to a restroom in a small stone building that looked like a tomb. She didn't come out for ten minutes. When she finally reappeared she was laughing. She was laughing at herself. A few minutes earlier she said, she had been inside the dim dank building pushing at the heavy oak door, unable to move it.   She had yelled and pounded on the boards. She was sure she was about to die in a graveyard toilet.

In our last two days in England she let go of the family search and turned to the one event that surely banishes depression--love. Love is nothing if it is not hope and optimism and joy, or at least the expectation. I was not surprised that at 75 my mother still had that hope. In fact, 25 years later reading her diary for the month before our trip, I found this entry:

Sweet, exciting dream. Who is he? No stranger. He is hometown. Well-respected gentleman. I am young & single. He is employed by Gov. He has promised to marry me. This is a promise before he goes on a gov. Mission. He returns – I have not seen him & a dinner is being given in his honor. I await his coming to speak. I am with Helen & Elmer Conklin. Nervous waiting. Will he come to me? He enters the hall, seeks for me, kisses me, takes my arm and has me sit beside him on the platform. Much to his host's surprise. He tells all, we are inseparable. – Then –

We go to fertilize pecan trees. They are in a huge circle. (Forgot a small incident before this – it also pertain to his holding on to me.)

Oh I hated to awaken as I was happy and warm.

Could this kind of love happen to a 75 yr, older? Wouldn't it be a comfort?

The next entry, a few hours later, begins, "what shall I cook today in the micro oven?"

The one unfinished love in her life had sailed into the finger of Long Island Sound called Hempstead Harbor and then into the final nipple of that harbor where tidy little Roslyn Village offered docking, repair, and services for the yachts visiting F. Scott Fitzgerald's "Gold Coast" estates as well as the skiffs of oystermen, clam rakers and flounder fishers. My mother thumbed through the London phone book looking for that "proper Englishman," Wilfred Hill who had sailed into her life in 1929 on the yacht of financier Henry D. Walbridge.

Like many of the American nouveau riche, Walbridge created the air of established wealth by hiring English servants. For my mother all things English were from the Golden Age. In that age her own mother had been a beautiful and happy young woman who took strolls along a colonnaded walk of The Pantiles; who ate rich steaming dishes like "toad-in-the-hole" and "roly poly," Yorkshire pudding, and plum pudding. Her mother had gone to London to watch the grand carriages at Picadilly Circus. From that English world, aboard the Waldbridge yacht, had arrived a lanky young steward in his creased slacks and starched shirt. The English language had rolled sweetly from his tongue like the unpolluted headwaters of a river.

He and my mother began taking long slow walks along the streets of Roslyn Village. That was her version of romance. She didn't know much else, either because she had grown up in a photographer's darkroom or because her parents were strict Victorian Anglicans. Both environments can weaken the eyes of romance. My mother and her Englishman in his creased white slacks walked around the millpond and through the park across East Broadway from her house. Her father, who had risen from immigrant stable hand to storekeeper and civic gadfly lay in bed dying cheerfully of stomach cancer, at least when he had outside visitors. Her brothers Art and Jack, however, were young men with a sense of right and wrong, at least for baby sister. Curly haired, hot tempered Jack worked as a carpenter in a shop near Roslyn Harbor and he knew sailors and yachtsmen. Nothing about Englishmen enchanted him. His father was an Englishman, after all, and a little tyrant of a man who had worked his family, especially his boys, like slaves. Jack and Art followed the lovers like a pair of hired detectives. They permitted my mother no privacy until Wilfred sailed away. They must have succeeded in keeping the romance from blossoming into love. Romance is hope while love is a sacrament whose severance is as painful as the severing of Siamese twins without anesthesia. Her sins of romance were venial, not mortal, and she loved her unobtainable boys the rest of their lives just as she carried the hope of meeting Wilfred through five decades.

Fifty-seven years after Wilfred sailed out of Roslyn Harbor my mother and I sat in our stuffy little room on the third floor of the Atlas Hotel, thumbing the telephone directory. I couldn't say who was more world weary, the hotel or my mother. We found the name Wilfred Hill. Unashamed to have me listening, my mother dialed. She introduced herself to a woman and said, "I am looking for a Wilfred Hill who visited America in 1929."

At the other end of the line a very cautious woman said, "Yes, Wilfred Hill is my father, and he did go to the United States in 1929." She did not remember, however, that he had ever said he worked on a yacht, and maybe it was Boston he had visited, not New York.

My mother smiled, one of her few smiles during our trip. "I would like to talk to him," she said in her usual direct way.

"He's here, but I'm afraid he is not very well," the woman said in her indirect British way. He could not come to the phone and "his memory is very bad now anyway, you see."

Was she saving herself the trouble of chaperoning aged lovers, or was she telling the truth? Did she have any idea what she might be doing to my mother's last hope or illusion? My mother said meekly, "I understand." My mother left her name and address. Wilfred Hill's daughter promised to talk to her father when he was "up to it." He never was. My mother would never again try to find the loves she had lost.

The depression whose roots would find and pull out had been her curse since she was a young girl, the tenth and last child, bearing her mother's first name and maiden name: Emma Hasell (spelled as it was in her mother's childhood—Hazel). She believed she shared this depression with her mother and at least four of her brothers--three of them quick suicides and one a slow suicide by alcohol. Her father had worked his way up from a railroad trackwalker to rich man's stable boy, to respected storekeeper, photographer, community volunteer, and civic activist. Her mother, however, almost never went out in public except on household errands, to church, on a rare family outing, and when she did volunteer work during WWI. None of the several newspaper features about her father mentions any fact about my grandmother except her existence and ten children born over 18 years. My grandmother at age 46 looks out of photos like a human mule—patient, resolute, enduring. That year she lay down again and gave birth to my mother.

My mother herself tried suicide once with an overdose of pills, and a second time she committed herself to a mental institution and submitted to electric shock treatment which she forever after claimed had erased from her mind and memory whole periods of her life. Electric shock had been a selective rather than a total suicide, an amputation of memory. What those memories were she could never say.

For the next 50 years and more, with varying success, she held depression at bay by daily devotion to pills and prayer and by small unsolicited acts of kindness to neighbors. Her ambitions were also a defense. Her personal ambitions, at least after the destruction of her knee, did not rank among the world's exotic or great ambitions, but like all ambitions, they were made of hope, and hope is the opposite of depression. Even as the calcium leaked from her bones and she became ever shorter and more shapeless, her ambitions did not shrink with her. As a young woman her hope had been to become a respected stenographer. Her last professional hope was to become a writer. Her one success was a short article in *Mobile Home Journal* about the Florida trailer park where she lived for eighteen years after my father's death. The sparkling title was, "I Found A New Life." She didn't publish another article for 30 years and finally gave up literary ambition the year she moved out of her townhouse. She didn't so much give up as give over—passing it on to me with the question, **Why**?

Her ambition, if just the ambition to defeat her own demons, is why she notoriously sandwiched her acts of kindness between a prologue and epilogue of criticism: *That Emily, why doesn't she get up off that couch and do something? I can't understand why she doesn't call her daughter to help.* My mother gave generously of what little she had in things and time, but she gave no mercy or pity to those who gave away their lives to the darkness and despair that had stalked her from childhood. She kept her psychic door barred to those attackers as meticulously as she kept the door to her apartment locked and bolted day and night against swindlers, thieves, and rapists.

As I cleaned up after her move to Massachusetts, in the hall closet of her townhouse I found a clear plastic box where she had once kept balls of wool and knitting needles. She had given up knitting in her late seventies. Since she did not have what people now call a "warm personality," knitting and giving away afghans, socks, sweaters, and gloves was her way of keeping the people she loved warm. She understood, as many of the recipients did, that the warmth of wool lasted far longer than any words. The Chilean poet Neruda says at the end of his ode to a pair of wool socks,

> Two times is beauty
> The beautiful
> And what is good is doubly
> Good
> When one deal with two socks
> Of wool
> And it's winter.

My mother's intuition was right, at least in my case. I remember several pairs of wool socks she knitted for me during high school and how they kept my feet warm and well padded inside my ice skates or the work shoes I wore hiking the beach in winter. She had been a skater on Roslyn's Silver Lake (Mill Pond), and she knew how much warm feet contributed to the pleasures of skating. In these later years when I have come to understand her and to understand mothers better, those socks, long gone, warm my heart.

In her last ten years in Pittsboro my mother had gradually filled the knitting box with papers. Folders full of letters from brothers, sisters, cousins from America, England and Australia responding to her questions about her father and mother and aunts and uncles. She had written and typed hundreds of notes about her life on the backs of envelopes, notebook pages and the blank sides of junk mail. She wrote the story of my father's death in an automobile accident at least ten times. She wrote the main facts of her father's life four or five times. Other lives she described in two or three sentences on one scrap of paper, a few more on another.

She was unable to write a chronological story about her family, so she wrote brief sketches about each brother and sister, character sketches for a story she could not put together. In some way the total package, the effort of her last twenty years or more, was an ongoing attempt to answer questions that had roiled her peace of mind since she had become a young woman. No, *roiled* is too mild. The questions kept erupting into her mind and soul like chronic acid reflux. In her moving she had become either reckless or too depressed to care who might find these scraps of a life she had always kept quite private, though she expected I would be the finder. She did not hand them too me like passing a baton. In my absence she threw them at me. Take that, Smart Aleck. I took it, all the pieces scattered about her vacated townhouse.

'Why?' is the question that must have dawned in the human mind more than a million years ago in the very earliest gauze of consciousness, and it is the question most often asked by children becoming conscious of cause and effect. *Why?* is the question every suffering person asks of God or nature or his tormentors. Science, as it answers a million questions about the how and when of the fission of amoebas or the cosmic sucking action of black holes, has never once answered the question *Why?* In the Bible's story of Job, a man afflicted despite all his good deeds, the beautiful answers given by God come down to that most hated non-answer every parent gives in good measure—because I said so.

Yet it is not a useless question. It is like a whip that drives the carthorse, the hope that leads us around yet one more curve. My mother had been following it her entire life, with rest stops in love, in work, in hospitals, in prayer, and in Scrabble. Along the way she had shrunk from five-foot-four to four-foot-ten. In the thousands of games of Scrabble played in her last years, she must have often spelled out the word WHY, each letter being a high value, four pointer and the word giving her a silent satisfaction among the longer, fancier and less meaningful words of life.

The papers in the box are the baton she passed to me, the one of her three sons who is a writer. If I want to continue where do I start? When I had gathered them all and brought them home, one night I skimmed through the papers, throwing out the many repetitions. I made a list of questions and sent them to her in a letter. She scribbled a few short notes on the same letter and sent it back to me with two sentences at the bottom. "I get confused! Yes, you better pick my mind now!" I understood. The past was fading as she was. When she had left all of her notes, she had also given up trying to see and understand the past. The mess in her townhouse was the mess of a surrender, the stuff a final retreat from which there is no return. By leaving all of her notes behind, she was saying, *I will chase the answer no more. Here are some clues. It's your turn.* She would pronounced *It's your turn* with a stinging irony, and also like a command. She had left that to me, left me the driving question, *Why?* She had passed it on to me, and what I will never know about that act is, why.

The people who study genetics and evolution are more and more convinced that the code for the spine not only of our back but of our psychic backbone can be traced to our genes. The genes of a culture or a family are like a shelf full of spices. They flavor each bowl of soup, a limited shelf of flavors, but added in different proportions and different constellations to each bowl.

It is possible that the ecstatic and usually joyous act of procreation passes the tendency to depression from one generation to the next. It is possible that along with my height, the color of my mother's eyes and hair, and this generally average body, I received some measure of her family's curse, depression. I have also received its nemesis—ambition or hope. As life sweeps along like a strong river with no eddies, I've been pulled under many times, and I always beat my way to the surface again, moving on, convinced that if I stay afloat, I will find in the flow of things those invincible depression killers—not valium or Prozac, but success and love.

"We Americans worship the almighty dollar! Well, it is a worthier god than Hereditary Privilege." (Mark Twain, Notebook)

CHAPTER 2. THE FUTURE IN 1939

In late September of 1938 the worst hurricane in the history of New York City roared into town, blew out the lights, killed dozens of people, and mowed down 250 million trees in New York and New England. I was there. Inside my mother I had just become a fetus the size of a golf ball with the barest suggestion of eyes and ears, useless stubs of hands and feet, but I have fingerprints and a brain, but no mind. Truly I float mindlessly in the warm amniotic darkness. For most New Yorkers struggling through the ninth year of the Great Depression the storm was a passing inconvenience. Farther out on Long Island where my grandmother and uncles and aunt lived trees came crashing down and even little Hempstead Harbor swelled with the storm tide and flooded estates and nearby roads. If my mother worried for her mother in Roslyn Village I could not know, not even if her fear spilled unfamiliar chemicals into her blood that was also mine.

For me the storm would provide both great convenience and comfort, but not for another seven years (and a few dozen pages farther on in this book). In the following cold fall days of 1938 and the raw gritty city winter of 1939 I stretched, kicked, turned and slept in the thick darkness while the body around me, my mother, exhausted itself feeding and cleaning and answering the needs of my twin brothers whose infant cries came heavily muffled and faint into my comfortably flooded sea cave.

In April of 1939 the nation was awaiting an imminent birth but not mine. I interested no one outside the family except four or five of my parents' close friends and their trusted Dr. Fierro. Since thousands of potential presidents are born every day, America did not even blink in my direction but continued waiting for the birth of a new entertainment a few miles away in the same New York City borough of Queens. Thousands of workers had recently finished hauling away mountains of coal ash deposited on 1,200 acres by the Brooklyn Ash Removal Company. This toxic waste had accumulated from hundreds of thousands of coal furnaces that heated homes, apartments, schools, offices and factories. As some workers were hauling, others were building. They were building the greatest commercial exhibition the world had ever seen, the 1939 World's Fair. It covered the old ash and garbage dump, and it covered wetland marshes whose mosquitoes had plagued residents for a mile around the site. The Fair was government and industry's answer to the pessimism of the Great Depression that was then ten long years of misery old. As the economic depression defied all of the remedies applied by America's cheerful president, FDR, it had become a spiritual depression too.

The Great Depression the World's Fair was more than a diversion or fantasy. The programs launched by Franklin Roosevelt to fight The Depression had changed nothing for people like my mother and father, aunts and uncles. The transformation of this New York dump and swamp was real and rose up over Flushing Meadows with its obelisk piercing the sky and its giant sphere pregnant with what the Fair's promoters called "The World of Tomorrow." This birth would not have to be fed and clothed like my brothers and I. Quite the contrary--it promised to spring into existence full of ideas and power. And it would immediately feed and clothe everyone in America. It was business and industry—capitalism, Sandburg's "hog butcher, steelmaker to the world"—with a promise much larger than the government's real but impotent charity.

I offered no such promise. For being born I received two presents—a blanket from a German friend of my Austrian grandmother and five dollars each from my mother's mother and her brother Jack the carpenter-storekeeper. That is to say my mother received the money on my behalf. My mother began the record of my infancy in the baby book padded in pink satin, an extravagant $1.20 cent gift from my grandmother. My grandmother's choice of colors says she was playing the odds or trying to seduce fate and expecting a girl. She herself had given birth to seven boys and three girls. At age 46, deep into that chronological zone that produces a high proportion of retarded Downs Syndrome children, then called "Mongolian Idiots," my mother had been her last. My mother and grandmother believed in keeping records. "Baby's Book" would serve for three years—vaccinations and illnesses noted, growth figures, gifts, progress of limbs and "Development of Character."

If my mother had known I would want to be president, she might have kept a fuller diary more narrowly focused on my verbal development and negotiating skills. Or she might have put me out for adoption since throughout her life I never heard her speak even briefly about politics without concluding, "Stay out of politics. They're dirty."

Two days after I was born my father came home from work and set down his black, humpbacked metal lunchbox on the kitchen table. He kissed my mother and he kissed the twins who were playing on the floor. I lay well wrapped in my crib in the narrow kitchen, crying. I now had both a brain and a mind, but I was entirely too self-occupied to eavesdrop. I heard about that evening many years later—many times.

"Em," said my father to my mother, "I have bad news. They cut me back from nineteen dollars to fourteen." Now, for a potential presidential candidate, this is the next best thing to being born in a log cabin like Abe Lincoln, Andrew Jackson, or Senator Robert Byrd. People in log cabins, of course, had hunting rifles and gardens, and children were valued labor by age five. My father had only his brains and he was thinking hard.

Three weeks after my birth Mayor Fiorello LaGuardia and his commissioner of public works, Robert Moses, opened the gates on THE WORLD OF TOMORROW. The fair not only promised more than Roosevelt's minimum subsistence, it showed Americans how they would live; how I and my twin brothers, born a year earlier, would live. My father began to save money to see the future.

Americans paid seventy-five cents to walk through the gates into THE WORLD OF TOMORROW, and once inside a reasonably full tour and a meal for two people ran the tab up to $7.00. In wages or buying power, this was the 1939 equivalent to $93 in the year 2000. Even without the meal or the rides, the entry fee and a few exhibits for my mother and father required a week's wages. They had to go. Hope is an irresistible magnet. Leaving me and my brothers with our jolly Aunt Annie and her two doting girls, my father took my mother to the Fair, spending a week's wages for their entry and less than the full tour of the pavilions, exhibits and amusements.

The stars of the Fair were not from Hollywood. They were born as a complete family from the imagination of corporate America, a family created by Westinghouse and named the Middletons. (America's poor may envy America's rich but in the practical wisdom and self-control necessary for successful poverty, they have always limited their aspirations to being America's Middletons, its middle class.) Mother Jane Middleton and Father Tom Middleton, eighteen year old Babs and fourteen year old Bud and Grandma

appeared in films and exhibits encouraging fair visitors to explore the hope of the future. The Middletons rode in the latest cars, dined in their tidy dining room, prepared food and washed dishes in their bright kitchen, and enjoyed the reliable clean heating system that used electric instead of coal. No hauling buckets of ashes for the Middletons. Mrs. Middleton was not beautiful and Mr. Middleton was not handsome. They were my mother and father, aunts and uncles and most Americans, washed and combed and dressed in sensible clothes. Or as Westinghouse called them, "the Middleton Family, from Everywhere, U.S.A.!"

Many writers and academics pooh poohed or condemned the WORLD OF TOMORROW and its sales pitch for technology, and they told Americans that the commercialized world dreamed up by corporations and their industrial engineers should not and could not be their hope. The respected literary essayist Joseph Wood Krutch called it bread and circuses. Sci Fi novelist John Crowley would write, "It seemed so urgent that Tomorrow be dragged out of the Future where it lay, peacefully unborn. But why was it so urgent? Why?" My parents and all their friends could have told him why. The historian Francis V. O'Connor said the fair was "latent fascism" because its powerful advertising sought to mesmerize and enslave Americans as consumers as Hitler had already done in his brutal economic revival of Germany. O'Connor worried about the average American as only those who don't know them can worry. Ignorant people like my parents would never figure out why they were suddenly lusting after modern kitchens, highways, and imported food and might accept any compromise of principles to have these things. Rutgers historian Warren Susman said the Fair helped develop "psychological conditioning to foster artificial demand" for products people didn't really need.

The people who worried about Americans being enslaved to technology were almost always sons and daughters of families long ago emancipated by money and consuming plenty. They did not need hope. Some felt they had too much of everything already and that the philosophers were right—people without wealth were happier with their simple lives. The literary lights among them assured Americans that wealth was wrong and a spiritual burden. Politicians, then as now, talked of the "working people" and called them "the salt of the earth." Perhaps this explains why voters like politicians born in log cabins, but it doesn't explain why most successful politicians come from rich families. Who read these brilliant commentaries? Not the "salt of the earth." A Gallup poll showed that 85% of the people who attended liked the show and its message. And women liked it more than men. It didn't mean women were more gullible. It meant they felt the Depression through their washing boards, in their ice chests, while darning socks and patching trousers, and listening to children who wanted more to eat when more to eat didn't exist. Women are always the most enslaved by poverty, and felt most urgently the need to call forth the Future.

When my mother and father went to the Worlds Fair I was still years away from having ears keen enough to hear either the siren call of consumerism or the warnings of wealthy consumers. I was fated to rise in life, however, and join their ranks and live many years among the Fair's critics. I have come to recognize them as the Puritans of Plenty. Historians and essayists might have spurned and reviled the World's Fair as they do most popular entertainments. Their learned arguments were no match for the enthusiastic but fictitious words and home of the Middletons.

People like my mother and father paid a nickel a day for the popular tabloid *The New York Daily News*. Magazine subscriptions were for the *World of Tomorrow* and the *Home of the Future*. *The New York Times* might proclaim it contained "All the news that's fit to print," but people like my parents called their paper, "*The News*." It far outsold *The New York Times*. The year I was born 1.7 million people read it every day, 3 million on Sunday. It could be read in the time a laborer rode the subway or knocked off for lunch. *The News* was a loud paper that spoke clearly and simply to people who lived and worked in loud places. *The News* declared the day's most important story with big headlines and told it with a writing that sounded like talk. It offered as much sports as news. Sports were hope by proxy. Your team would win, your horse would finish in the money. And *The News* had comics, something you could bring home to the kids, someone else's troubles to laugh about.

My parents were average Americans. Although my father had dropped out of high school, it had been necessity, not surrender. When he left Public School 30 bound for high school, his teacher, Ernest Merkelson, awarded him an Honor Certificate for "regular attendance, invariable punctuality, persevering effort and excellent deportment." The stern blue seal in the corner of that certificate carried the motto, "Perseverance Wins--Self Control." My father could not persevere his way through high school, but Ernest Merkelson had been right. My father never got to work late. He occasionally took sick in a noticeable way, but never took a sick day. His self-control was like an iron cage; the bars would sometimes shake terribly and anger would boil behind his eyes and in his clenched jaws, but he seldom lost his temper, and he never lost a friend.

My mother and father, high school drop-outs in the twenty-eighth year of their lives, paid their admission and walked into the World of Tomorrow. The future looked pretty good to my mother who had started her working life washing photographs in a dark room and folding papers when she was five and delivering them at six. My mother identified with Mrs. Middleton in the Westinghouse ad in which she tells her mother-in-law how fine it would be to have a robot do "all the household chores." Smiling, Grandmother Middleton replies, "Isn't that what all our Westinghouse appliances do?" Washing machines, steam irons, vacuum cleaners, and electric refrigerators might be unnecessary consumer goods to historians and literary critics, but they were great and even necessary hope to my mother.

By the time my father took her to the World of Tomorrow, she had been washing her clothes, my father's work clothes, sheets and towels, and for the last eighteen months the twins' diapers on a galvanized washboard. She hung them out over an alleyway to dry. I thought the pulley and rope that ran the banners of our clothes out over the alley the most interesting mechanical device of my early childhood. Every back window in every building had a pulley screwed into the kitchen or bathroom window frame, and from them lines zig zagged across the open space between buildings. The laundry hung out to dry--white underwear and sheets, blue overalls and work shirts, and flowered house dresses—flapped like banners in the wind that scoured the alley. That was the first landscape I knew and enjoyed. Each line testified to one woman's endurance and her conquest over the world's grime. Each washing was an act of perseverance, a conquest, a modest and silent confirmation of hope. My mother still kept food in a box cooled by a block of real ice. She cleaned with a mop and broom and on her knees with a brush. She ironed clothes with a solid heavy flat iron heated on the stove. Who knows but the iron that pressed my father's good shirt may at this moment be painted red and used as a doorstop in a home of the future.

Holding my mother's hand, my father shuffled along in line toward the gates of The World of Tomorrow. He was then a twenty-eight year old bread winner who sometimes could not buy a loaf of bread with the $3.80 a day Seligsburg's brokerage paid him as a clerk and runner on Wall Street. Every day my father handled and delivered hundreds of thousands of dollars worth of stocks from one broker to another, but that was as high as he had risen in the twelve years since dropping out of Stuyvesant High School as a sophomore. He was a thin young man of average height, a slightly week chin, wavy black hair and the small dark eyes passed down with Semitic genes from the Middle East. My mother had the brown hair, soft face and hazel eyes of the northern European genetic stewpot called England. Together, as they inched toward the future in the line along Corona Avenue, they were a fair enough representation of average America, Mr. and Mrs. Young Bluecollar going to peek in on the Middleton house.

At the gate they parted with half of a day's wages and were released from the tight line into what seemed a lifetime of choices. Ahead of them rose the two central buildings of the Fair, the gleaming 700 foot needle of the Trylon, and next to it, as wide as a city block, the globe of the Perisphere. First they visited the General Motors pavilion that stood directly before them. Inside they sat in the padded chairs that moved along a track above a model of the United States and its cities of the future where streamlined cars cruised along wide highways and citizens living in small towns and suburbs strolled over the roads on elevated walkways. In a few minutes they had "flown" across the United States of the future. "It would be nice if it were like that," my mother said as they walked out. My father held her hand and said, "I could learn to drive a car." His people were city people who had never owned a car, and he had never sat behind the wheel, moving or still.

The line for the Perisphere stretched for several blocks, and they decided to come back later to see Democracity. They walked slowly around Main Street, Petticoat Lane, Rainbow Avenue. They went in to see the free exhibits and the new electrical appliances, and the General Electric Robot. They stared at the fuzzy ovoid television screen showing pictures of the crowds they had left just outside. They walked by the rides and amusements on the Great White Way. They made the circuit around Liberty Lake and came back to the Perisphere and stood poised to join the line. "We should save the money," my mother said.

"I have it if you want to go," my father answered.

"I guess the babies will be okay with my sister Annie and the girls," my mother said.

A man who stood near them lighting a cigarette for his wife said, "You are crazy if you don't go see it. Absolutely amazing. I don't know how they did it."

"Let's see it," my father said and guided her into the line.

They moved in the slow stream of people up the ramp on the side of the great sphere and through the doors. Inside a walkway circled the wall and beneath lay the metropolis Democracity, scaled in every fine detail—skyscrapers in the center, suburbs and parks and rivers around it and the country beyond that. There were no rows of drab brick apartments, no grimy factory districts, no canyons like the canyon of Wall Street. Democracity was more than they could look at in a whole afternoon, but they kept moving along with the crowd and soon found themselves outside again,

They walked slowly back toward the gates and Corona Avenue. They walked back out onto the poor streets of Queens, back into the world of their day. My father said, "Well, that was worth it."

My mother said, "Do you think it will ever be that way?"

My father shrugged. "We'll get by, Em," he said. They walked away wearing the small white pins that someone handed out when they left the General Motors Building. Each pin bore the italicized sky blue words:

I
Have seen
The
Future

"We hold these truths to be self-evident, that all men are created equal, that they are endowed by their Creator with certain unalienable Rights . . . " The Unanimous Declaration of the Thirteen United States of America, 1776.

"For not to know your place is perhaps a deep-seated American tradition. That's what democracy and equality is about, isn't it?" Thomas Griffin.

"I never had a strong attachment to my family. . . From early boyhood I remember my family as a quarrelsome lot of women who were always getting me into trouble. The nearest I came to liking my family was a romantic notion of the family in ages past, based on Auntie Dot's fantasies." Second Cousin Rev. Edwin White, Nedlands, Western Australia.

CHAPTER 3. MY FIRST INHERITANCE

Somewhere in the penumbra of the Declaration of Independence and Constitution lies the right of American parents to endow their children with a noble pedigree. This right may not be 'self-evident,' but we act as if it were 'unalienable.' But in which shadow do they find it? In the shadow of that right which the Declaration calls the "pursuit of happiness." Before Jefferson and colleagues laid this foundation stone of America, the three unalienable rights had appeared in other political declarations, and in them, life and liberty were followed not by pursuit of happiness but by "property." A pedigree or a coat of arms seem like scant bits of property, but in fact, for most people while castles and fortunes come and go, pedigrees and coats of arms cannot be destroyed or stolen. However, they can also be created, especially in the pursuit of happiness. To this right I owe my middle name.

My right to a pedigree was first exercised on my behalf not by my parents or by anybody's parent, but by a great great aunt born in the sleepy village of Doveridge, Derbyshire, England in 1875. She was the fifth and last child of Ann and Henry Fenwick Pickering. She was the last because Henry died three months before she was born. She never married, never had children, never set foot in America, and never knew me. That did not stop her from creating a pedigree for her family, past and future. I first knew her as a picture in my mother's photo album, a four-inch thick book of coarse brown pages with photos pasted directly onto the paper. Auntie Dot is a small woman, less than five feet tall. She wears a long black skirt and a simple striped blouse buttoned high around the neck and its shapeless sleeves buttoned around the wrists. Her half clenched hands hang awkwardly at her side, and she stares slightly squint-eyed into the camera demanding silently, "Tell me when I can move." She was a mover and a shaper—of the truth.

My great grandparents named her Sarah Jane, but she became known to the nieces and nephews and grand nieces and nephews she often took care of as Auntie Dot. She worked her whole life as a nanny in the homes of English gentry in the soft green countryside south of London in Tunbridge Wells. Before and during the First World War she lived with a niece and cared for her niece's five children while their father was in the army for ten years. In defiance of Anglican England she was a devout Baptist. Baptists in 19th century England were what American politicians today call "working people." She and her sisters and her nieces all served proudly as chambermaids and cooks. Her brothers and her nephews scraped by on farms, delivering mail, and serving as foot soldiers.

My closest connection to her was a boy she helped raise, my great Uncle Ted White. We met only by mail when he was retired, an avowed 83 year old agnostic Congregational pastor in Western Australia. He cast aside the notion that he was a "hearing impaired senior citizen," and introduced himself as "a half deaf, half blind old man," and "rather cynical," but he allowed that "I can still get excited by ideas or causes or people, indeed, it is exciting to recall my old excitements." He also remembered his boyhood and Auntie Dot.

He had once shared her evangelical enthusiasms, maybe because he was often left in her charge as a young boy. He recalled her having "a spirit and will of iron--or perhaps Sheffield Steel." Sheffield being an English city not far from her birthplace. When Edwin entered the ministry as a Congregational pastor, Auntie Dot said she would support his calling by naming him her sole heir. As a single woman throughout life, she had saved more than anyone. When she died her favorite nephew inherited "a few pieces of furniture and a pile of receipts for donations she had made to the 'Baptist Tabernacle Building Fund.'" And her stories.

She was a game-playing and story-telling Baptist with a vivid imagination. She made up stories for her niece's children and her clients' children. From her family stories the nieces and nephews learned that they had descended from the nobility in the north of England by the Scottish border where her parents had been born. Auntie Dot's stories included how the town of Pickering in Yorkshire and Pickering Castle had been named for her father's ancestors, how in medieval times we were kin to Robin Hood, and of course, how her mother had descended from the Vickers nobility, those Vickers whose family made the famous rifle and later airplanes. Her brother William, my grandfather, named one of his children Thomas Vickers Pickering. My mother passed on Vickers to me. And via her favorite brother Wallace she gave me a double dose of that wild northern England heritage. If Auntie Dot were alive she would probably have connected me to William Wallace, the Braveheart.

Ted's younger brother Jack replied to my mother's first family history inquiries in January 1957. He was not sure who had gone to America to become my mother's parents, but he was sure about one thing. "Great Grandma by the way was a Miss Vickers of the great Vickers Aircraft Co., but apparently her family objected to her marrying Mr. Pickering, so they disowned her—did you know this?" His "Big Auntie Ada" also told this story to my mother and she added that when Ann's husband died, the Vickers family renewed tried to embrace their once-rejected daughter, but she refused their help. When I took my mother to England as her 75th birthday present in 1987, we visited Jack White and a few others who had been under Auntie Dot's care, and they were also under her spell. I heard how one remembered a Mr. Vickers coming around at Christmas time to give each child a shining shilling.

To the disappointment of several family members, Auntie Dot invented the story that engendered and ennobled my middle name, Vickers. The incriminating evidence lies in public records scattered around the English provinces—ordinary Vickers families as common as rocks in that rocky land and without the least tie to the family that made the 19th Century Vickers rifle and the 20th Century planes. No one had bothered to fact check Auntie Dot.

The family has a singular lack of tall members, and perhaps my Uncle Ted was right when he said, "It is only since WW2 that the British have grown longer. When I was a boy it was 'the gentry' who were tall." Whether the gentry acquired their height from French genes brought over by William the Conqueror in 1066 or by superior diet, little Auntie Dot was not to be deterred from lifting the family to gentry heights. Ted White said he had seen no evidence at all that the Miss Anne Vickers who married my great grandfather had any connection to the famous Vickers.

When he was one year old his father went to France as a sergeant in the Machine Gun Corps and Auntie Dot became his frequent overseer and entertainer. This continued until he was almost ten because when his father returned from the war badly wounded and suffering from the effects of a gas attack, he tried his hand at business in London while Ted's mother took in washing and ironing. Ted and Auntie Dot often visited "Big Grandma" who lived with Auntie Dot in a small apartment and dressed every day in black. Big Grandma was my great grandmother, Anne Vickers Pickering. "Big Grandma meant Great Grandma. In his memory and in a photo of Big Grandma standing next to Auntie Dot, herself a small woman, Big Grandma is tiny. She was then in her eighties and had shrunk considerably. Her husband, Henry Pickering—teacher, versifier and stock clerk—had died 40 years earlier, but like her sovereign Queen Victoria mourning the early death of Prince Albert, Big Grandma always wore black.

Uncle Ted had grown up under fire, or rather an occasional hail of stones thrown at him and his father, a Salvation Army evangelizer. (The English establishment, always fond of its upper class privileges, may have a historical mistrust of internal armed forces, like those that forced the Magna Carta on King John in 1250 or Cromwell's roundhead Puritans who beheaded King Charles in 1649.

After ordination in England, he had sailed for Western Australia as a missionary in the Congregational Church. By way of ministering to long lost relatives, he sent me a paperback copy of physicist Paul Davies book, *The Mind of God*. That came along with a note saying he had never been excited about the working class family he grew up in, with one exception. "The nearest I came to liking my family was a romantic notion of the family in ages past, based on Auntie Dot's fantasies." He is the only person I talked to or heard from who remembered Auntie Dot well and knew her family stories to be fantasy. They believed in the Vickers connection.

The darker and more unshakeable doubts about our noble origins were uncovered by my American cousin Catherine Pickering, born in Roslyn, and a lifelong resident of the nearby north shore. Not willing to settle for Auntie Dot's well told, well sold, and oft repeated oral literature, Catherine retired from service as a school librarian and embarked on family service. She dedicated her formidable clerical and archival skills to finding lost ancestors and resurrecting those who had faded into little more than ghosts of names. Early in her research she made a trip to England and became the first Pickering to visit Henry Pickering's grave in 125 years. She also became a frequent visitor in the greatest of all unified genealogical archives, those that have been gathered against the final Day of Judgment by the Church of Latter Day Saints, the Mormons. She pieced together a convincing record of our origins.

The facts as we now know them, are that Auntie Dot's mother had been born Ann Vickers in the village of Hensingham, hard by the coast where Solway Firth joins the Irish Sea. Just east lies that northwestern part of England known as the Lake District where I would one day, still innocent of family history, spend a month gathering material for my graduate thesis on the poet William Wordsworth. I took long walks on some of the same roads and footpaths that my great grandmother and her brothers and sisters used.

The north of England is also where enterprising English craftsmen forged Sheffield steel, and where in 1828, six years before my great grandmother's birth, three men formed Naylor, Hutchinson, Vickers and Company. The company prospered and went public in 1867 as Vickers Sons & Company Limited. By that time Anne had been married for nine years and had two sons by a popular school-master and versifier, Henry Pickering.

The bare facts of the connection between the Pickerings and the Vickers families are documented in a wedding certificate and a few other documents. The story begins in the 1850s with the love affair between the 24 year old Miss Anne Vickers and the 22 year old "schoolmaster at High School" Mr. Henry Fenwick Pickering. Nothing indicates the affluence of steel makers; just the opposite. Henry and his twin brother Jacob were fourth and fifth of the eight children of the stone mason William Pickering. Anne Vickers had been born near the Lake District center Keswick, the youngest of six children.

The lovers both lived in the village of Hensingham. The record lists Anne Vickers's profession as "servant" and her father Joseph's as "husbandman" or farmer. Henry signed his name and Anne signed her mark, X.

When my mother had me christened Wallace Vickers, Auntie Dot's version of history held sway in both England and America and had been part of family lore since my mother was a child. In those days, however, it had been nothing more than the rumor of an undisclosed scandal. The slight skeleton of the story as my mother first told it to me included her Aunt Ada's claim that Anne Vickers had married a commoner. In outrage, her noble family cast her out. Who might have said what to whom and what other events may have tainted the marriage remained for the imagination. Only two other ties to the Vickers family survived alongside Auntie Dot's unverified stories. My great grandmother, Anne Vickers Pickering, did keep a small card edged with printed black drape and sent to her in 1892 to notify her of the death of her seventeen year old niece, Florence Lillian Vickers. Add to that the memory of some English relatives that in the early 1900s when they were children, "a Mr. Vickers would sometimes come by and give each of us a shilling." That philanthropic or guilty Mr. Vickers disappeared before they were old enough to know who he was. He was probably one of Ann's brothers or one of her nephews.

When I was old enough to ask about my middle name, my mother wrote to her cousins in England and politely asked what they knew. They were happy to tell. Ada wrote about the wealthy Vickers kin. Another letter said that Henry Fenwick Pickering died in 1875, when a train he was riding in went over a bridge. In short, I grew up believing that long before my birth we had come down in the world, or at least we had lost a connection that would have had me born into the British upper class. At the same time, I was proud that my great grandmother had not gone groveling back to the family that, according to inherited legend, disowned her. I much preferred Robin Hood to rich business people, even if they did make guns and airplanes.

In fact, the Pickerings would never have appeared in Roslyn, New York if they had been wealthy or if they had accepted their position in the British class system. In Victorian England each class had its place. A hard working family could improve its comforts and future, but it had little hope of real wealth, and no hope of rising into the ranks of the landed gentry. Improvement through hard work for an illiterate single mother with four children was impossible. After Sarah Jane (Auntie Dot) was born the year after her father's death, the family moved south, toward greater opportunity within the scope of their class.

Anne's gradual migration south traversed only 300 miles, but it crossed a large cultural distance in a country where local pride and custom is still strong and distinct. With the family's greater distance from its kin and roots, the fatherless serving girl Sarah Jane chose to elevate the family by fabricating kinship to the wealthy northern gentry, a story which also portrayed their poverty as an injustice. Although Sarah Jane's mother had turned her back on the Vickers kin of the north, Sarah Jane's imagination would return and reconstruct the family in a way that served pride and ambition. This was a family destined to send out immigrants because, unlike so many European intellectuals and their followers, it did not want to pull down the rich, but to ennoble the poor. This is the stuff of both soap operas and the American dream. Our dreamer, Sarah Jane, remained single and grew into Auntie Dot whose children were her nephews and nieces. Her feisty and runty older brother William, a child of the Scottish border, would be the first to emigrate.

Out of that northern English heritage my grandfather William and his easy-going southern wife Emma named one of their children Wallace and another Thomas Vickers. My mother began naming her children by splitting the difference with my father when their first children were twins. One of my brothers they named Arthur Emmett after my father and his father. The other William John after my mother's brother Jack and one of her brothers or her father or both. They abandoned the symmetry the next year when I was born. I don't know why they did not give me one name from each side. I received Wallace for my mother's favorite brother and Vickers, for the family's claim to entitlement. My English great grandmother Anne Vickers had been dead for 17 years by that time, and Auntie Dot's stories had become established as fact. Auntie Dot was also dead when I came along. Her spirit and mythology lived on, however, and it colored my childhood as it had colored others.

Why should truth be any more important than a noble or wishful lie? Auntie Dot had sewn onto the spiritual garments of the family a noble crest. None of the scores of Pickering and Vickers descendants had earned the heritage, but then what child born into even the highest family has earned anything yet? I'm sure that knowing what one's family has overcome is a far more useful heritage than knowing what luck has settled on us. Yet I cannot fault my Auntie Dot for inventing the story or my mother and others for believing it. She invented and they believed because they aspired. Maybe they felt they had earned the right to a title because in their humble, nobody-special lives as servants, mail carriers, rag pickers, miners, carpenters, stable hands and factory workers they had seldom complained, had brought up honest families, had overcome and endured more than most members of noble families have to do. Auntie Dot's invention and their acceptance of the story was their way of saying, "We are somebody too." Whether their belief in aristocratic ancestors was a claim on nobility or an instinctive affirmation of the unalienable right to the pursuit of happiness and equality is a difference without a distinction—both said we are entitled to be free and respected.

Like Auntie Dot, I have set out to create for the family yet another history of its origins. If this story were solely for the family I might, like Auntie Dot, create an inspiring tale of noble and wealthy origins from whence we fell and to which we might hope to return. But I intend this history for both a narrow audience and a wider one. The narrower audience is two people, my mother and me. Our debts to our parents do not end with their deaths. Somewhere in this history is the WHY she asked for. Also, as with all stories, real and imagined, somewhere in this history is the Why that drives me to write it. The wider audience, of course, is anyone beyond our family who might be reading these words now, because we all seek the answer to a WHY.

CHAPTER 4: HAPPY SEEDS OF DISCONTENT

Who shall judge a man from manners?
  Who shall know him by his dress?
Paupers may be fit for princes
  Princes fit for something less;
Crumpled shirt and dirty jacket
  Maybe clothe the golden ore
Of the deepest thought and feeling—
  Satin vests could be no more.
(from an anonymous poem pasted in a scrapbook from my mother's teenage years)

"Psychiatry enables us to correct our faults by confessing our parents' shortcomings."
Laurence J. Peter

"You are just like your grandfather." When my mother began saying that to me is a marker lost in what psychologists now call "childhood amnesia." I did not acquire this handicap the time I dove off a chair arm at age three and split my head open on the cast iron radiator. Childhood amnesia handicaps all humankind. It is the period before four or five years old of which we later remember only a few scenes and events. Our early childhoods are rare memories strung out behind us like widely separated beads on an invisible thread of time—our amnesia. Amnesia is followed by the brain rapidly starting to remember whole episodes, which coincidentally coincides with rapidly distinguishing ourselves from other kinds of animals.

"You are just like your grandfather." I was proud to hear her say it. To me it signified that I was like an adult, like her father. I should have taken caution from two clues—one grammatical, the other facial. Notice she always said *your* grandfather, not *my* father. Second, my mother never smiled when she said that. It was not a compliment. It was a bag of mixed emotions from which I chose the best. Her father had owned his own newspaper, magazine, candy, and tobacco store, branched out into photography, then junk, used books, and antiques. He and his wife Emma had ten children, my mother being the last. "The baby of the family," she often called herself. To the child who was me she was the most beautiful and accomplished in her family. Until I was a teenager, being like my grandfather I heard and received as a compliment. Later it became a humorous irony because her father's curiosity and entrepreneurial ambition led him in too many directions, and he sometimes ignored his family. Despite his business expertise, he fell in love with his books and antiques and wouldn't sell the best of them. It would lead to an embarrassing death, not unlike his own father's. (Later in this narrative each in his own time shall die in some detail.)

The full meaning of her father and being just like him took me decades to comprehend. My mother was not sophisticated or well read, but she had a strong sense of what children should and should not hear. (Or perhaps my conjunction should be "therefore"—my observation being that well read and sophisticated people often think children can be told anything.) To hear the full family truth about the Pickerings of Roslyn, she still judged I contained too much child in me at age 30, and less at age 40 but still too much for the whole truth. I would not learn how deeply wounded she was by her father's darker side until my mother was old and I was middle aged, that is to say when she judged me mature enough or when she felt she wanted to get in the final lick before death called time's up.

Like human beings from the dawn of language I learned who I was or who I should be from stories, a fragmented family scripture. Before I could recite my street address and phone number, these stories had become part of my social address. At birth parents give us names that pretend we are discreet and independent new creations. This is a habit carried down through the millennia of ignorance that preceded the discovery of the double helix and the following revelation of genetic research that we are 96% ape and 50% fungus, genetically speaking. As everyone who has followed the abortion debate knows, no one can say where one individual ends and another begins without resorting to metaphysics and faith. From the perspective of biology the genetic material that uttered its first cry in Maspeth, New York and immediately bore my name and appearance has existed from humanity's "African genesis". And before that was the animal genesis. Our convenient definition of individual and the whole abortion debate rests on when one believes that a combination of genetic materials has been endowed with a soul or, for some, when it becomes endowed with human rights.

When my mother said, "You're just like your grandfather," she was acknowledging at least the suspicion that my life began in places and times before I was born. For centuries before our births, family members who precede us in the world are carrying around our genetic materials, shuffling and reshuffling. Generation by generation that two barreled, maternal-paternal funnel of time gathers, assembles and reassembles the pieces for us. Once born, each of us must live a life formed by accident and purpose. Our genetic heritage is the biological hand dealt to us out of the mile high deck of genetic playing cards possessed by the human race. (Okay, now and then some epigenetic event might slip a new card into our cells, but this is not a biology textbook.) With the cards dealt at conception we have to play the game of life. Some of those cards may even determine how well we can learn to play the game.

It's a biological fact, of course, that my great grandparents' oldest son William Henry carried part of me in him as surely as he carried his father's and grandfather's names in public. We are not the exhuming kind of family, so science shall never examine his remains and say what in me was in him, which of my cards were his cards. My mother, however, was very sure we were playing with almost the same cards. The English and Scots among whom my grandfather and his parents had been born had seldom moved far during their short lives. I can assume that my grandfather took from his father Henry and his mother Anne Vickers many doses of genetic material from farmer hands and stone masons, ragpickers, servant women, miners and school teachers in the English north country and Scottish border lands. These lands were once the farthest outpost of the Roman Empire, then the kingdom of Rheged ruled by King Urien. Briefly, after the Saxon king Edmund had conquered King Dunmail the lands were ceded to Scotland under King Malcolm. The waves of battle that washed across these hills and mountains included the fiercely independent and murderous Border Reivers who pillaged and stole livestock for a living. Somewhere in that seething northern soup of Celtic, Briton, Norman, Saxon, Pictic, and Anglo tribes began the families called Peckering, Puckering, Pickering and Vickers.

By the late 1700s when our Pickering part of this history first appears on the records, the region had settled down to farming, quarrying, and mining. My great great great grandfather William Pickering was born in 1763 at Souly How, a nobble of sheep farming land northeast of the village of Gosforth, and a few miles from the Irish Sea and near his wife Jane.

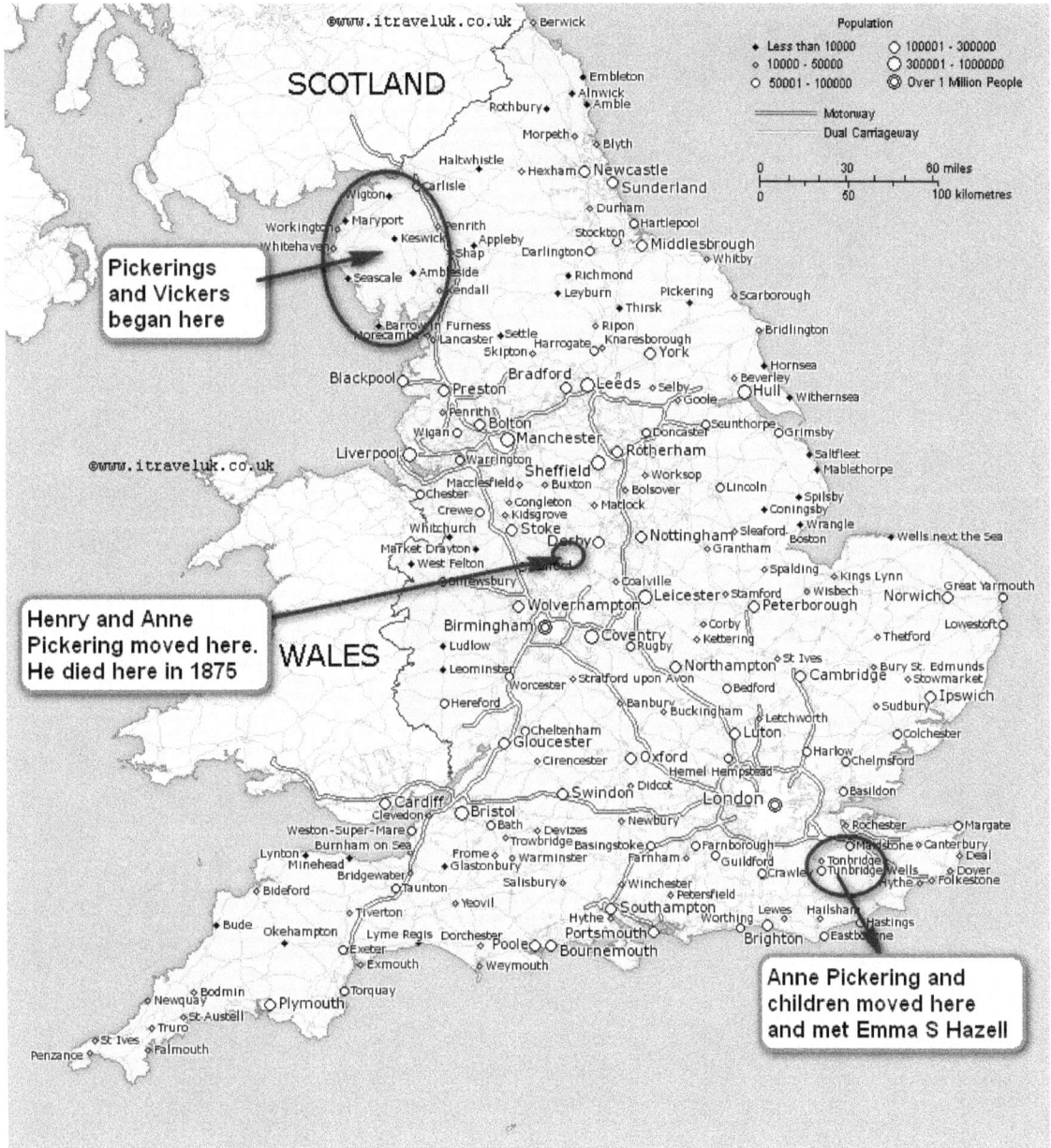

©www.itraveluk.co.uk

SCOTLAND

Pickerings and Vickers began here

Henry and Anne Pickering moved here. He died here in 1875

WALES

Anne Pickering and children moved here and met Emma S Hazell

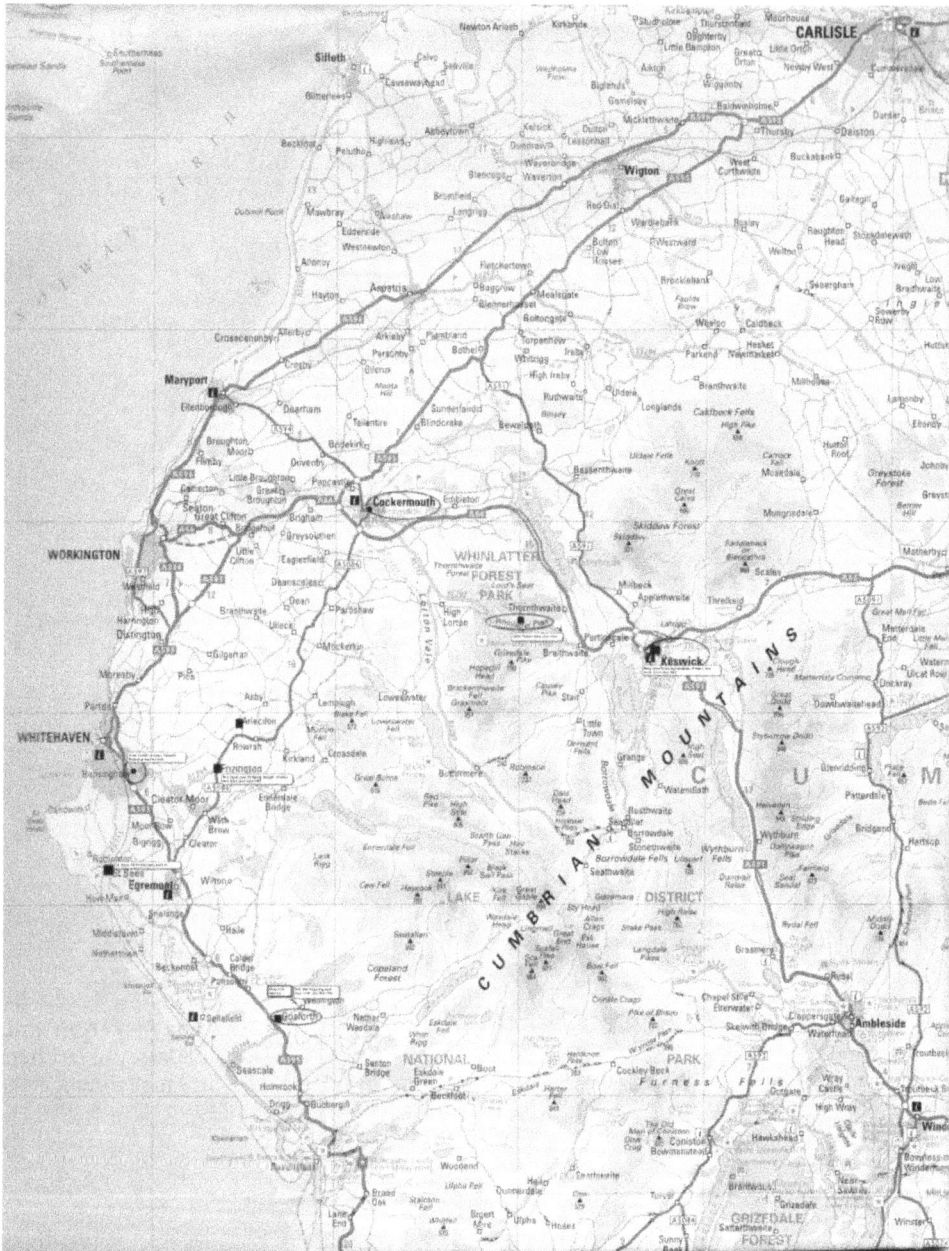

Cumbria and the Lake District, showing sites for births, marriages, deaths and work for Vickers and Pickering families in the early to mid 1800s. The area then was devoted largely to lead, iron, coal and other mining and sheep herding. The poets Wordsworth and Coleridge also lived here. Also the writers Southey and DeQuincy.

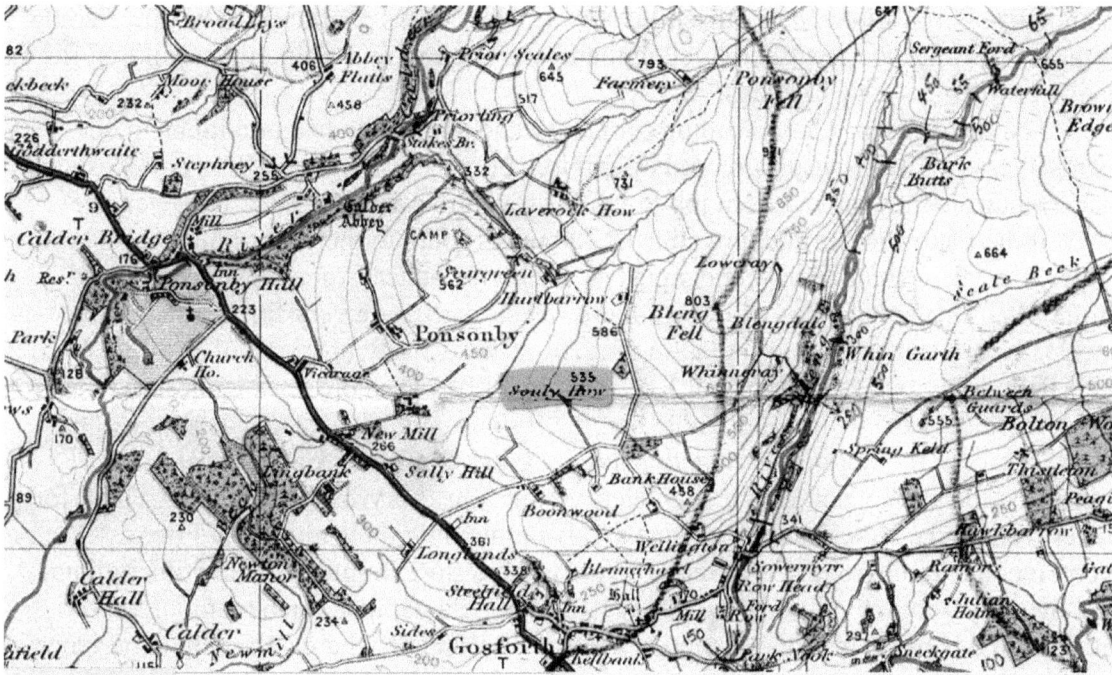

This map shows Souly How, a noll of land near Gosforth where William Pickering was born in 1763, the first record I've found of this family name and the Pickering ancestors

In 1792 he gave the name William to his son, my great great grandfather who broke with the pastoral tradition and became a stone mason in the mining town of Hensingham perched just above the little port of Whitehaven. That second William married a 16 year old local girl named Elizabeth Smith. She bore the first of their six boys, another William, before she turned 17. The other seven, two girls and five boys, came almost regularly, every three years until she was 40. In 1836 she bore twin boys, Jacob and Henry Fenwick.

Except for those static facts on the census records, our Pickering part of this history does not appear on any public records that I or others have found until the moment this part of the family and its share of my DNA began to move. The known part of the story begins in that village of Hensingham with the marriage of Henry Fenwick to the 24 year old serving girl, Anne Vickers on July 27, 1858. The farmer Joseph Vickers gave his daughter, a 24 year old serving girl, to stone mason William Pickering's son, the 22 year old Henry Fenwick Pickering. On the marriage certificate Anne signed her X below Henry's perfect signature. They could hardly have imagined their own future and certainly not that one day in America a great grandson would carry the name Vickers and the Jewish name Kaufman. 1858 was the year England emancipated her Jews, and the day before the Pickering-Vickers marriage the first Jew took his seat in the House of

Commons--Baron Lionel de Rothschild. Nevertheless, Jews continued to be unwelcome in most of British society, often lived in their own ghettos, and forbid their children from dating or mating with Christians.

None of this had any meaning for Henry and Anne who had ambitions to better themselves. For a few years a record of children born in Frizington (1859) and Keswick (1862) indicate they moved from job to job for several years. By 1864, however, they had left the Lake District and moved over 200 miles south to the coal mining town of Silverdale where Henry had found a post as a school teacher. Anne's twenty year old brother Wilson came to live with them there. That made for a very full house. Almost as soon as Henry and Anne had settled in, tragedy struck. Early in spring of 1864 on April 2 their first child, four year old Sarah Jane, died in a fire. The coroner's inquest two days later closed the case with its only note being, "By burning."

Perhaps the full house, tragedy, and the gritty conditions of Silverdale's coal mines and the nearby potteries moved Henry after fourteen years of teaching to look for better work and a better home for Anne and his remaining three children. Friends recommended him strongly to manage a cooperative store in the green and quiet village of Doveridge some 30 miles east. Henry had become a popular teacher among both students and parents, but he was then in his mid 30s, an age where sufficient experience combined with ambition moves many people to reinvent their lives. The human animal is said to be an "economic animal," and studies show that those who have economic ambition typically make their first independent moves in their early thirties. A teacher had both a very limited salary and a clearly defined future. Silverdale was a poor, sooty, crowded little town of mining families.

Doveridge with a population of less than 1,000 had seen little change for almost a century. It seemed an unlikely place for an ambitious family. Managing a general store also does not sound adventuresome to modern ears, and modern cooperatives in America are generally supported and patronized by affluent white collar professionals. In Henry's time, as the Industrial Revolution had stirred great hope and great rebellion against the factory system as well as against changes in the English countryside. The Cooperative Movement was part of working class rebellion against powerful forces that seemed to be taking over their lives and pocketbooks. When Henry and Anne had been children, labor law reformers launched the violent rebellions of the Chartist radicals. Blood flowed in towns across England.

The cooperative movement aimed at economic empowerment by taking on ownership of retail operations and their profits. It began with flannel weavers near Manchester who, inspired by the principles of mill owner and reformer Wilfred Owen, opened a part time grocery for their members. Instead of voting according the size of one's investment as in a corporation, the humblest and the richest member of a cooperative each had one vote. Forty years before English law allowed women to control their own possessions, cooperatives gave shares and the vote to women. Each member received a share of the profits in proportion to his or her purchases.

Doveridge in Henry's day was a small village on the quiet waters of the River

Dove. A turnpike through the midlands and its growing pottery industry had by-passed the little village, but it had a few claims to history. One of them was the church Henry, Anne and the children attended. The church had been built of local stone shortly after William the Conqueror sailed from France in 1066 and took over the English throne, but it may have been built on an even older foundation since it is dedicated to the Anglo Saxon saint Cuthbert.

Less than five years before the Pickerings moved to Doveridge, the church had received a fine pipe organ and a new clock in its tower. The same organ plays today and the same clock keeps time. Inside the church the dark wooden pews in which the Pickerings sat have been improved only by seat cushions. Outside the church along the path to the main door stands a giant yew tree older than the church itself. Its gnarled trunk is over 22 feet in diameter and the dense branches spread over 30 feet around, forming a tunnel over the walkway. A legend associated with this tree may have inspired Henry and Anne's last child, "Auntie Dot," to tell later generations that they were related to Robin Hood. A medieval manuscript in the British Museum tells this story:

> Said Robin Hood, lady fair, whither away,
> Oh whither fair lady away?
> And she made him answer, to kill a fair buck,
> For tomorrow is Titbury day. [Titbury = present nearby Tutbury]
> When dinner was ended
> Sir Roger the parson of Dubbidge [Dubbidge = Doveridge]
> Was sent for in haste;
> He brought his mass book, and
> He bade them take hands,
> And he joined them in marriage full fast.

Unfortunately Henry had only three years to enjoy his new freedom and his place in reforming the English economy. As his wife Anne began to grow noticeably with their fifth child in 1875 Henry began to have bouts of digestive problems. Over the weeks the pains became more severe and more frequent. Toward summer he began to have fits of vomiting and often found blood in his stools. A fever came on and by late June he could no longer work. On June 29 he died of an intestinal problem that frequently occurs in children but seldom in adults. Perhaps because of polyps in his intestine or a growing cancer, one part of his intestines had been slowly drawn into a lower part in a syndrome called intussusceptions.

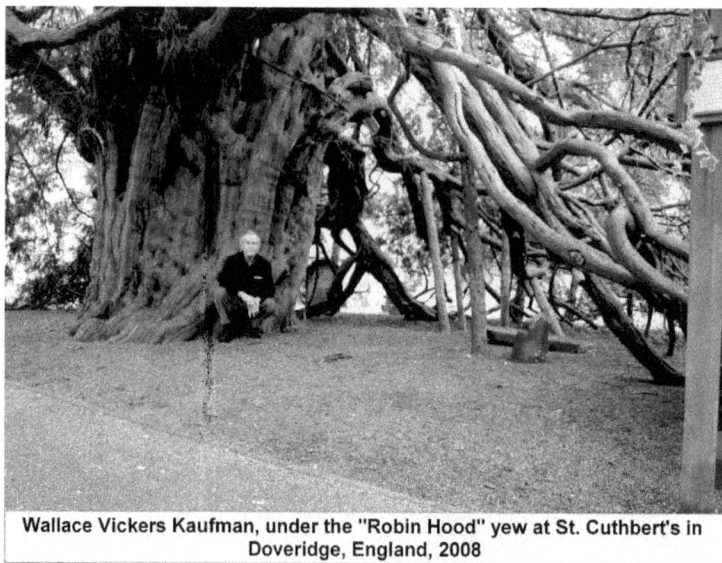

Wallace Vickers Kaufman, under the "Robin Hood" yew at St. Cuthbert's in Doveridge, England, 2008

Although the cooperative he managed in Doveridge was part of important reforms that upset a good part of the established powers, Henry's ability to transcend rigid class lines was proven by his sudden death and the celebration of his life embodied in his funeral.

In Henry, with the aid of two fulsome obituaries, I can see the first dim reflection of myself. I don't believe in reading broken lives out of broken lines on the palm, and I don't have the slightest proof that I have a single gene from Henry. Nor do I put much muscle into wringing meaning out of coincidence. Some coincidence, however, demands attention, especially in light of my mother's insistence "you are just like my father." Then why not like her grandfather Henry? Consider:

Begin even with Henry's father, a stone mason. My hobby of choice long before I knew of Henry and his father, was stone masonry.

Henry began his career as a teacher. So did I.

Henry left teaching and went into business. So did I.

Henry's business was part of an economic experiment aimed to bring to lower income people some of the fruits of commerce. I went into business with the same motivation.

Henry had a small reputation as a poet and loved poetry. Me too.

Henry died at age 39. Not me. At age 37 I did fall out of a tree with a roaring chain saw, crush a vertebra, and for a moment I believed I had sawed off my head. That was pure coincidence. I was responsible for my own near death experience.

Henry's fulsome obituaries from Silverdale and Uttoexter make no mention of how he died. The beige slab of his stone in St. Cuthbert's churchyard is set next to the main path and under the sheltering branches of the ancient yew where Robin Hood and maid Marian were said to have been betrothed. Some of those branches, blowing across the stone in the winds or laden with snow have worn away part of the inscription on the soft stone:

> In Memory of
> Henry Pickering
> Three years st[ayed?] in this parish
> Died June 29th 1875
> Aged 39 years
> His ready store of love, and care for the ____[o]f all

The rest is indistinguishable except for the notation that part of it came from the Gospel of Matthew, chapter 25.

At the bottom of the stone in small letters, however is a footnote of sorts that is revealing. "Erected by public subscription." None of the other stones in that cemetery bear these words. The wife of a humble store keeper for the local cooperative, widowed with three children and a fourth on the way, probably had little money for any stone. For this man the people of the village bought a stone.

He was humble but unusually respected and befriended by both rich and poor. The Silverdale paper and the *New Era* from the nearby town of Uttoexeter printed detailed obituaries. In Silverdale where he had taught school for almost ten years, residents called him "Poet of the Village." Moved by their poet's death, many people from Silverdale made the thirty mile trip south to Doveridge by coach, horse, or wagon.

The *New Era's* obituary is the longest, although the Pickerings had been in Doveridge only three years. It says the death of the "worthy store keeper" came suddenly and "a sad gloom has this week been cast above pretty village [Doveridge] . . ."

In the style of journalism that tells us the news but none of the reasons for it, his untimely sudden death is more important than the cause which the reporter never mentions. So too we know nothing of why he had built in a few years a fine reputation which brought to his funeral service and procession "the whole village from Lord Waterpark [Sir Henry Anson Cavendish] and A.W. Lyon Esq., to the humblest individual, and even the children, assembled to do honor to one whom they had learned to love." Almost a hundred school children, each with a bouquet followed the coffin to its grave at stone church of St. Cuthbert. The obituary tells us, again without details, that he had had a "great and increasing interest . . . in everything which had contributed to their happiness."

Let the paper tell the rest of his funeral service:

> Distinguished ladies of the village alike contributed to the general feeling of respect by making some beautiful wreaths and placing them on the coffin. The highest ladies in the village brought wreathes they had made and laid them on his coffin. The burial service was impressively read by the esteemed Vicar, who afterwards spoke most feelingly of the departed, showing how the most humble individuals may honour God in

their daily lives, and thus win the affection of a whole community. The children sang that now well known hymn, "Safe in the arms of Jesus," and then marched by the grave and threw in their floral offerings, thus literally burying their friend with the flowers he had loved so well. No one could witness the many sorrowful faces, of the numerous instances in which the people strove to show their respect and affection for the departed, without being convinced that he who could in such a brief period draw forth such general, deep and sincere feelings of sorrow, could have been no ordinary person."[1]

Allowing that this had the flourishes and sentimentality typical of Victorian prose, simple facts bloom in it like flowers in a rock garden. He loved children and they loved him. He loved flowers. In a rigid class society he had friends from highest to lowest. Maybe this bridging of class bonds was appropriate for the village where Robin Hood was said to have proposed to Maid Marian. Maybe it was the first indication that some members of this family would rise in the world. And some would repeat parts of his own life. His son William Henry, only ten when his father died, would also become a shop keeper, an avid reader, and a writer of some humor and eloquence in civil causes and public letters. And his friends would have to raise money for his burial. Two of William's sons would also come to own their own stores. Whether the similarities in our lives may be genetic or the results of family culture or coincidental, I am glad to make this small note about an unusually good man. He had no foreknowledge of his own family's future, no less of mine, but while it is everyone's inevitable function to pass on the DNA of their descendants, I am happy to fulfill one of a writer's most important functions—passing on the memory of lives well lived.

The yew tree at St. Cuthbert's. Henry Pickering's grave is to the right of the path, inside the tunnel formed by the branches. Lower photo: Pickering grave to left of the walk.

CHAPTER 5. MOVING ON: STABLE BOY TO STOREKEEPER

Why, how and when Anne decided to take her children to the south of the country and Tunbridge Wells, I have not discovered. Maybe she had a connection, a friend or family member who invited her. Tunbridge Wells also appealed to her as a place where she and her children might all find work with rich families more concentrated and affluent than the estates of the Lake District or Derbyshire. And maybe the history and character of the place also appealed to her.

Tunbridge Wells had begun life as a place of healing waters and landscapes, and it was still a peaceful country town. Its iron rich, reddish spring waters were discovered in 1606 by the young Lord Dudley North. North, a dissolute member of King James I's court, had gone south of London to stay with his friend Lord Abergavenny at Eridge Castle. On a trip back to London he discovered the springs flowing from a wooded crease in the land. His physicians advised him that the restoring powers he had noticed might return him to health, and the following summer Lord North became the first Englishman on record to be cured by the spring waters. Other nobility soon followed. Lord Abergavenny had two of the springs surrounded by wooden fences. In 1630 Charles I's wife Queen Henrietta set up camp at nearby Bishop's Down and took the waters and enjoyed the scenery for six weeks. By 1659 the prominent local lawyer and magistrate Richard Kilburne noted, "In this parish are those famous waters called by some *Fant Wells* and by others *Tunbridge Wells*, so much resorted unto and drunk by the nobility and gentry of this nation : coming hither for that purpose from several parts yearly in the summer, and more especially in the months of July and August." [2] By 1684 Tunbridge was graced by the Church of King Charles the Martyr.

Only in the 1800s with the advent of good roads and the railroad did Tunbridge Wells become a residential town. By the time the Pickerings had arrived in Tunbridge Wells it was more like the place described by another noble visitor, Count Hamilton. "All that is considered handsome and gallant in either sex resorts here in the water season; the company always numerous is always select, for those who only seek diversion always exceed in number those who come hither of necessity. Everything there breathes pleasure and joy. Constraint is banished; intimacy is established at the first acquaintance. People . . . assemble in the morning at the wells - a large alley of thick bowering trees, under which they walk while drinking the waters. On one side of the alley stands a long row of shops (booths ?) stocked with all kinds of trinkets, laces, stockings, and gloves, where you can play as at the French fair. On the other side of the alley is the market, and as every one goes there to choose and buy provisions, you never see there any offal of a disgusting kind. But you meet pretty village lasses, fair and fresh, with linen very clean and white, little straw hats, and neat in shoes " and stockings, who sell game, vegetables, flowers, and fruit. You get as good living there as you can desire. As soon as night falls, every one leaves the little palaces, for the assembly on the Bowling Green, where you may dance if you like in open air, on turf more soft and firm than the smartest carpets in the world."

When Anne decided to take her family to Tunbridge Wells the village had become a fashionable place for rich business people to live. Town homes and country houses boasted designs by the best architects. It was a green and quiet haven within easy coach or train distance from London. Like all rich towns it needed a serving class. Anne and her oldest daughter Mary, now called Polly in the family, seized the opportunity. Anne, perhaps having learned during her marriage to Henry how to read and write and manage a business, became the manager of a local dairy. As a girl she had worked on country estates and knew livestock and dairy production.

Her son Willie, who I am "exactly like," was eleven or twelve when he arrived in Tunbridge Wells. The odds of being a success were against him. The odds in this case means largely the not very odd British class system. For American readers who might think I exaggerate, I'll note that even when I studied in England finding a real working class student at Oxford was difficult. When I brought to a college dinner a Scottish friend working as a construction laborer, the other graduate students acted as if I had brought in a load of manure. When I worked on a hops farm one summer, the prosperous owner of the estate almost fired me when he learned I had gone to a local pub to have a beer and sing country music with the men and women I worked with in the field. Upper class English still frequently talked about working people "not being one of us." And I passed through England a century after my great grandparents married.

Victorian England for all its wealth, power and commerce had a class system that gave little hope for a working class Englishman to rise above his class. There was no glass ceiling, but there were very high social walls. While Horatio Alger in America was writing his optimistic novels of opportunity, in England Karl Marx had been sitting in the British museum working on *Das Kapital*, writing tracts to urge working men and women to recognize that the upper classes were engaged in a conspiracy to keep them poor and in their places, and that their only hope was to overthrow the upper classes. In Paris in 1848 and 1871 revolution had briefly produced working class communes that took over government. The English establishment kept a tight lid on their working class and did not appreciate their upstart religions—the Baptists, Methodists, and the Salvation Army. The upper class considered these religions naïve at best, subversive at worst. William's sister Polly (Mary Anne) had married a grocer who had been one of the first men in Tunbridge Wells to join the Salvation Army.

"The Army," founded by "General" William Booth, the son of a bankrupt small time builder, took inspiration from America's backwoods preachers who visited England. The army of salvation aimed its message squarely at working class people who found

British Anglicans stuffy and unworldly. "The one thing you had to avoid was 'churchiness'. For the church was felt to be a middle class, formal, snobbish affair, while the mission was a working-class, lively and loving concern." (Coutts: 68) Tunbridge Wells was very much a town run by and for the gentry and established middle class. The establishment looked the other way when town rowdies, themselves unskilled laborers, broke up one of the Army's singing and prayer sessions by pushing their carts and barrows through the group. One attacker, using his massive hawker's barrow as a battering ram, ran down Mary's husband Charles, crushed his leg and left him limping the rest of his life as he sometimes walked ten or fifteen miles to preach and work for "The Army."

Class and caste were not written into English law, but everyone knew his or her station—his superiors and inferiors. Instead of the Indian color dot of caste on the forehead, in Britain accent and vocabulary marked one's caste, and if these were not enough, one could always be properly categorized by the answer to the question, "What did your parents do?" Thus the famous scene in Oscar Wilde's "Importance of Being Earnest" when Lady Augusta Bracknell's questions the young man who is courting her daughter:

Lady Bracknell: Are your parents living?

Jack Worthing: I have lost both my parents.

Lady Bracknell: To lose one parent, Mr. Worthing, may be regarded as a misfortune; to lose both looks like carelessness.

By the time my widowed grandmother started life anew in the south, maybe she was telling son William, "Willie, you are exactly like your father." In that case it would have been a compliment--at least if we believe the accolades of the two obituaries. Except in the cases of tyrants and mass murderers, obituaries are inclined to speak well of the dead, but they are seldom inclined to speak as well of a man as they did of Henry Fenwick Pickering.

History documents what became of Willie much more generously than it treats his father. One reason is time, the other is America and the village life of Roslyn. That public story of little William Pickering, however, shows none of my grandfather's dark side. He was a living illustration of the vastly popular dime novels by Horatio Alger the Harvard grad turned Unitarian minister. In all Alger novels poor boys like Ragged Dick and Paul the Peddler rose to success and wealth by honesty and hard work. While William was still in his teens he began to strike out on his own, disappearing from home for days or weeks at a time looking for work.[3] The family had settled in Tunbridge Wells and his older sister Mary Anne had married the grocer Charles Norman. With the help of Mary Anne's in-laws, William entered the postal service as a telegraph messenger boy.

Soon his brother Ted followed. Ted would make a career of it, and was still carrying mail when his nephew and namesake Ted White was a boy. Ted recalled, "He was not much bigger than his mother or his sister [Sarah Jane called Auntie Dot], but for many years he carried a postman's heavy bag through the streets of Clapham, South London." Ted had none of brother William's outgoing personality. "He had a lively wit and sense of fun; he was gentle and tolerant, but somewhat withdrawn: his face hidden in a great bushy beard, he was a man of few words."

Postal work might be okay for his in-laws and his brother, but for William it seemed a dead end job with the only exception being that in this job he might save money for a ticket out of English society and its high social walls. The easiest way out of the system was the one that ambitious Englishmen had been taking for over 200 years—go to America. The cheapest passage for a healthy young telegram clerk was to sign on as a seaman. At age 20 or 21 William Pickering registered as a seaman. He was not a seaman for very long. America takes note of his presence in 1887, a date written on his naturalization papers as his entry.

His public story is sketched in *The Brooklyn Daily Eagle* for September 26, 1908. The anonymous writer compares "Billy" Pickering to a character from Dickens' famous novel *Martin Chuzzlewit*.

A MODERN MARK TAPLEY IS "BILLY" PICKERING

He is as Optimistic as Ever Dickens' Character Was

HIS INTERESTING LIFE STORY.

Sailor, P.O. Clerk, Track Walker, Stable Boy--Now He's a
Successful Artist Photographer

Like most Dickens characters, the essence of Mark Tapley can be captured in one sentence. Young Mark Tapley sees the best side of people, events, and life. Like Henry Pickering's oldest son, he sailed for America in the 19th Century. To the world beyond his family William Pickering was a modern Mark Tapley. He guarded family and personal matters within the fortress of English reserve. As far as the *Brooklyn Daily Eagle*'s details go, the writer is faithful to fact, except no one in the family ever called William Pickering an artist photographer, and he never thought of himself as one.

The young seaman who left England in 1886 waved good-bye to his ship in New York in 1887. He immediately left the city swarming with impoverished immigrants and headed for Texas following the famous advice popularized by *New York Tribune* editor Horace Greeley—"Go west, young man." In Texas William took the first offer of work because he didn't believe in waiting for opportunity to knock again. He became a track walker for the new lines of the Southern Pacific Railroad.

Track walkers had lonely tedious jobs that numerous immigrants took up. His duty under a broiling Texas sun was to walk the tracks looking for obstacles, loose spikes, and anything else that would threaten safe passage. He did his job well and he used the time to think about his future. And in Texas where hundreds of thousands of cattle had to be driven to Kansas for shipment East, the railroad was the future. William was expecting a promotion when suddenly the water that had kept him alive also gave him typhoid fever. He lost his strength. He had frequent headaches that threatened to explode. For days on end he had a raging fever. He lay near death for several weeks. In the 19th century typhoid from water and food contaminated by sewage or the unclean hands of a typhoid carrier commonly struck Americans. It killed one out of three of its victims. Ten years after it felled William it became the biggest killer in the Spanish-American War (1898-1900). 85% of the men who died were killed not by bullets but by typhoid.

Few things turn a man's heart toward home and family more than being sick unto death in a foreign country. When William recovered enough strength to travel, he went to the port of Galveston, Texas, and on September 4, 1888 he signed onto the British ship HMS Charrington as a seaman to work off his passage home. The Charrington carried a variety of cargoes between Northern England, the Mediterranean and North America. One voyage it might take European wines to America. An existing record shows it being the first ship of the year into the St. Lawrence River after the ice broke, carrying 20,000 boxes of lemons and 10,000 boxes of oranges to Montreal. We don't know what the ship carried from Galveston to England or ports in between, but a month after William signed on the ship docked in Liverpool where William received his certificate of discharge. The reverse side of his discharge records both his "Character for Ability in Whatever Capacity" and his "Character for Conduct" as "very good."

William returned to convalesce in Tunbridge Wells where his mother and sisters were still working. His mother made room for him in the house she shared with Sarah Jane in the railroad district, 59 Goods Station Rd. The neighborhood teemed with working class families and their children. Their neighbors were mainly household servants and laborers, a dressmaker, a brewer's clerk, a cart driver, and several old widows scraping by on what had been left to them. William's sister Mary Anne and her husband Charles Norman lived nearby. Brother Ted, now 20, had also found work and moved to his own lodging.

The post office offered to hire William again, but the taste of freedom and opportunity was too strong for him to settle into a job with no future. He stayed in England only three months—long enough to recover his strength and fall in love. His older sister Sarah Jane (soon to become Auntie Dot) introduced him to a sturdy serving woman who attended the same Baptist church and who lived at the large brick Baptist Tabernacle on Calverly St. Emma Susan Hasell (sometimes Hazell) may have lost her parents early in life. By age five she was living with her widowed great aunt, a miller named Maria Howard. Some years later Maria Howard probably placed her as a servant girl and child's nurse in the home of the prosperous Essex businessman, Thomas Wedlake. Wedlake had taken over his father's iron foundry and shop in the 1860s and produced modern farm implements. He and his wife Anna had moved to their own home called White House where they had three children. At age 13 Emma left them and perhaps Hornchurch to make her living as an adult. She took with her a copy of *The Book of Common Prayer* bearing the inscription, "Emma Hasell, A parting present from

Master Sidney and Miss Hilda Wedlake, November 30th 1880." Since the oldest of the three Wedlake children was 8 year old Robert, and Sidney was 3, Hylda only a year old, the evidence suggests that Thomas or Anna or both gave Emma the book as thanks for her care of the younger children.

Emma was native to the mild south of England and, in a variety of forms, so was her family name—Hasell. Like Sarah Jane Pickering, she was enough of a non-conformist to be a strong Baptist in a very Anglican country. Or perhaps their affiliation was as much with the British working class as with the Baptist church, since the church's members were largely working class people.

William went out walking with Emma who enjoyed both the famous Pantiles with its shops and sheltered walkway lined by white columns and the famous spring water and walks to the edge of town. In her free time she often enjoyed walking to the Southborough neighborhood taking in the stately "cottages" and places like Hamilton Lodge and its adjoining Hamilton House private school.

After three months being nursed and fed by his sister and her friend Emma Hasell, William decided to return to America. He had also decided that his nurse should also become his wife. He had seen enough of America to be sure he would be able to find work and earn money to start a family with Emma.

Emma Hasell, was a quiet, small, straight backed and sturdy woman with sad eyes, a small mouth with thin lips, her brown hair always drawn back tightly across her head and parted in the middle. In all the family photo albums to follow in the next fifty years there would never be a picture of her by her husband or by anyone in which she is genuinely smiling. Contentment is the strongest joy that registers in any picture.

Like many lower class English who had differences with the Anglican establishment, Emma had left the Queen's Anglican faith and become a Baptist. Whether those who choose a minority religion that challenges social order know it or not, they often convert to or adhere to the new church because it offers them a haven from a fixed and low place in the establishment religion. No matter how ordinary and dull their lives may seem, somewhere in their hearts they are nonconformists. Nonconformist, in fact, is the very designation often given to them in official British records. William may have been drawn to Emma for this reason.

Despite William's near death in America and his lonely days walking Texas railroad tracks, the country had nourished his dreams of being someone. He was a convincing talker, and Emma agreed to join him in America when he could send money for her passage. His confidence also convinced his friend Thomas Fearns the harness maker and a laborer named Ted Lewington to accompany him. Fearns had been in the British cavalry and served in the first Boer War of 1880-81[4] in which the South African Boer descendants of Dutch settlers successfully preserved their independence from Britain.

On February 9, 1889 the three young Englishmen were among the hundreds who lined the rails if their steamer as they coasted past the three year old Statue of Liberty with her torch held high above Ellis Island. That island had not yet opened for business, however, and their ship docked at the Castle Garden immigration center at the southern tip of Manhattan Island where Bowery Park now stands. Like all the immigrants, William received a Bible. In it he wrote his name and "Given to me at Castle Garden, NY, 9th Feb. '89". He was in his "promised land." He would never leave America again.

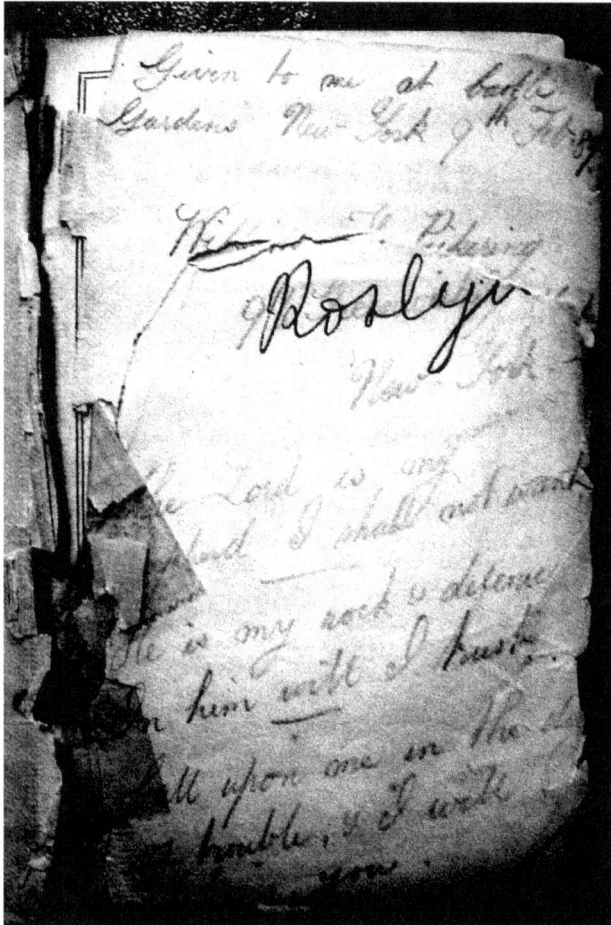

Inscription on Bible given to Wm Pickering at Castle Garden

Whether by chance or purpose, he made his new start in America where the money was, on the estates of the eastern establishment. He took his first job as coachman and gardener on a small estate north of New York City on the Hudson River. By May of 1890 he had already sent Emma the money for her passage. The price for steerage was about $20 (equivalent to $457 in 2006). The average worker earned twenty cents an hour, so William could have saved up enough for Emma's passage in a few weeks or months. In the spring of 1890 he found new work on a Long Island estate as a coachman for socialite Nathaniel Gibbs Ingraham. Ingraham's lineage went back to a prominent New York judge in the early years of the US and he is listed as one of the visitors to ex-president Chester A. Arthur's house the day after Arthur died in 1886. He may also have been a social climber and gold seeker. Some years after he employed William, and when he had won the wealthy Edyth Ward Newcomb away from her rich husband, a copper baron, Ingraham extracted a prenuptial agreement from her promising him $4,500 a year if they ever parted. (In 2006 dollars that is about $106,000 per year.) When they divorced in 1906 after three years of marriage, Edyth claimed he had used fortune telling to lure her away from her husband and then duped her into signing the agreement.

Whatever Ingraham's condition and character when he hired William Pickering in May of 1890, William stayed with the man only three months. William left in August with a brief letter of recommendation in which Ingraham wrote, "I have found him honest & sober & a fairly good man." William soon had work with wealthy young lawyer and future judge, Townsend Scudder whose home lay on the west side of Hempstead Harbor just north of Roslyn Village. William would always remember Scudder as a man who treated him with respect and kindness and who actively tried to make his work lighter.

Ten thousand years earlier a retreating glacier had gouged the harbor out from of the north shore of Long Island. It was broad at its entry from Long Island Sound and narrowed to a hundred yards or so at its inland end. The village of Roslyn straddled that narrow end of the harbor. It had all the amenities America's nouveau riche could desire. The village was already 200 years old but still quaint and occupied by hard working boat builders, fishermen, clam diggers, crabbers and oystermen, and surrounded by a patchwork of forest and farm on its glacial bluffs. It was the perfect pastoral retreat from the booming businesses and banks and their fierce competition in Manhattan.

The railroad had established a commuter line from New York City in 1864, and a telephone exchange had come in 1887. The steamer Seawanhaka put Roslyn on its schedule sailing to and from New York. The tight harbor sheltered by tall hills on the east and west offered a quiet anchorage for the yachts that had begun to fill it. The rich could now live in country estates and telephone their firms. To rush to their offices they could jump on their special Parlor Car of the Long Island Railroad, relax with the paper in their swivel chairs, and order a drink from the steward. Within an hour they would be on Wall Street or Fifth Avenue. To leave worldly cares behind, their yachts lay at anchor five or ten minutes from home. They quickly converted the lands along the harbor into sprawling estates with colonnaded mansions. Even larger estates claimed the higher glacial hills above the harbor. These lands became what novelist F. Scott Fitzgerald called the "Gold Coast."

By the mid 1890s both Roslyn and neighboring Sea Cliff, once a Methodist campground, had become fashionable resorts where city people came for the fresh air and a cooling swim. *The New York Times* on August 10, 1895 summed up the summer season in Roslyn.

> There is a large number of people who enjoy the combination of beautiful scenery and the quiet home life here. The cottages are always occupied in the Summer, and the hotels and boarding houses enjoy a liberal patronage. . . . Roslyn enjoys all the attractions that make the north shore of Long Island a favorite spot. Here you find the Summer girl in comfortable ease. She is not called upon to make frequent changes of costume each day. Instead you find her swinging in a hammock under a shady tree or upon the water, manipulating the oars of a graceful boat, or perhaps wandering through the woods in a manner that indicates a full enjoyment of nature. . . . Wheelmen [bicyclists] make Roslyn a stopping poace during north-shore runs. . . The social side of a Summer existence in

the country is not forgotten by any means. Progressive euchre [a partners card game] parties and other forms of entertainment are of almost always nightly occurrence. [p. 12]

In that day when losers were losers *The New York Times* could also report that at the card party the previous Saturday "the booby prize for ladies went to Mrs. Giriff Conklin, and the men's booby prize fell to Dr. William A. Seimel of Brooklyn."

The most prominent estate of all lay a few miles north of Roslyn, just inside the mouth of the harbor on the eastern shore protected by a half mile finger of boulders reaching into the harbor. This was the estate of banker J.Pierpont Morgan, one of the richest men in America. William Pickering wanted some of this wealth for himself, but he also wanted and earned their respect. William had liberated himself from the English class system, and as soon as he made enough money, he would begin his campaign to keep America's upper crust from acting like the landed gentry back home. J.P. Morgan would be no exception.

Between the wealthy on their estates and the merchants and trade people of the village lay a large economic divide, but it was a divide across which money flowed freely. In little towns like Roslyn a good laborer or intelligent merchant could make a comfortable living. The gentry were happy to provide work for both William and Emma. On the first of June 1890 Emma left her place as a member of the growing Baptist Tabernacle on Calverley Road in Tunbridge Wells. She carried with her a recommendation letter from Samuel Hunt, Sec. of the Tabernacle, writing on behalf of the church and certifying her a member of the Tabernacle. ". . . we can cordially recommend her to any Christian Fellowship she may seek to join. We wish her God speed in the new country." She traveled north to docks of Liverpool and her berth among the many immigrants traveling below decks on one of the fastest and most modern steamships in Britain's White Line, the SS Majestic. The ship made the passage in six days. Later that summer it would set a speed record for crossing the Atlantic. The ship would also take on as her second captain an officer who would later become famous as the captain of the Titanic.

Passenger #356 at the top of the page is "Miss E. Hasell," spinster, age 24.

In New York City Emma took a room arranged for her in the safe confines of the Salvation Army. The Salvation Army, of course, was thoroughly English in origins, a working class movement started in 1865 when William Booth scandalized many staid Anglicans by dramatic preaching in the poorest streets and workplaces of London. With his flowing white hair and beard and his understanding of the poorest classes, he recruited thousands of "soldiers" for his Army of Salvation. In 1880 Booth had sent his trusted 31 year old aid and first Commissioner George Scott Railton to "invade" America "for God and the Army" with seven Hallelujah Lassies. They disembarked from the steamer Australia at Castle Garden in March and immediately began recruiting. The Army established an office at 73 Beekman St. in lower Manhattan, and the year Emma arrived that center sent its first pairs of "slum sisters" among the city's poor. They dressed like the people they served, feeding the hungry, bathing and tending the sick, visiting tenements teeming with humanity to wash and comfort babies or make beds, mend clothes, cook, and sober up drunks. They paid for coffins, washed the dead and dressed them in their final suit of clothes. Although the Army grew rapidly, they were often jeered, mocked and at times physically assaulted. Nothing discouraged their faith or optimism. Emma's English life had been a hard one since going to live with her aunt at age five and going to work in her mid teens as a serving girl. If she was afflicted by depression as my mother believed, she most likely found comfort in the Salvation Army's conviction that no misery was too deep to overcome. The shy and quiet Emma Hasell found safe haven in this Army's camp.

Soon she started work as a waitress and chambermaid for the family of Charles M. and Maud Perry. The Perrys spent most of the winter at 111 Eighteenth St. in New York City's tony Gramercy Park neighborhood, and they had a summer home on the shores of Hempstead Harbor near Roslyn Village. The next summer the Perry's hired William to look after their horses at the summer house. They quickly grew to trust the little Englishman and left him in charge during their winter absence. On November 19, 1891, as Long Island slipped into a crisp autumn, William went to New York City in his best clothes. He wore a stiffly starched white shirt, a white tie with a broad knot, and a dark vest and jacket with a white handkerchief tucked in his pocket. Possibly for the first time in his life he was wearing light gray pin striped trousers. His hair had been pomaded and combed with a sharp crease on the left. He had his mother's high broad forehead, thin straight lip line and intense eyes. He was a short, muscular, compact young man who posed for a picture looking very much as if at any minute he might leap up to catch a runaway horse.

William's destination was the large brownstone church on Stuyvesant Square, St. George's Episcopal Church. It was a church whose congregation included many of New York's wealthiest people. Its choir featured the regular solos of J.P. Morgan. William waited in the vastness of the church for his fiancé, Emma. She arrived with her employer, Maud Perry who lived only a few blocks away. In a quiet ceremony William and Emma said their wedding vows before the assistant priest with Maud Perry and Josephine Nielson as witnesses. They returned to the Perry place on Hempstead Harbor to begin married life in the same building with the horses William tended. Their rooms were in the Perry stable building.

The next few years are almost blank in both family and public records, but for a stable boy and a serving woman the real money and the best estates were on Long Island. Roslyn was also a good place for a man starting a family, and just a year after their marriage, Emma was pregnant. The old village offered rooms for rent and the estates often had their own servants' quarters. By 1893 William and Emma had a room in a boarding house known as the Hayes Homestead. There in June of that year a midwife delivered their first child, a boy. They had him christened in the humble Trinity Anglican church in October. Maud and her husband Charles M. Perry sponsored the baptism of Edward "Ted" Pickering, the first Pickering child. Nine more would follow.

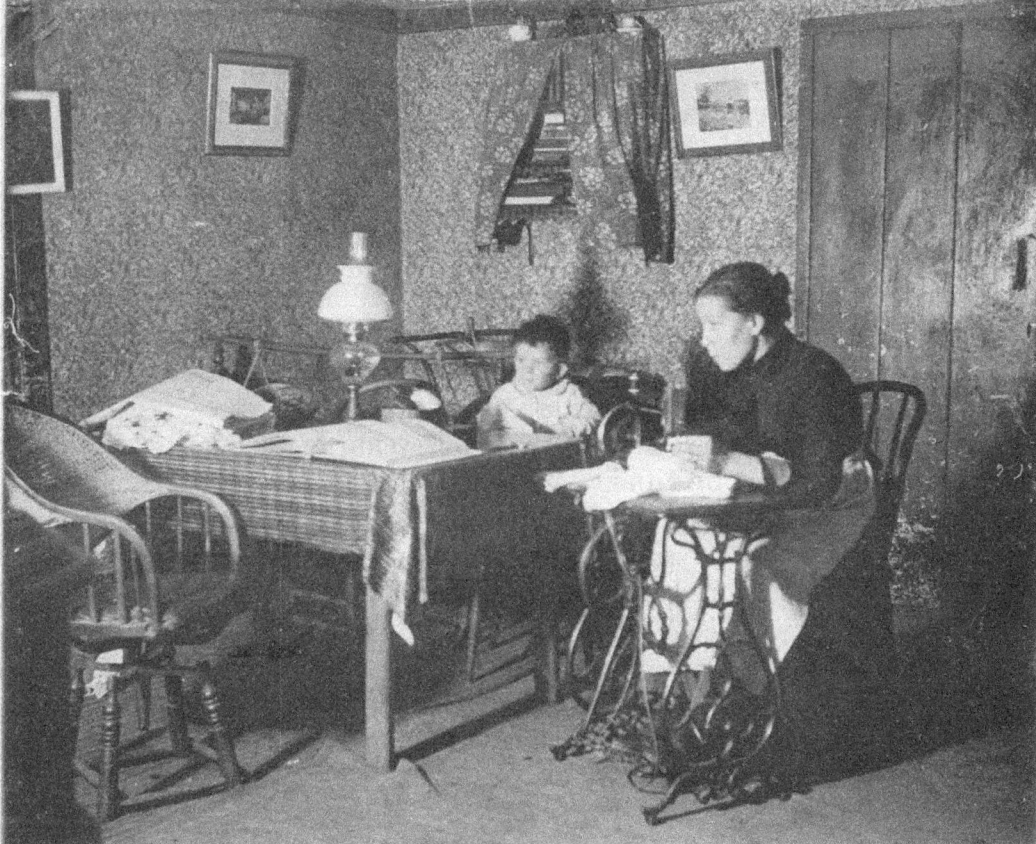

Photo of Emma Pickering and son Ted, by her husband

CHAPTER 6: FOR RICHER OR POORER

William probably never left the Church of England as his sisters did. He brought his Baptist wife back to the church when they were married and when they christened their first child at Trinity Church. They had both put England and Anglican social hierarchy behind them, but in America the Anglican (or in America Episcopalian) Church suited him fine. In England a working man had little hope of claiming the best pews, but in America the pews were not bought or reserved. If Emma objected, she said nothing.

In the late 19th Century, of course, the Episcopal Church in America included many of the wealthy and famous families—the ruling WASPs or White, Anglo-Saxon, Protestants. Most of America's founding fathers and families maintained ties to the church even while declaring independence from its nominal head—the King. Although George Washington's inner religious life remains unclear, he was baptized and buried as an Episcopal. Lincoln was married and buried in Episcopal services. Great men of finance and industry like Cornelius Vanderbilt and J.P. Morgan worshipped as Episcopalians. Two weeks after William and Emma's first child, Bishop Littlejohn, who presided over the baptisms, marriages and funerals of the rich and famous, heard William's Episcopal confirmation vows in Roslyn's Trinity Church.

Trinity Church would soon be endowed by wealthy families and rebuilt into a large church with windows by Tiffany. William, or Billy as he had become known around Roslyn, planned to build his own family and its future on that wealth too. Good horse handlers, carpenters, servants, and grounds keepers who spoke English found ready jobs. The rich preferred white help to black. A literate stable boy or maid who could say a crisp British *Yes, sir* and *No, Madame* had more status than a Negro who said *Yassuh, No M'am*. Billy started where he could and began to work his way up. He was as tough and crude as any working class Englishman. All his life he would blow his nose by pinching his nostrils and snorting the snot onto the ground. He also had the working man's respect for money and class. To that he had quickly added an American's ambition to have it too.

In the next twelve years he would have at least three different estate jobs. Maybe he was restless or ambitious, or just intolerably independent, but more likely his job hopping says the market was good, especially since he never said a bad word about his employers, and no record exists of his being fired. He was doing what he set out to do, work and save and become someone. In the first ten years of life on Long Island he worked for Ingraham, the Perrys, and then as a stable boy for a rapidly rising young lawyer Townsend Scudder. William would later say that his time with Townsend was full of good memories of an understanding man who never overburdened his employees. Nevertheless, he worked for Scudder little more than a year when he and Emma moved to the estate of former Democratic Congressman and ambassador to Netherlands, Lloyd Bryce. This estate had originally been owned by poet William Cullen Bryant, and on Bryce's death the land with a new mansion on it would be bought by steel magnate Henry

Clay Frick. Although Bryce moved in the highest echelons of New York society, he was also a journalist, politician, diplomat and a champion of new American sports for their power to unite "the different classes of society in bonds of friendship, of reconciling the poor to the apparent injustice of social order as it exists, and of exorcising the demon of discontentment . . . " [1] He was an employer Billy Pickering could admire.

The Bryce Estate

Bryce had bought his estate the year Emma and William were married, then later spent $300,000 to turn the eleven room two story hodgepodge into a four story 23 room imitation of a French Loire Valley chateau. William by now, thanks to Maud Perry and lawyer Scudder, had learned to handle horses and carriages. He became Bryce's coachman. Family memory says Emma served as cook, but a multi-millionaire diplomat's estate with a 23 room house had more than one cook. And a sophisticated, well-traveled family would not very easily settle for English peasant fare—toad-in-the-hole, meat puddings, stews, roast beef, and blackberry roly-poly. No one in the family remembers Emma cooking more aristocratic dishes. Bryce's chief cook would almost certainly have lived on the estate, but William and Emma rented a room in one of the boarding houses in "the landing" near the boat docks and the swamp-fed pond that until a few years earlier had powered Long Island's first paper mill.

Bryce's too was a rung on the Pickering ladder. From Bryce's Billy went to work on the other side of the harbor for the family of advertising agent George Card Pease. During the first years in America Billy had begun to take photographs and learned to develop and print his film plates. While he and his family were living on the Pease estate, Billy began to make postcards from photographs. With his children in tow, he would walk up and down the streets of Roslyn Village selling the cards to tourists and shoppers for ten cents each. That was a fancy price in the early days of the picture postcard.

---

[1] Lloyd S. Bryce, "A Plea for Sport," *North American Review* 128 (May 1879), 523.

Billy had also begun to invest in real estate. In 1893 he and Emma bought a 25 ft by 112 ft tract in the countryside beyond Mackay's estate along the main road from Glen Cove to New York City. If they planned to build there one day, they never did.

The 48 acre Pease estate called Wildwood was in fact 40 acres of wild woods rising up almost 170 feet from Shore Road and spreading over the top of the bluff. A curving road led up the hill to the secluded house that Pease kept expanding. The land included a wildlife haven known as Black Swamp where Pease would sometimes take friends from the city who came out for nature watching excursions. He also prohibited all hunting on his property.

Emma and Bill, Tom, Ted, Dorothy, Jack in carriage, Pease house, 1899

Billy did not stay with Pease long before he left there to join some three hundred men building the grandest estate on all of Long Island—Clarence Mackay's "Harbor Hill."

Billy joined other English and Irish immigrants serving the Mackay family, including the sedate Mr. Heckler who supervised the farming operations and Mr. Mercer, the superintendent. Ironically this job as assistant gardener put the young Episcopal Englishman in the employ of a once poor Irish Catholic immigrant family. Clarence's father John had sailed from Ireland to New York with his family in 1840 at age 9. At age 20 he sailed out of New York with others hoping to cross the isthmus of Panama by horse and then sail north to California and join the Gold Rush that had started in 1849. He dug and sweated and lived lean for nine more years before packing up to try his luck in Nevada's rough new mining camp, Virginia City where miners were lifting silver out of the mountains. Mackay began as a carpenter earning $6 a day shoring up mine shafts. After rising to supervisor in the Kentucky Mine and saving enough money, he and partners began buying small mines that they operated as the Bonanza Firm. Four years later in 1872 Mackay's partnership hit the "Big Bonanza" deposit in the fabled Comstock Lode. He married a destitute, nineteen year old girl who had been taken west and then

Harbor Hill: the Clarence Mackay Estate

abandoned by a shylock pharmaceutical salesman. By 1877 Big Bonanza was turning out $19 million worth of silver (over $360 million in 2007 dollars). Within a six year period Mackay and three partners shared almost $300 million (over $5 billion in 2007 dollars). In an age associated with monopolies, combinations and trusts that combined potential rival businesses, John Mackay was a competitor. He used his fortune to form a transatlantic cable company to compete with the monopoly held by John Gould's Western Union. His competition quickly ignited a two year price war that dramatically lowered the cost of international telegrams.

John Mackay remained a shy and generous man and honest employer. He often rescued desperately poor families and gave generously to churches and colleges. Christian good works were not enough to win him a place in society dominated by Anglican Christians, the WASP social world. John had tried to settle his wife and boys in New York City to take their place in America's high society. New York's establishment, however, turned its back on newly rich Irish Catholics. Irish Catholics, especially common ones, were almost as unwelcome as Jews. John's wife moved to Europe to enjoy high culture and fashion, and during their lives she returned to America only twice.

Mrs. Mackay brought her two sons, John and little "Clarie," to Europe and educated them in England. In 1895 a race horse pounding around the track in hot competition threw twenty-five year old John Mackay, Jr. The fall killed him. His father brought 21 year old Clarence to New York to learn the telegraph cable business. Clarence was as different from his father as Bordeaux wine from Guiness stout. Clarence married Katherine Alexander Duer, the Episcopal socialite daughter of a wealthy New York lawyer. When the estate that Clarence had leased burned down seven months after their marriage, John bought as a wedding present for Clarence and Katherine the 648 acre Harbor Hill property, a forest covered glacial moraine 387 feet above the village of Roslyn. The undeveloped land straddled the second highest point on the 110 miles of Long Island. Fitting for a wealthy couple at the peak of American business, the site could be seen from both Long Island Sound to the north and from the Atlantic Ocean twenty miles south across the Island's girth.

Clarence had already begun to parlay his father's great American fortune of the 19th century into one of America's greatest fortunes of the early 20th century. Katherine Mackay commissioned America's leading architect, Stanford White, to design their Harbor Hill mansion in the style of Maisons-Lafitte near Paris. The stone building and the landscaping, barns and other buildings took five years to complete. It set a new standard for the homes of the rich.

All over the New York and New England area architects abandoned the grand country home covered with wooden shingles like Teddy Roosevelt's home in Oyster Bay. Shingles and wood elaborated on an old American motif of the sturdy frontier family. Stone and brick reflected the new sense of power and status of America's industrialists and bankers. In the Great Depression thirty years later the eventual loss of Harbor Hill was called one of the "10 greatest losses to Long Island in the 20th Century" by the director of the Society for the Preservation of Long Island Antiquities.

While lesser men were content to monogram their shirts and handkerchiefs, Clarence monogrammed his mansion. The colonnaded main entry bore a pediment which in turn bore a large royal oval bearing the monogram M. This cartouche, of course, imitated the Egyptian cartouches which usual bore the name of emperors and empresses. Mackay furnished his chateau with hundreds of crates full of European tapestry, paintings, and medieval armor. Harbor Hill could entertain over 1,000 guests at a single party. No other Gold Coast mansion was as large or as modern. Its forty by eighty foot main hall could have swallowed three average Roslyn village homes.

When Clarence's father died in 1902, the year Billy Pickering and other workmen put the finishing touches on Harbor Hill, the $500 million in silver mine property and the cable empire that John Mackay left to Clarence made his son one of the richest and most powerful men in America. Society may have spurned Clarence Mackay's Irish immigrant father and the French wife he saved from poverty, but it could not ignore the expanding Mackay empire. Nor could New York's social elite ignore Clarence's Anglican wife, Katherine Duer whose family history was woven into New York's high society.

To entertain their children or maybe with a mind to expanding the horizons of Roslyn's village children, Mackay's wife Katherine would send word to the village that their delicate daughter Ellin Mackay would like certain children to come to the estate to play. The parents of the chosen knew they had to have their children at Trinity Episcopal Church at the appointed time. The Mackay governess would arrive in the Mackay carriage driven by the chauffeur Donahue. The son of a poor Irish immigrant did not object to his children playing with the sons and daughters of an English immigrant. William and Emma's second daughter Annie Pickering went to visit several times but remembered in her later years little of the visits except the luxury of the house, Ellin's fabulous toys, and the life sized statue of a horse in the Mackay mansion.

Like most wealthy men of his generation, including the most reviled "Robber Barons," Clarence Mackay gave millions to education, religion, and public works. In Colorado, in gratitude for the origins of his fortune, he provided over $2 million for the Mackay School of Mines building and the Mackay Science Hall at the University of Nevada. His wife Katherine Duer Mackay, friend of English royalty and herself from a wealthy family, employed Stanford White, to build the Trinity Episcopal Church parsonage as a memorial to her father, William Alexander Duer. Befitting a woman known for her independence, within a few weeks she announced that as a memorial to her mother, Ellin Travers Duer, she would replace the old 1862 wooden church with one designed by Stanford White. (White had just finished the plans for the church when millionaire Harry K. Thaw, enraged that the architect was having an affair with his wife, shot him to death at a rooftop dinner theater performance in New York City.)

Billy felt no shame in working for once poor immigrants, even Irish Catholics. He had little respect for the "shanty Irish" who lived in squalor and drank hard and sang and fought loudly, but success was stronger than heritage. That was America for Billy Pickering, a place where poor immigrants could transform themselves from Englishmen, Germans, Jews or Irish into Americans; where a poor immigrant could become a rich businessman and employ poor immigrants. American lore says that when Cornwallis surrendered to Washington after the Battle of Yorktown the British band played "The World Turned Upside Down." For Billy Pickering America was England upside down. It was everything that England had not been for his once illiterate mother and for his brothers and sisters and uncles, aunts and cousins still employed as mail carriers, laborers and servants.

Among the employees at Harbor Hill that Billy would come to know well would have been Henry Hechler to whom Clarence gave the job of estate manager in 1907. Mackay recruited Hechler for his university training in animal husbandry. Hechler's three boys went to the Roslyn school with the Pickering children. The youngest son, Ken Hechler, born in 1914, would go on to become a special advisor to President Truman, then Congressman from West Virginia. As a young Army officer at the end of World War II Hechler was assigned to interview Hitler's number two man, Hermann Goering for the Nuremberg war crimes trials.

To document life at Harbor Hill, Mackay would make his one time gardener Billy Pickering the estate's official photographer. Billy would be summoned for baptisms and weddings and the visit of royalty. He worked under one condition: if he sold a single picture to the press, he would never sell another newspaper on any estate. Billy's second son, William Hasell, would later accompany his father to the Mackay estate and said that his father and Clarence Mackay became good friends and Billy's straight laced Anglican ways played a big role. "He never drank or nothing, see, and they could trust him."

By the end of 1901 when Clarence Mackay had completed his Harbor Hill mansion, down below Harbor Hill in the village of Roslyn, Billy Pickering had accumulated the funds for his own nest egg. As the summer petered out in September Billy made a deal with John L. Craft, an elderly widower, to buy an old house on the dirt road along the east side of the swamps and creeks above Roslyn's mill pond. This had once been part of the Kirby lands, a family that owned a large piece of land at the head of and along the upper flanks of the swamps. To pay the $1,700 price and a few other bills, the Pickerings borrowed $1,800 from Miss Alice A. Hicks at 6% to be repaid twice yearly until 1904. The payments stretched a budget that had to feed and clothe six children under ten years old. But with the house he also bought three acres where they would have a vegetable garden.. The house had been built as a simple settler's cottage around 1827 and added to over the years. The dirt lane would never become more than a two lane blacktop, but it also had ambitions in its name—East Broadway.

To meet their mortgage they would have to sell the small tracts that they had bought over the past years. In 1905 they also sold part of their land near the house to Julius Becker of New York City. This begins a pattern of borrowing to grow the business or pay debts or invest in more land. Each time they borrow from Alice Hicks and use their home as collateral. Hicks clearly considered them good for the money.

Few immigrant laborers earned the price of a home quickly. At the turn of the century the average working person earned $428 a year for full time labor. That $1,700, for the old house was equivalent to $129,550 in 2006 money. Widower Craft might have been glad to get rid of the old house. The gravelly land on the hillside had little value. The clapboard house sat a few feet above the lane. From the lane the family climbed a set of wooden stairs to reach the middle floor where most of the living took place. The kitchen was served by a hand operated water pump next to the sink. It lifted water out of the clay foundations of the bluff. A large iron cookstove that burned wood and coal occupied one wall and kept the house warm. In the hot and humid summers instead of heating that mass of cast iron, Emma put a portable, tin kerosene stove on top of it. A small room for wood and coal opened off the kitchen and also a small pantry. In wooden boxes on the floor Emma kept her potatoes, flour, lard, and other staples. A large room next to the kitchen served as both bedroom and living room. A smaller room in the rear of the house on this floor was Dot and Annie's bedroom.

The unheated garret rooms upstairs with their eyebrow windows looking out over the swamps the boys had their barracks. On the coldest winter evenings Emma would heat clay jugs of water on the stove and give them to the boys to carry upstairs for footwarmers. Once they had shut the kitchen door behind them, in the narrow stairwell their breath created a cloud of fog through which they climbed. During the summers the low ceiling of the boys' rooms radiated an oven-like heat into the spaces. The older boys escaped and slept in a tent behind the house. Like most Roslyn homes at the beginning of the 20th Century, the Pickering home had no electricity and no indoor plumbing except the pump. Kerosene lanterns and candles provided light and an outhouse just uphill and behind the house served as toilet.

The boys' summer bedroom tent

The bluff behind the house rose up steeply with trees and brush barely holding the old glacial till in place. The neighborhood wasn't ideal either. Most of the land lay on the hillside overlooking the creeks, ponds and bogs. During the summers mists of mosquitoes rose from these swamps. In the next two decades the mosquitoes would strike several of Billy and Emma's children with malaria. Cut into the bluff at the top border of Billy's land ran the tracks of the Long Island Railroad whose coal fired steam engines sometimes caused brush fires. Along the lane to the north of Billy's purchase lay a small sand mining operation from which the Irish Connolly brothers sold sand for concrete and masonry cement. The brothers also operated a blacksmith forge where they shoed horses, made nails, forged wagon wheel rims, and drank large quantities of whiskey or beer, depending on the season. In summer they eased their ferocious thirst with gallons of beer. In winter they kept themselves warm with quarts of Irish whiskey. Billy and Emma were both teetotalers.

Pickering House on East Broadway, Roslyn Village, about 1910

Billy had bought not for the present but for the future. He was and always had been, both boy and man, someone whose mind was fixed on the future, and he could see it plainly. The land Billy Pickering bought was nobody's ideal home site. Billy, however, again exercised his optimism and his vision of the future. East Broadway, narrow as it was (and still is) served as the shortest of two roads from Roslyn Harbor to the train station a half mile from Billy's new home. The railroad had already made Roslyn's picturesque village and its rolling hills a rural haven for some of the most prominent New Yorkers. Billy and Emma had worked for them and knew the course of their affairs. And the same year he bought his land, on top of the bluff above him Clarence Mackay and his wife had just finished Harbor Hill on its 648 acre estate.

Mackay's grand estate was soon imitated in various sizes. The Brooklyn Eagle for Oct. 7, 1902 ran a story on a new estate being built near Mackay's by businessman A. Cass Canfield. "Brick to be used for the lodge entrance gates and outbuildings are arriving at Roslyn Town dock by the million and farmers about the countryside are kept busy carting them from the dock to the grounds. So much building is going on in and about Roslyn that contractors are put to their wits' end to secure transportation for their men and supplies." America's great fortunes were lifting the fortunes of most Roslyn families, including the Pickering family.

Far more important, but unsuspected, to the future of the Pickerings and to history in general was Clarence Mackay's wife's fierce independence. Katherine Mackay and several wealthy friends poured their status and their money into the movement for the woman's right to vote and for greater independence for women in general. A fellow suffragette who welcomed the resources and attention Mackay brought, wrote, "here was a beautiful and charming young woman, a society leader, longing for a greater stage to move upon than the usual outlet given by fashionable society."[5]

Clarence and Katherine Mackay's Harbor Hill above the Pickering house

Although New York State would not grant women the right to vote until 1917, Katherine Mackay put her name on the ballot for one of two open seats on the Roslyn school board in 1905. Her candidacy fomented something of a local revolution. She had been in Roslyn only 3 years, but she shrewdly sought out a local livery stable owner and brother of a prominent judge to run alongside her for the other open seat. In tandem with John F. Remsen, from whom Billy Pickering sometimes rented an extra cart horse and wagon, she took on the good old boys and their 83 year old incumbent Dr. P.D. Leys. Leys was a formidable Scotsman, a distinguished Civil War veteran, a founder of the Roslyn Congregational church, and Secretary of the local Republican committee. Leys declared, "I can afford to retire but I don't care for those new notions which Mrs. Mackay is bringing into school affairs. Mind you, I'm not saying a word against her, but she's young and impulsive, while I've seen the school children grow into manhood and womanhood."

For a while the election threatened something close to a civil war. Local coach driver Hike Snyder summed it up in words quoted by The New York Times: "Are we goin' to have the old-fashioned schoolin'—readin', 'ritin', an' 'righmetic—or a Noo York fad trainin'?" The report says that Snyder had a loud public argument with one Tom Rivers, but that within an hour Judge Cornelius Remsen, brother of John the stable owner, had convinced both to back the Mackay-Remsen ticket. The judge gathered them and other supporters in the stable, gave them instructions, and soon had them out on the streets preaching for their candidates.

The New York Times said, "It was the greatest election that Roslyn has had in years—perhaps ever. A record vote was certainly cast."[6] Remsen ran on a "3 Rs platform". What reforms Katherine Mackay proposed, the *Times* did not say. Billy Pickering probably joined the record turnout on that balmy summer day with the temperatures in the mid 70s. It was a beautiful day for him to cast his first vote in an American election. Clarence Mackay himself appeared at the opening of the polls, chugging down the main street in an automobile. Women, not yet able to vote in national elections, turned out in unusual numbers. Ninety year old Jane Verity voted for the first time in her life. She said, "I'm not so old but what I know a good thing, I'm not where I was fifty years ago, and neither's the world; so that new fashions in teaching seem quite natural to me."

Roslyn voters gave Mackay and Remsen 253 and 254 votes respectively, 219 of them on a straight Mackay-Remsen slate.[7]

Katherine Mackay would also cause a great public scandal in 1912 when she ran off with a surgeon who was a good friend of her husband's, gave up her three children, and asked her husband for a divorce.

The contrast between the two immigrant family homes—the first generation Pickerings and the second generation Mackays—could hardly be greater, but the next few decades would show that Mackays were on the way down and Pickerings were on the way up. Billy Pickering may also have understood the principle of real estate practice that is an economic version of the law of gravity—that valuable houses pull up lesser homes and the lesser pull down the greater. In this case, of course, Billy's home and the other ramshackle and modest homes on East Broadway had about as much influence on Mackay's as Pluto has on the sun. Both, however, shared in the growing affluence of the village. In 1900 Mackay joined with other millionaires, Morgan and Whitney, to form the Roslyn Light and Power Company to illuminate their mansions, but within a year they had also brought the Edison Magic Candle to light the streets in Roslyn Village.

The new century was a good time to go into business. In the November 1900 election Republican President William McKinley campaigned for reelection on the slogan "Four More Years of the Full Dinner Pail." At his side was a new vice presidential candidate, the Governor of New York, Theodore Roosevelt. The young, dashing and rich Roosevelt was famous for his charge up San Juan Hill in the recently concluded Spanish-American War. Most of America shared his version of the war:

> "Four years ago the nation was uneasy because at our very doors an American island was writhing in hideous agony under a worse than medieval despotism. We had our Armenia at our threshold. The situation in Cuba had become such that we could no longer stand quiet and retain one shred of self-respect…. We drew the sword and waged the most righteous and brilliantly successful foreign war that this generation has seen."

The Democrats fielded once again, the great fundamentalist orator William Jennings Bryan. Bryan was also the anti-war candidate who drew support from one of the country's richest immigrants, steel magnate Andrew Carnegie. Bryan covered 18,000 miles of the country by train but Roosevelt logged 21,000. Billy Pickering could not yet vote, but he had already become a great admirer of Teddy Roosevelt and his populist stand against the super-rich and monopolies. Roosevelt, however, was a frequent dinner guest at the Mackay estate and enjoyed the tennis courts and the pool.

What Emma thought about Billy's purchase of land and the house no one has said, and probably no one knew. His children would always refer to it as the place "Pop bought." She must have welcomed even this little house for her rapidly growing family. When they moved in Emma had four boys and a girl running energetically around the house as well as Wallace George who was not yet one and Robin toddling toward two. In early January of 1902 Robin broke out in measles. He was one year and seven months old. Families expected measles to strike older children without dire consequences, but in New York one in eight children under five died after coming down with measles. It struck down children under two at the rate of one in five. Most died when measles led to pneumonia. Emma nursed Robin and prayed as his body blistered and his fever climbed. In the third week of January he began a rasping struggle for breath. He had pneumonia. As he grew rapidly weaker, Emma rocked him and sang to him and recited nursery rhymes she said for all of her children. With a precision found nowhere else in the 36 years of Emma's "birthday book" diary, for January 22nd she wrote, "Dear Robin died, 10 minutes to 1 o'clock, Wed morn," the moment of his death. They buried him the next day. (He would be the only child to die, and he had been the only child not named for another Pickering, Vickers or Hasell.) For the rest of Emma's life she kept his baby bottle and the two slim books of children's verse sent by his English grandmother when she received word of his birth.

Emma certainly must have known that Billy intended to set up his own business on their land, but whether the prospect of self-employment gladdened or frightened her no one ever knew. She was a quiet woman who had gone from being a servant to the rich to being a servant and nanny in her own home. What she did think would have made no difference to the little Englishman fixed on his own independence. They were both the children of Victorian England, and while they might have been glad to leave behind the English class system, they lived a Victorian family life.

In America "a man's home is his castle," and Billy had one domain where he was monarch as absolute as William the Conqueror—his business and his home. In his work as a track walker, horse handler, gardener and coachman he had been part of a rough and often coarse fraternity, but he ruled his own home in Christian Victorian fashion. He started every meal with a prayer and demanded good manners and respect from his children. If they did not like something put on their plates, he brooked no complaint, and ate what their mother put on the table or left hungry. Every morning he got up, dressed, opened a small cabinet by the kitchen door, and using the mirror that hung inside the door, he shaved with a straight razor. For as long as he lived, he wore white shirts, starched collars, ties, and a vest and kept his high-ankled black shoes shined. He was a small man and the sleeves of his shirts always doubled over the arm garters he wore to shorten them.

Emma continued as a servant in her own home. As soon as she was dressed she slipped on a long white muslin apron over her dress. All of her children remembered their mother in her working uniform—the apron. It appears in most of the photographs that her husband took of her and the children. With the apron on, she began her routines that were framed by the "daily bread." She stoked the big cast iron stove in the kitchen with wood or coal and put inside the oven the bread dough that had been on top of the stove rising overnight. Soon the comfortable smell of fresh bread filled the house, and by evening the bread was gone. She finished each day by putting a new pan of dough on top of the stove to rise. She considered a store-bought loaf of bread an insult to her cooking.

Annie and Bill Pickering at wood cutting, about 1910

Although she limited her menus to the English working class food she knew best, her children would remember throughout their lives several favorites including 'toad-in-the-hole,' a casserole of sausages baked in Yorkshire pudding batter. Meat was often kidney stew. On Sundays she cooked a hot lunch, and in the evenings the meal would often be cheese and onions. The most likely desserts included raisin cake, rice pudding, and cornstarch pudding flavored with lemon peel. In summers the children gathered blackberries and raspberries in the swamps and on the hillsides, and Emma rolled them up into tubes of pie dough and sliced the "roly-poly" into sections, one for each child. In winter she unwrapped and steamed hearty plum pudding and served it with a dollop of rich buttery hard sauce.

Almost as soon as the children could walk they were expected to help in and around the house. Emma cooked and heated the house with wood that had to be sawed and split and piled by the boys after school. Once ready they stacked the firewood in a small room that opened off the kitchen where they also stored bags of coal and where the dog slept. In the summer she would use a small metal oven on top of the four hole wood stove that burned continuously most of the winter. Younger children sifted the ashes to pick out the still usable charcoal or unburned wood. The stoves themselves had to be cleaned and polished. So did the lighting. Dorothy, and later her sisters, learned to take apart the kerosene lamps, trim the wicks, and carefully wash the glass chimneys. Billy put each child to work at five or six years old, prohibited all alcohol, enforced church attendance and Bible reading on Sunday, and felt "cleanliness is next to Godliness." As soon as Emma made sure after the Sunday papers were out, she dressed the younger children for Sunday school." "We only wore our best clothes for Sundays and special occasions," Annie recalled. "We had to keep our shoes shined."

Emma washed both clothes and people in large tin and wooden tubs. The boys would man the iron pump inside the kitchen, and from a shaft that pierced the kitchen floor and the hillside beneath the house they pumped clear cool water. After the wood stove had heated part of it, the bath or the laundry water was ready. To keep her husband's shirts, her aprons and the boys shirts white and crisp Emma made her own bluing from a commercial concentrate. (Adding a little blue to laundry had become a common way to make whites seem whiter.) She also mixed her own starch. Before ironing she placed heavy flat irons on the stove. She taught the girls how to clean them with rubbing wax. Clothes for the entire family she boiled in tubs and scrubbed by hand over a corrugated zinc coated washboard.

1913. Emma bathes little Emma as Annie watches.

Every autumn as the last leaves fell from the trees and the weather turned cold, Billy would gather his children for a trip to one of the local general stores. It was one of the great domestic events that meant each child who had outgrown his or her boots and coat and wool pants would receive a new set. The old clothes, of course, were handed down from older to younger children. Emma patched and sewed and pulled old socks over her marble-smooth maple-wood darning egg to mend them with a woven patch of tough sewing thread. Wallace George remembers that "though often mended and old, our clothes were always clean." Gradually new clothes became clothes for work and play, then rags stored in a box and used around the house or sold to a man who came down East Broadway now and then with his horse pulling a big wagon, ringing little bell and shouting, "Rags, rags, rags."

On cold mornings the children rose before dawn, dressed in front of the kitchen stove, and warmed their feet on its iron fender before they pulled on their shoes and started their chores. They had to carry the chamber pots from the night up the hill and dump them carefully through the outhouse hole. Then they fed the cats and dogs and chickens, gathered the eggs and now and then collected the manure. Dead animals they buried in the hillside sands along with the daily garbage. The carpets that covered the drafty floorboards indoors quickly absorbed the grime of heavy traffic despite daily sweeping. In winter the children periodically hauled the carpets outside to clean them in the snow, then hung them up and beat them with a wicker paddle.

Chickens also provided the cheapest meat. Billy or one of the boys would wring a chicken's neck and Emma would soak it in a pail of hot water before plucking the feathers. Billy raised a pig one year but decided against it as a regular part of the family economy. He had enough money to buy staples in bulk when they were cheap and store them. In the fall Billy bought big sacks of potatoes and onions to store in the cool cellar. The children spent hours wrapping apples and pears in old newspapers, then layering them in a big wooden box alongside the potatoes. In spring when the potatoes in the cellar began to sprout, Emma sent several children into the cellar to sort them and dig out the eyes with short paring knives while others cut the green sprouts from the onions.

The most perishable food Emma kept in a large wooden icebox, supplied every other day with a fresh block of ice delivered by the local ice and coal dealer. As the ice melted it dripped into a collecting pan that had to be checked regularly and emptied before it flooded the kitchen. Despite her growing work load, every afternoon Emma would take off her work apron and house dress, put on a black skirt and a clean white "waist," a short apron that covered the front of her skirt. Then she would engage in an English tradition she never gave up—sitting down for a few quiet minutes with a pot of hot tea.

The number of children and the work necessary to maintain them and the house they lived in required discipline, and Billy enforced rules and routines with stern and uncompromising determination. Defiance boiled his temper, and he glared over his rimless glasses. When his temper exploded, he whipped his boys with his belt. If Dorothy or Annie broke the rules flagrantly he gave them a stinging slap on the cheek. When order reigned, as it usually did, Billy immersed himself in his work, often whistling hymns and at times pouring his confidence into "A Mighty Fortress Is Our Lord." Billy and Emma were held together by four important bonds—their mutual commitment to abstinence, work, family, and faith.

The Pickerings had no sooner moved into their new home than Billy began building a one story concrete block building next to the house. Its front wall was flush

with the edge of the road, the rear wall buried in the sandy hillside. He put a large glass window on either side of the central doorway and over the doorway he hung a wooden sign advertising newspapers, candy, cigars, and Kodak developing. Soon he would advertise himself as a photographer. Besides his early sales of postcards even before opening the store, his first commercial success in photography came from his pictures of a local disaster.

In November 1902 on the east side of the harbor one of Roslyn's grand old homes burned in a spectacular fire. Hundreds of citizens came out to watch or help. Several crews of firefighters pumped water into the flames hour after hour and finally saved some of the exterior and the foundations. In a day when many people read and quoted poetry, this home was revered for its deceased owner, William Cullen Bryant, a bestselling poet. School children into the middle of the 20th century read "Thanatopsis" and "To A Waterfowl," both poems about the approach of death. Bryant had purchased his 40 acres from a friend who not long before had bought this land and other pieces from Roslyn farmers. The building Bryant bought had been built in 1787 by local Quakers. Bryant, who was also a lawyer and part owner of the *New York Evening Post* had come to Roslyn in the vanguard of the rich businessmen who, by the time the Pickerings arrived, had transformed the area from a quiet farming and harbor town into a landscape dominated by the elegant estates of New York business people. The uncontrollable fire nearly destroyed the famous landmark. In February 13, 1903 *The Roslyn News* carried this small advertisement: "Photographs of the Bryant Place after the fire, are for sale by "Wm. Pickering. Mail orders promptly filled."

The beginning of William's passion for photography is marked by only a few photographs. Less than a half dozen photographs date from before the purchase of his house. His passion for photographer may have been the strongest motive in opening his store, and he had started taking pictures and making postcards while working on the estates. His first camera was an unpainted wooden box not quite big enough to hold a baseball and his son William passed it on to his sister Annie who left it to her daughter Anne Claire. The pine wood is light and thin, dovetailed at the corners. The wooden top slid open and a glass plate of film could be slipped into two parallel slots at the back of the box, ready for exposure. To expose the plate, he removed a cap from the lens, counted sufficient seconds, the replaced the cap.

Sometime after he advanced to better instruments Billy wrote in an arc of bold white letters above the hole for the lens, "MY FIRST CAMERA" and below the hole, "W PICKERING." The camera is the same in almost every detail as the first cheap handheld camera invented by William Fox Talbot around 1839. Fox called his cameras "mousetraps." Billy Pickering was trapped by photography for the rest of his life.

Wm Pickering's "My First Camera"

Even as Billy worked on his store, his former employer George Pease wrote to him in mid December of 1902 offering him not only his old job but a place to live on the newly expanded estate. When Billy refused, politely, Pease's regret letter had a bite to it. On December 28 he wrote:

> Dear William,
> Of course I too am sorry you will not come to us again but I dare say you have decided for what appears to you to be best.
> I thought when you left last March it was because I could not then guarantee you steady employment and that you said you would gladly take up your old work again if a way offered to accommodate your large family. When I wrote to you the other day I did not anticipate such an upheaval as we have had here, but I thought in good faith that my letter would be a Xmas proposition that would be pleasing to you. Especially did I wish to show you my interest because of a rumor that you are getting out of favor at Harbor Hill and that a change of management is contemplated there which will be prejudicial to you.

Your photography is very good as a pastime but I very much doubt if it is in your interest to try to make such a business of it. However, this may be because I know so little about it and it is none of my business now any way. I shall not refer to it or any other like subject again. I am not sorry I wrote you because seeing my way clear at last to get my cottage where it would save you all and us further question about your children I merely kept my word by suggesting the idea to you. I have had this in mind ever since I bought on the shore as I told you when you were here last summer.

It takes time to bring these things about, but it seems to me that I now have no further obligation in the matter and can only wish you all good luck and freedom from worry. These recent events show us how far you have drifted from us in a season. "Out of sight, out of mind."

With our best wishes for the New Year.

Yours truly,
George Pease

Pease did not understand the young Englishman. Billy had been taking photographs and printing them on postcards for at least a year while he was working for Pease. His son Bill remembered, "My father would make up these postcards. And us kids would go with him and walk up and down with the people selling those postcards. I think he figured a dime a piece and that was a lot of money then." To Pease's chagrin, Billy's profit from his hobby held out a hope of independence with which Pease could not compete.

If Pease didn't understand Billy, Billy may have understood Pease very well. Pease was not a man to stay put for long, and despite his economic success, he often suffered depression. Pease had come to New York in 1889 to write for *The New York Times*. Two years later he switched to *The New York Sun*. Two years after that he went to England to work for the printing company Scott and Browne. He was back in America in 1896 and soon began work on his Roslyn estate as he grew richer on advertising income. In 1906 when Billy had become an established and popular shopkeeper, Pease sold his estate to a nephew of the great steel baron, Scottish immigrant Andrew Carnegie, who in turn found it too small for his great ambitions and sold it to Countess Yarmouth. Her brother, brother socialite Harry Thaw, had recently stood trial in one of America's most famous murder cases—the shooting of architect Stanford White. White, of course, had designed Mackay's Harbor Hill and Roslyn's Trinity Church for Mrs. Clarence Mackay and Thaw's bullet put an end to his supervision of new church.

Pease left Roslyn for a new estate in Vergennes, Vermont where he could keep a stable of thoroughbred horses. They had no sooner moved than a sleigh ran over his wife and left her crippled. Eighteen months later, on June 26, 1910 at age 50 Pease raised a pistol to his right ear, pulled the trigger. [8] Nevertheless, on August 13th of that year the social notes section of *The New York Times* about the Vanderbilts, Whitneys, and other members of high society carried this note: "Mr. and Mrs. George Card Pease are at Vergennes, VT for the rest of the summer." George Pease had already decided to stay for eternity.

A few years later a reporter spelled out the reason for Billy's success. "He has the bulldog tenacity of the typical Briton, holding fast to a purpose until its fulfillment." Pease had either manufactured the rumors of Billy's disfavor at the Mackay estate or the rumors were wrong. Billy would soon move up from being a gardener to becoming the tycoon's chosen photographer and supplier of newspapers and magazines. First, Billy had to establish his store and darkroom.

By the time he had opened his store in 1904 he was using a camera with flexible cloth bellows that allowed the photographer to move the lens backward and forward on a track for more flexible focusing. Over the windows of his new shop a sign proclaimed:

WILLIAM PICKERING GENERAL PHOTOGRAPHER,
KODAK DEVELOPING & PRINTING . SODA . CIGARS AND SOUVENIRS.

The window itself was half pasted over with signs for newspapers and magazines. Inside the shelves under the glass counter and the shelves behind the counter overflowed with candies, cigars, cigarettes, drinks, and magazines.

    With his business open and making a profit, on December 3, 1904 Billy went to the Nassau County Courthouse in Mineola and before the County Clerk Thomas Cheshire the little Englishman put his left hand on the Bible, raised his right hand and took the oath of U.S. citizenship. Had he waited 14 years because he equated owning a business with America? With his business he would both support and transform his wife and children into unpaid labor. With his citizenship he would challenge the richest men in America to deny his freedom. At this point in the story onto the stage emerges the dark side of the man who my mother so often said I was just like.

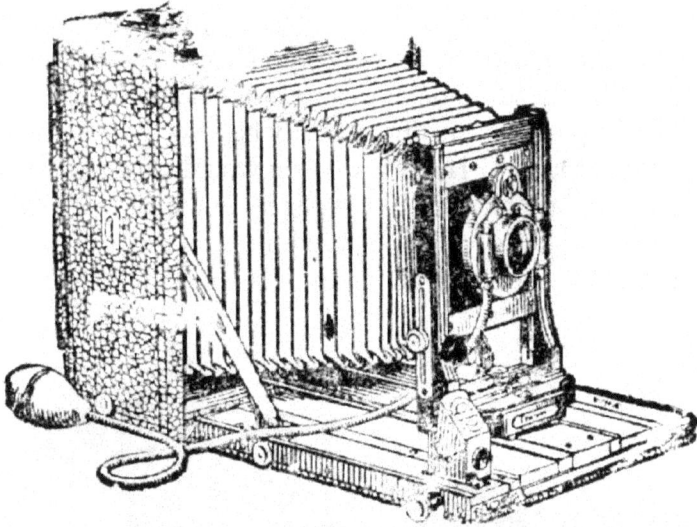

WILLIAM PICKERING
GENERAL PHOTOGRAPHER

Developing and Printing   News Agent
Cigars, Candies, Tobacco, Stationery
Sheet Music, Curios, Novels
Old and Very Rare Books Bought and Sold
Trolley Stop 35, Kirby's Corner

Tel. 31-J   -   -   ROSLYN, N. Y.

CHAPTER 7. WILLIAM OF ROSLYN

"His life's story is interesting because of his varied life and pursuits, but it is an example which counts for much in a time when one is constantly hearing or reading of men who have lost courage, grown faint hearted, and are berating everything but their own lack of faith and persistent effort. . . " Brooklyn Daily Eagle story on Billy Pickering, 1908.

For an entrepreneur with modest means and heavy family burdens (seven children and more coming), William Pickering had chosen two good businesses for the future—photography and newspapers. His friend, Thomas Fearns, who had sailed with him from England, chose a business for the past. Like his friend Billy he also opened a shop, Thomas Fearns and Son, Harness Makers. Harness making would soon become a specialty niche as autos rapidly replaced horses. Newspapers in the early 1900s, however, reigned supreme as the source of quick, in-depth information about the world, especially the business world and the prices of hundreds of stocks upon which great fortunes rose and fell.

Pickering Boys loading baled papers

Billy had secured as customers the names of some the wealthiest families of the Gold Coast—Mackay, Whitney, Phipps, Scudder, Munson, Pratt, and Bryce. The big estates often bought as many as a dozen copies of a single paper. Billy had launched his business on a rising tide of American wealth.

In the first months, or even year or two, the newspapers and racing forms popular with the wealthy came in by train from New York City, tied or wired into heavy bales. Billy had the boys go up the hill with wooden sided wheel barrows and bring the papers to the store. The boys tried to arrive at the station in time to meet the coal fired, soot belching steam engines that brought both passengers and freight. From the baggage car a freight man tossed to the sheltered concrete platform bails of newspapers tied with wires--*The New York Times*, T*he Herald Tribune, The Morning American, The Mirror, The Telegraph, The Racing Form, The Evening Sun, The Journal*, and *The Brooklyn Eagle* along with Italian and German papers.

Famous magazines accompanied the papers. *The Saturday Evening Post* sold for five cents, and *Life* cost ten cents. The children and Emma sorted them and marked them with the names of subscribers. As soon as the special weekend inserts began arriving on Thursdays, Billy put the children to work grouping them, then inserting them in the papers. The boys, each with a delivery route, made local deliveries with their wheelbarrows or from sagging newspaper sacks slung across their shoulders. In winter they pulled their papers on sleds. On the west side of the harbor towards Port Washington they took shortcuts through the paths made by sand miners. On the east side they went two miles along the shore road to Glenwood Landing. They charged twelve cents a week for daily papers, eight cents for Sunday paper.

By any definition Billy Pickering ran his business with child labor, a practice abhorred today from UN to Uganda. In the 18th and 19th centuries, however, many families were de facto sweat shops. But that was an era when most family labor was farm work or home crafts and parents were considered compassionate employers. Americans believed conditions at home or on the farm either nobody else's business or healthy discipline.

This time was the crest of the great wave of European immigrants. Almost every New York City tenement building had one or two sweatshops, and families that did not work in someone else's sweatshop, often set up their own. In thousands of apartments the rattle of foot powered treadle sewing machines droned on from morning to night. Families of Bohemian cigar makers rolled two or three thousand cigars a week and sold them for $3.75 a thousand. Billy Pickering's store and darkroom were far nicer places to work than city tenements, though he was a hard driving boss, and having him as a father after work was no vacation.

He never took his children out of school for work, but after school when other children were roving the sandbanks, playing in the village streets, throwing baseballs or snowballs or skating, the Pickering kids were assembling and delivering papers or mixing chemicals and rocking trays of prints in the darkroom. On Saturdays and the free hours of summer days the boys liked to sneak up East Broadway to the blacksmith shop run by the two Connolly brothers. Bill Pickering, Emma and Billy's second son, used to play in the Connolly's sand bank with his brothers. They came come home with sand in their hair and clothes when their caves collapsed on them. The Connolly brothers were "rummies, drunks" Bill recalled. They were usually well lubricated with whiskey in winter and beer in summer and they welcomed young visitors. They allowed the boys to "blow the forge" by pumping the big bellows. After one of the Connollys had fitted a horse with shoes, he would reward the boys with shiny horseshoe nails that they bent into rings.

Emma could tell from the coal dust on their clothes and hands when they had been to the Connolly's. If Billy found out, "We used to get hell from our father," Bill says. Few things upset his thrifty father than grown men drinking away their earnings. He would lecture his sons on the evils of alcohol and drunkenness and possibly certain kinds of Irishmen.

Bill and his brothers and other boys would sometimes organize a foot race down East Broadway, up Main St, and back to East Broadway, or they would tromp around the woods or play on the sand banks. As they got older and automobiles became more common, "we'd play poker with the numbers on the cars for pennies." For more excitement they would follow the town's new motorcycle policemen to Judge Remsen's office when a motorist had been caught violating the law. "They'd chase them down the east turnpike up the west turnpike and then they would bring them down to Judge Remsen. Boy, that was some time. Well, here they come and we're having some fun laughing. And these city slickers come through town—aww they had their leggings on and you know bring them in to the judge. It was a circus. Well maybe there were half a dozen kids. Them days that was a lot."

Annie recalled that at home, "Most entertainment was a family affair. We had a stereoscope and enjoyed seeing the beautiful pictures, a lovely music box, a phonograph which used cylinder records. Later a Victrola with a horn on it. Also an organ. My brothers made toys. Sometimes they made dancing dolls. They used a jig saw. Wagons were made from old pieces of wood. And baby carriages or bike wheels. We would harness the dog to the wagon. He would also pull the sleigh in winter."

Pickerings and friends' goat and dog about 1908

Emma Pickering and dog Jud about 1915

A couple of years after Billy opened shop he bought a horse that his son Wallace said "had a permanent posture which gave the impression he was prepared to hurdle." He may also have bought a harness from his friend Thomas Fearns. Twice each day, beginning at dawn, Billy had one or two of his boys hitch the brown horse to a small cart sheltered by a canopy and lead it up the hill to the Roslyn station. The horse also extended their delivery reach into outlying estates. The Pickering children delivered their papers to Roslyn Village, Roslyn Estates, and two miles away in Glenwood Landing and Bulls Head (a name later changed to Red Ground). The boys coaxed and cajoled the horse, fed it scraps of bread and old apples. The horse quickly became fond of them. He soon became the family's chief mode of transportation for any destination that required hauling papers, supplies or photography apparatus. For the heavy Sunday papers Billy hired a second horse and wagon from the Remsen stables.

Ted and Bill began delivering papers "before we could read them." They collected twelve cents a week for the weekly papers, and for a Sunday paper eight cents. As soon as they could, the boys began to read what they delivered. Bill would remember that when he was ten he delivered the papers carrying the headlines that shouted the news of the great 1906 San Francisco earthquake that nearly leveled the city.

No natural disaster approaching this magnitude had ever befallen America. Natural gas mains broke and ignited fires while broken water lines turned firefighters into spectators. The city and the US Army collaborated on blowing up whole blocks of buildings to create firebreaks. Many property owners intentionally set their damaged buildings on fire to qualify for insurance payments from policies that did not cover earthquake damage. The natural catastrophe, aggravated by human actions triggered a social and political crisis that even Hurricane Katrina almost a century later could not equal. Mayor Eugene Shmitz posted a proclamation with these words:

> "The Federal Troops, the members of the Regular Police Force and all Special Police Officers have been authorized by me to KILL any and all persons found engaged in Looting or in the Commission of Any Other Crime."

Police, vigilante patrols, and army troops under mayor Eugene Shmitz's orders shot and killed about 500 looters. Twenty-eight thousand buildings were completely destroyed. Over 200,000 people lost their homes. Three thousand died. The catastrophe, coming in the midst of growing American prosperity and power, both at home and abroad, shocked Americans with the knowledge that their great cities were not invincible and their government had its limits. The rapid rebuilding and recovery of the city, however, more than restored America's confidence that it could conquer all adversity and adversaries.

The newsboys worked on the front lines of mass communications in that era before radio and the spread of telephones. They delivered the headlines that would be etched in the world's history and in their own understanding of the world. Billy Pickering sold the news and his children delivered it. The boys, and later the girls too, may not have liked the work, but they liked being part of something important, being first with the news. At times like the San Francisco quake public attention focused on their service as it now focuses on television. Most people in and around Roslyn first heard of events like the sinking of the Titanic, the outbreak of war in Europe, and America's entry into that war when one of the Pickering boys or girls delivered a newspaper with screaming headlines or when they went to the store to pick up a paper and soak up local gossip before it became news. Billy sometimes posted a flier with large letters in the window announcing a big event customers could read about if they bought a paper.

Billy's store, in fact, with its strategic location on the short route between village and railway station soon became a kind of community center where citizens rich and poor often met and discussed the events of the day and passed on the gossip and rumors from town and country estate. Delivering newspapers brought the kids into the top and bottom niches of Long Island society. Wallace George, called "Buster," never forgot the scenes of drunken men and women he saw when he delivered papers daily in Roslyn's several bars. His older brother Bill also delivered to the saloons that occupied each street corner around the station. His impression was that Roslyn then had, "more rum shacks than there were churches. All the corners were bar rooms. When Prohibition came they all became gas stations."

The boys also learned the petty power plays of the business world where a person often had to "go along to get along." Frank Cody who managed the Roslyn train station for almost 50 years commandeered the Pickering boys to help him clean the station. "Had to," Bill remembered, "Otherwise I couldn't sell the papers."

Just as the newspapers and magazines catered to all tastes, Billy's store also had something for everyone. Smokers had their choice of loose tobacco and papers for rolling their own or packaged Lucky Strikes, Camels and Chesterfield cigarettes at ten cents a pack. In those days the working man's cigar cost five cents. A "good ten cent cigar" included Sweet Capparil, Hassinan, Mecca and Honest Tobacco. Good panatela cigars went for twenty-five cents. Tobacco chewers could buy Mechanic's Delight or Ivanhoe for ten cents a pack. A variety of candy bars went for five cents each and loose candies two for a penny.

Those were his "penny profit" items. Photography immediately brought higher margins and more interesting work. The rapidly growing popularity of automobiles brought with it a state law requiring all drivers to have photo identification. Billy made chauffeurs' photos at four for a dollar, and he would photograph a bride and groom or wedding party and receive $3.00 for a dozen copies. For these pictures he had purchased a large wooden camera whose lens slid forward and backward on two tracks for focusing the image on the glass plate inside. Often Billy designated one of the boys as helper to carry the big tripod and the cases with his glass negatives, flash pan and the calcium carbide powder that he ignited for flash pictures. (His family knew what "a flash in the pan" meant.) His helper also prepared the horse and wagon and served as driver. Billy used his contacts to grab another new opportunity: he became the local coroner and jailer's chosen photographer, and his boys often took him to photograph the dead and the accused. *The Brooklyn Times* noted this new practice in an article announcing "Nassau Rogues' Gallery." By order of Sheriff Foster, the report said, William Pickering of Roslyn would take two views of each of twenty-six accused prisoners and pictures of those convicted would be retained for a permanent "Rogues' Gallery."

The Pickering Store and The Family, An Album

Ted, Dorothy, Tom, Buster, Jack, Arthur, Bill with Emma; Annie in cart
September 1908. Headlines read: "Mark Twain in Battle with Armed Burglar"

Emma and children with the family delivery horse

Dogs and handlers gather to search for murderer
(Photo by W Pickering, from Bryant Library Local History Collection)

Wm Pickering about 1905 with parrot

Emma with (from left) Annie, Arthur, Buster, Jack, Dorothy, Tom, Bill, and Ted

When President Teddy Roosevelt handed over the presidency to William Taft in 1909, Roosevelt's staunch supporter, Billy Pickering traveled to Roosevelt's Sagamore Hill home in Oyster Bay to photograph the grand homecoming. Roosevelt had served only one elected term because he had made a mistake he sorely regretted—he had promised not to run again. He kept the promise and left the White House with a national popularity enjoyed only by others who had or would depart in a coffin.

The owners of big estates would now and then summon Billy to take pictures of a wedding or for family passports, but his steady customer among the wealthy was his neighbor and friend Clarence Mackay on the Harbor Hill estate above the Pickering house. Young Bill remembers going with his father to Mackay's to photograph the wedding of Mackay's first daughter, Katherine.

The way Billy's son remembered the event is typical of how his father worked and of his relationship with Mackay and many other clients. "We used to carry big bags them days, them cameras, you know, I went with my father. I can see him now. He took exclusive pictures that nobody's ever seen since. Unless they got out of the Mackay house somehow. That was the agreement. He paid my father pretty well. He didn't want no publicity or nothing, see. . . ." He also remembered the night he tried some of the Mackay high life when his father's attention was elsewhere.

> Course the butler knew me, and they all knew me, and Mr. Mackay [too]. . . . You never seen such a spread in all your life. All this stuff in that big conservatory, and there's a bar room, and there's a bar there, these butlers and stuff, a lot of them knew me and I never drank much. [But] I guess I'd had a couple. I said to myself, 'You better watch out.' He'd [father] beat me right in front of them if he knew it. Finally I seen Mr. Mackay, and he said [to my father], 'Now Billy, this is one day I want to have a drink with you. I want you to have a drink with me.' I know my father. . . . But I think he put his lips to it anyway. And then he [Mackay] said, 'When you get ready to go home William, there's a box being made up for Emma.' Now that's my mother's name. He knew her well too. He said, 'There's a box being made up for you to take home to Emma.' Lord you should have seen what they put in that box. Cakes and oh, man, must have been a box that big. Because he knew there was a bunch of us kids. So anyway we go to the front door and John Mackay was there with the car and everything ready to go home. I can see it now. Away we went.

Emma Pickering in coat handed down from Ellin Mackay

As the photography business picked up, Billy began taking more and more pictures of his own family. Every year or two he propped a long wooden ladder against a morning glory covered wall and arranged his children on it with the oldest at the top and youngest at the bottom.

By far he preferred photographing his youngest children, often with their mother. Relatively few photos show the boys or the girls in their teenage years. The reason may well be that his strict discipline and enforced labor aggravated the normal friction between teenagers and parents.

Billy loved children, including his own, and as a man who knew poverty and hard labor he had compassion. As his children's employer, however, he either set aside his compassion, or lived by his own definition. At best, we can say that he made his way up life's ladder by believing no job too hard or demeaning for him or for the life he aimed to give his family. Therefore, no job and no hard labor should be beneath his wife and children. No matter freedom the children lost to the work demanded by their father, the children with their good manners and dedication to their work became daily ambassadors from the Pickering store to all corners of Roslyn and outlying areas. Both parents insisted on good manners, and the compassion that makes good manners genuine came from their mother, and possibly from their father's public sympathy for the underdog.

At the same time the store began to acquire growing popularity as a community gathering point. The chauffeurs, butlers and coachmen from grand estates not on the delivery route or whose owners were impatient came to pick up the papers set aside for their employers. For H.C. Phipps, the Scottish immigrant who grew rich in steel mills with his friend Andrew Carnegie, the genteel, tall and handsome Irishman Dick Mallon drove in from Old Westbury. From lawyer-stockbroker Charles Auchincloss' estate came a very different Irishman, a short chubby laughing, teasing man with an ever-present pipe sticking out under his fedora hat. The girls, the most frequent objects of his teasing, often forewarned the children with "Here comes that Paddy." From the estate of financier E.F. Hutton in Westbury came Percy, a tall, serious English chauffeur.

Chauffeurs, businessmen, servants, workmen, writers, and villagers mixed with each other, an informal news and gossip forum that became an integral part of Billy's store. Billy soaked it all in. Their talk became the new American's education in civics and politics. His working class English upbringing and his fierce independence matured into American populism and a disdain for the exercise of power through wealth.

By 1908 Billy thought he had finished his family and established himself in the center of Roslyn's civic and business life. He joined Foresters of America, a fraternal group inspired by England's Royal Foresters, who claimed their roots began with Robin Hood, that same Robin Hood whom Billy's sister Sarah Jane claimed for them as an ancestor. The Foresters dedicated themselves to "Unity, Benevolence and Concord" and pledged themselves to "Promote virtue, increase knowledge and to inculcate upon the minds of those who enjoy the privileges and the duties required of them as Ancient Foresters."

If Billy had been a wealthy man, he might have tried to rule the village as he ruled his family, but he knew his powers and his limits. His channeled his public efforts into leading civic organizations and promoting popular causes. He became an active member of the Business Mans Association, and The Chamber of Commerce. He served as president of The Roslyn Exchange Club. He helped organize and became President of the Long Island Newsdealers Association.

He became the official police photographer for the Town of North Hempstead, taking part in the modern innovations of law enforcement. On one occasion the county called him to take pictures of a Nassau politico who had just died. He took along his son Jack. Jack had often served as his father's subject when new film had to be tested, and his father was forever admonishing him, "Smile, damn it!" As they propped up the dead politician, Jack leaned over to his father and whispered, "Let's see you get that SOB to smile."

Billy had met Theodore Roosevelt and, like many Americans, he saw Roosevelt as a fighter against the arrogant power of wealth. Roosevelt had become president on William McKinley's assassination in September 1901. He was only six years older than Billy and about the same height--short. Roosevelt took control of the presidency with speed that shocked many people in the business and political world. One of his first acts to challenge what he called the "tyranny of wealth" embodied in the new Great Northern Holding Company, a railroad trust that included J.Pierpont Morgan. A few years later Billy Pickering would also confront J.P. Morgan.

A month after Roosevelt won his first elected term in 1904, Billy Pickering took the oath of American citizenship and became a voter. In 1912 Billy threw himself into Roosevelt's doomed Progressive or Bull Moose Party campaign for presidency. T

The Progressive Party and Roosevelt campaigned with a religious fervor for a "New

Nationalism" that included the vote for women, workman's compensation, a "Square Deal" for unions, and a national income tax. Billy went out recruiting for the Party. Other Roslyn Bull Moosers included Cornelia Bryce for whose family Billy had worked as a laborer.

Roosevelt beat his former Republican friend Taft, gaining 27% of the popular vote but losing to Woodrow Wilson's 42%. When Roosevelt lost the election, Billy's son Bill remembers several men gathering in front of the store and its Roosevelt posters, building a celebratory bonfire. Since the Pickering house did not yet have plumbing, Billy seized a bucket from the kitchen and marched a few feet across the garden plot to the store where son Bill watched as, "Dad took and threw a bucket of dirty dishwater on them." Roosevelt who practiced boxing and judo and carried a pistol in the White house might have approved. Roosevelt, despite his privileged upbringing, had become Billy's political hero and validated Billy's own disregard for inheritance, wealth, and privilege. All these activities led him to become, as he described himself, "Roslyn's bad boy and trouble hunter."

Billy's first successful civic crusade aimed at passing a bond issue to turn the swamps across from his house into a park. He could be accused of feathering his own nest because the park would increase the value of his property. However, the mosquitoes that emanated from the park had brought down scores of people all over the village with malaria. The bond issue passed easily. The swamps today would be a federally protected wetlands, but to the citizens of Roslyn in the early 20th century they were a reservoir of disease, death and muskrats. Young Bill Pickering found that he could put on his high rubber boots and earn a little extra money with a muskrat trap line from which he sold the furs.

William Hasell Pickering whacks
a newly trapped muskrat.

Although Billy had little time for recreation, he became active in the fight to preserve public access to "Barrow Beach" (now Bar Beach) on the west side of the harbor. Since the founding of the village almost two centuries earlier the shores and waters of the harbor had been used by oystermen, clammers, net fishers, crabbers, boaters, and swimmers. Now some of the estate owners, disturbed by the growing population and its intensifying use of the beaches, put up signs declaring the sands private property. The wealthy brewer Rudolph Oelsener built a tall board fence that blocked access to the 28 acres of shoreline that he claimed as part of his 300 acre estate. Enraged villagers showed up at a December 1908 public hearing and won the day for public access. Billy became a passionate defender of public access against the interests of the big estate owners.

Billy not only talked, he went to the beaches in front of the estates with his boys rowing and dared anyone to throw him off. His son Bill was with him when they rowed up the east shore of Hempstead Harbor to the J.P. Morgan estate in Glen Cove. Billy ordered his son to row straight onto the beach. They pulled their boat onto Morgan's beach and Billy, wearing his usual white shirt, and tie, vest and high top shoes, stepped out onto the sand. Morgan's men had come to confront him. His son remembers, "The gardener—Morgan used to hire all ex Marines in his banks and everything--he hollered at my father. He knew him. 'Get off Billy. The Old Man's up in the house watching. He [father] says, 'You tell the Old Man I want to see him.' Oh, my father was, everybody tell ya, he was a fighter."[9] If Billy's hero, Teddy Roosevelt, could confront Morgan, so could he. Like Roosevelt, he would not stand for the "tyranny of wealth." After all, hadn't he come to America to leave behind the English class system?

Billy, of course, shared J.P. Morgan's business credo: "Do your work; be honest; keep your word; help when you can; be fair." (Aldrich, 216) Fairness is what Billy also demanded of others and why he had come to Morgan's beach. Fairness was the theme of his community activism.

The rich landowners along the west side of the Harbor found the beaches below their estates increasingly populated with village residents and visitors. They began to post Private Property signs and build walls or fences to keep people off the beach. Behind the political scenes they worked to have their beach claims officially recognized. Billy Pickering joined the fight to keep the beaches public. He encouraged people to go by car, bicycle or boat and use the beaches. The estate owners and the owners of vacation bungalows or their hired help would try to chase them from the beaches. The bungalow owners often paid the Town of North Hempstead for their space, then received a handsome rent for their houses—rents that Billy's son Bill said often reached $1,000 a month. Bill says he got his start in the real estate business "meeting people on the road wanting to know where you could find a bungalow for rent."

Billy Pickering had also hung out his sign as a real estate agent, but neither his nor his son's Bill's business gave him any hesitation about fighting to keep the beaches public.

He wrote a rousing letter to *The Roslyn News*. He began by calling readers' attention to a meeting the night before, noting that the audience included "half a dozen public spirited citizens of Roslyn and at least 50 representatives of various corporations, and private individuals whose main object seems to be philanthropic projects for the benefit of their fellow citizens." About the philanthropy he was being sarcastic. The letter goes on:

> Probably one or two may have been sincere in this object, but, the
> majority, on the other hand were generous enough to give a few crumbs to

us poor little sparrows while they grabbed the whole loaf, meaning the entire shore front, (or what is left of it) for their own personal gain.

Glenwood is practically isolated now and will be completely so as soon as the plans of one or two other corporations are completed. Roslyn comes next for wholesale obliteration – no more fishing, swimming, skating, or 'clamming'; you will be boxed in as tight as h___, and if you do not wake up your beautiful Lake will disappear entirely. We are not opposed to any improvement for the public benefit and which will be progressive, but, we are opposed to false philanthropy and generous offers with strings to them. The Town of North Hempstead and Long Island generally has had a few deals handed them lately, which benefited private parties more than the citizens at large, including the disappearance of their shore rights in wholesale quantities.

What use are the beautiful state Boulevard doing us if we have no shore views or outlets to the shore, no parking spaces in our one horse town, Incorporated villages of a population of about a dozen privileged persons and a few dependants, with dead-end roads and a sign, 'Private Beach, No Bathing,' facing you?

Are you aware that in about a continuous 12 miles of shore front in Hempstead Harbor, and Cow Bay, the people have a bare 200 feet of bathing beach with a parking and bathing limit of 20 or 30 minutes? The rest is all gobbled up by the favored few and the people do not get a view of that particular shore front in their drive, except a bird's eye view from the top of Beacon Hill.

Wake up and back up the people that are fighting [for] your rights or lose the balance of Hempstead Harbor shore Fronts.

William H. Pickering, Sr.

Politicians who knew where their money and votes came from didn't appreciate the scrappy little Englishman who accused them of selling out. His son Bill accompanied him to a public hearing in Manhasset about whether the beaches should be kept open to the public. Bill remembered, "He got up and he told 'em off. They knew him and they hated his guts."

Billy concluded his attack on privilege and politics by saying, "Now gentlemen, I got nine children. They're all gonna grow up. They're all gonna have a car. They're going to get married and they're going to want a beach to go to."

One of the commissioners replied, "You're nuts, Billy."

He was nuts in the sense that anyone who has fallen in love is nuts, and Billy had fallen in love with American freedoms and his adopted home town of Roslyn. He was willing to risk scorn by displaying his love for his new home town in biblical Mosaic form that reflected his faith. Preserved in his papers are typed pages, the tablets on which he wrote "Ten Commandments for Roslyn." They have somewhat more humor than the commandments Moses brought from Mt. Sinai.

TEN COMMANDMENTS FOR ROSLYN

1. Thou shalt love Roslyn above all other towns, for Roslyn is thy hometown; thou shalt speak no evil of her; thou shall be loyal to her people, worthy of the great men and women of her past, confident in her present, and full of hope for her future.

2. Thou shalt guard Roslyn from the hosts of evil that would invade her and destroy her soul. The saloon, the gambling den, and the House of iniquity shalt thou crush under thy heel, for they are enemies of both God and man. Thou shalt keep the good name of Roslyn clean and without stain or blemish.

3. Thou shalt elect as thy public servants in political office men of strong character, without fear of favor of the boss or the ring, eager to conceive the best interests of thy people. And when thou hast elected such a man thou shalt stand by them and support them and encourage them, for their temptations are many and their burdens are not light.

4. Thou shalt exalt thy public school and honor it all the days of thy life with the best of teachers, buildings, and equipment, for the school is the cradle of democracy. Thy children are here and they shall be the citizens of tomorrow. No training is too good for them and no preparation superfluous.

5. Thou shalt defend the health of Roslyn from the death that lurks in marshes, swamps, and heaps of filth. Thou shalt swat the fly, and kill the mosquito before she is hatched. The tubercule bacillus shalt thou drive before thee with the sun and fresh air as thy allies.

6. Thou shalt build good roads and keep them good. For by her roads is a village known for good or ill on Long Island. Thou shalt not be content with sand in thy cup [pot] holes, but only with oil in stone and tar. Eternal watchfulness shall be thy motto, that the roads may not unravel nor their supervisor forget thee.

7. Thou shalt keep the Roslyn beautiful. The hills, the trees, the waters that nature hast given her thou shalt preserve in sacred trust. No hovel of man shalt thou permit to to disfigure them. Thou shalt keep thy homes and thy dooryards clean and cheerful. Thou shalt burn the caterpillar in his tent. The waters shalt thou purify that they may bring thee life and strength. The future of thy town shalt thou plan with care and diligence that thy growth be not haphazard but full of thought and loving care as the plan of a mother for the growth of her child.

8. Thou shalt go to church. Thou shalt not consider thyself too wise nor too busy nor too good to spend an hour or two on Sunday with thy neighbors in the worship of God. Thou shalt not send thy children to church, thou shalt bring them there. Thou shalt offer thyself to the minister and the officers of the church with the service of God and your community.

9. Thou shalt honor thy neighborhood house with thy support and presence. Thou shalt meet thy neighbors here on equal footing. Thou shalt work together here for the common weal. Thou shalt play together here with all thy heart and strength and mind. Thus shalt thou know each other better and thy friendships shall multiply.

10. Thou shalt not take unto thyself any graven image of a community secretary. When thou findest the man thou desirest thou shalt make him thy lord and master. Thou shalt obey him. Thou shalt do as thou art bidden. Thou shalt serve on committees where thou art put and not intrude on committees where thou art not put. Thou shalt encourage thy Secretary with thy service, thy loyalty, and thy friendship. So shall ye win many battles together.

Maybe it becomes clear why his love of his new home and his activism never led him to run for office. He was too plain spoken and too committed to speaking what he thought was common sense. In the last month of World War I, with Americans flush with pride and imminent victory, he had the guts or the gall to object to a monument to WWI veterans. In a letter to the editor he noted that he and other business people already contributed to the building of "the finest Memorial Hall on Long Island" and that building was already falling into disrepair. A few passages from his broadside against the memorial vouch for what modern activists call "speaking truth to power."

"It is the most outlandish project in Roslyn in some time and we have had some bughouse propositions handed to us in the past."

"Yes, by all means let us have another monument, paid and erected by these very generous gentlemen, not as a memorial to our brave sons, but a memorial to the egotism, aggrandizement, and conceit of these very generous men." [The promoters would do better to] "fill up the mill pond, and turn it into a cemetery, in charge of said gentlemen, with the stipulation that all graves should be surmounted by a monument or memorial," [and to] "use the Memorial building as a mausoleum, and mortuary chapel: as by their action these gentlemen take it to be useless as a Memorial, and start the project with one or two first class funerals of these said gentlemen, as we could well be rid of them and they would also be out of harm's way."

Billy Pickering championed the underdogs against the growing power of wealth, but the rich also respected him as a self-made man who knew what he was talking about. As a businessman risen from the rank of immigrant and former coachman and gardener, he straddled two worlds and easily made friends in both. Many of the rich moving to the North Shore gold coast, like Clarence Mackay, were themselves immigrants or first generation Americans who were still plain spoken and often undiplomatic.

In September of 1908 Billy had become a public figure, and a major New York newspaper, the *Brooklyn Eagle*, sent a reporter to write a story of Billy's success and the character behind it. The September 26 full page article on Billy and his family showed Emma and eight of her children lined up in front of the store on which Billy had already added a second story framed with wood. The caption below Emma and her children declared, "All Are Hustlers and All Are Cheerful." This was the front that Billy orchestrated for the rest of the world and that may have been his dream, even while the way he enforced his iron will was assuring that it could not be.

The article is an accurate picture of the surface of family life into which Billy and Emma's last child, my mother, would soon be born:

To-day, of the nine children born eight are living, and it is as amusing as it is interesting to see how each has its place in the working plan for their mutual benefit.

The writer happened in the store late one afternoon, just as the news wagon stopped to deliver the big bundles of evening papers. Before it came to a standstill it was surrounded by young Pickerings, and the way the great packages were handled by these little laddies was a lesson in industry.

Every load was a staggering one, but it reached its corner safely, and the work of untying and sorting and folding was begun at once. There were two who seemed only just beyond the baby age, but what they lacked in size and years they made up in spirit. The elder of these two [Wallace, 7] was inclined to give orders, and, dumping a big package carelessly where the littlest one [Arthur, 5] was gravely folding and counting, said: "here get this ready for the wagon." The little brother looked up with eyes that betoken anger, but after a steady, reproving glance, said: "You tend to your work and I'll tend to mine," which he certainly did.

      If the children are at school and Pickering away photographing on the big estates where he has a steady patronage, his wife wheels the baby [Annie], awake or asleep, into the store, and is as cheerful over the interruption as if she had nothing else to do. . . .

      There is always a lot of work to do developing for amateurs, and the eldest daughter [Dorothy] is an able assistant here, as well as in housewifely duties.

Among the reporter's conclusions we read:

      Pickering's life is a lesson for it teaches that the family bond is an important factor in success; that children may be helps and not hindrances; that sobriety, good temper and optimism hasten one on the road to prosperity. . . .

      "These factors, with an unfailing cheerfulness, seem to explain why William Pickering of Roslyn, L.I. locally known as 'Billy' Pickering is at last having success meet him more than half way."

      Reporters are easily fooled or easily fool themselves when they arrive with the outline of their story already in mind. The reporter should have spent a few minutes investigating the import of a sentence he tossed off as complimentary: "Therefore, no job and no hard labor should be beneath his wife and children." Perhaps this is too much to expect of a reporter doing a story on the man who had rights to distribute *The Brooklyn Eagle* to some of its wealthiest readers. The reporter, like all reporters, was here today, gone tomorrow. He would never know that five of the boys and the two girls would slip away from home without telling their father, often under cover of the night and find their own work, rooms, and eventually their wives or husbands. Four of the boys would become suicides and one of the girls would try twice.

Emma with (left to right) Ted, Dorothy, Tom, Buster, Wm, Arthur, Jack, Annie in wagon, 1908

Sunday papers required two horses and wagons, one rented

Annie Pickering driving family delivery car for a beach outing (others unidentified). About 1922

CHAPTER 8. THE BEGINNING OF THE END

In the winter of 1910 after only eleven years in America, Billy's store provided reasonably well for his wife and eight children. Those eleven years of hard work had aged both of them. At 45 Billy's hair had receded from his high forehead, but he was still a trim and sturdy man with a bit of fire in the eye. He stood straight and talked straight. His wife Emma at 43 looked older than her husband, her wrinkles deeper, her face wore a full time tiredness. Her once fine skin had thickened. Time, gravity and the care of children and a husband had pulled down the corners of the eyes and mouth. Both Emma and Billy had developed those two vertical lines that run from the bridge of the nose and inside terminals of the eyebrows up onto the forehead. Billy's daily uniform continued to be his vest and white shirt with high starched collar and a tie. Emma's uniform was her ever present ankle length, white or checked apron over a long skirt that ended over high topped laced shoes.

Emma Pickering now working by electric light

Their oldest child, Ted, had turned a strong and sturdy eighteen. The youngest, Annie, had turned into a long haired, big eyed, beautiful five year old and was already folding papers and mixing chemicals in the darkroom. The full work force now numbered eight plus Emma when she had time from cooking, cleaning and washing. They still used the outhouse perched on the sandbank behind the house. Emma still cooked under a shed in summer. In the evenings she tidied the kitchen, kneaded the dough, patched trousers, darned socks and read the Bible or her prayer book. The children studied by the light of oil lamps. Yet W.H. Pickering, Photographer and News Dealer, had expanded his store with a second floor where he kept old books and a few antiques, and he was indeed the success celebrated in the *Brooklyn Eagle* two years earlier.

A picture taken in the fall of 1910 and printed on an advertising flyer shows him and Emma standing by the ladder full of eight children, Annie at the bottom and Ted at the top. Until that time they both believed they had completed their family and knew their future. In the picture, however, the top two rungs of the ladder are conspicuously empty. Annie Pickering would later say that one of the empty rungs was in memory of the baby Robin who died. The other rung was for the child that had just begun to stir in Emma. If Emma did not yet know of the unexpected child of her 43rd year, she certainly knew by the time the family sat down for Thanksgiving dinner.

On July 13, 1911 July 13 Billy sent his sons up East Broadway to the number 35 trolley stop at Kirby's Corner and told them to take a trolley to Port Washington a few miles up the west side of the harbor from Roslyn. When they returned that evening, their mother was lying in her bed holding their newest and last sibling, a girl. The name Emma gave the new child suggests finality. She named the child after herself—Emma—and after her family-- Hasell. (Her father and mother appear in English records as Hazell, but that's not unusual.) The mother could not have known that this last child would also be the one who most strongly resembled her.

Years before I began writing this story my mother, a woman of few superstitions, had clipped from a newspaper an astrological prediction for her birth date: *"You born today are endowed with a fine mind, a great love of home and family and talent for mathematics and science. Your loyalty and sense of responsibility are outstanding, as are your conservatism and conventionality. You are extremely versatile and, if you do not lose confidence in yourself (it's a Cancerian tendency) can become highly successful in any career you choose. You could turn to a literary career and shine at it, or a business connected with books; could excel in real estate, or geology, music, medicine, or architecture. Traits to curb: jealousy and overpossessiveness."* She had scrawled a note on it, "most true but not math."

I have no more respect for astrology than I do for voodoo, but I have great respect for my mother's ability to recognize herself in a mirror. She was always very conventional and conservative. She underlined the passage that said she could turn to a literary career and shine at it, but she made no comment in the margin. It was one more encouragement for her to continue trying to record a life she had struggled futilely to understand.

From this point in the story, with apologies to others in the family and to readers who prefer a broader brush, I will report events and people largely through my mother's eyes. Practical reasons also call for this narrower story. From my mother I first heard the stories of Pickerings and Vickers. From her hundreds of bits of unfinished thoughts and scribbled memories I can mine the facts for the most coherent story. That story will be, of course, her version of the family, elaborated from and checked against many other records and memories. The personal reason for following this final member of Billy and Emma's family is that in a biological sense when the second Emma was conceived, I too was half created--half my genes resting in each cell of this new Emma Hasell.

Long after her father's death and her own suicide attempts, my mother spent much of her life trying to construct and reconstruct the story of the forces that had shaped her character and her life, especially those forces that had settled within her the well of melancholy and depression that never went dry. Most of her pondering was bounded by her childhood in Roslyn. Since she was looking for the source of trouble, her memories dwelled more on her father than her mother.

Like all children's impressions of their parents, my mother's picture of her father survived in vignettes of those habits which made him stand out in the family and in his community. Photographs of him in earlier years show a slim handsome man with sharp eyes and a serious set to his jaw and a wrinkle of concern in his forehead. This man had long disappeared by the time he became a force in my mother's life. She remembers her father as "a short, chubby man with yellowed teeth." When he was engrossed in work he had a habit of sliding his tongue over his lower lip. When he was in a good mood he whistled religious hymns. The little man of great faith in himself and his God particularly liked to whistle, "A Mighty Fortress Is Our God."

The loud arguments between sons and father and the whippings terrified her. One argument in which her father threatened her brother Jack with a knife left her terrified of all knives and their possessors. When the traveling knife and scissors sharpener drove his horse and cart down East Broadway ringing his bell, in the night that followed little Emma would dream of men with knives and wake up trembling or screaming.

Open doors at night frightened her. In summer the window and the door from the girls' room to the wooded hill behind the house were opened and the openings hung with an airy curtain to keep out mosquitoes. Little Emma lived in terror of something or someone coming in and had nightmares about this room and the open door and window throughout her life.

This life of childhood fear, however, did not fill all her hours. She found a safe place from this terrifying world of the huge figures that crowded the little house, from her brothers' teasing, and her father's moods. She took possession of a low but large closet under the stairs that led from the living room to the upper bedrooms. It had a small square window that looked out on a rock garden. She made that closet the room in which she and her few dolls pretended a future full of flowers and kind people.

The dozens of surviving photos that her father took of her do not show a frightened or even a shy child. In these she is a pleasant, sturdy little girl playing in the snow, romping with the family Newfoundland dog Jud who she came to think of as her own dog, posing placidly with her brothers, playing on a makeshift see saw, posing in adult clothes. In a few of the pictures she wears a smile, but in none is she laughing. In most she is posing dutifully. Smiling for the camera, or at least the family camera, did not come easily to her mother either, in fact only one of hundreds of surviving photos shows her with even the hint of a smile. As one of her granddaughters who knew her well said, "What did she ever have to smile about. She had ten kids and no washing machine and a husband who loved to run away and buy antiques and then come home with a barrel and say, 'Look what I have here.' He would have just what Mr. So and So wanted." That find would pay for his entire trip, but did nothing to relieve his wife's burdens or lighten her soul.

Emma and daughter Emma and dog Jud

The growing tensions between Billy Pickering and his older children may be reflected in words he wrote on the back of his wife's *Book of Common Prayer* on January 6, 1913. "This book is the property of the most faithful wife and mother in America, always the same in trials, troubles, and joy. God prosper her and bless her. I make one request of my boys and girls, love your mother always and never forsake her, she is your best friend and adviser."

The inscription is a coded admission that he now knew he was neither their friend nor adviser. They hardly had to be reminded of this, or the fact that their mother was often the peacemaker and their protector. Her daughter Annie would one day look back and say, "I will never know how my mother was able to be so cheerful. I know she had bad days keeping peace in the family." She was the savior of all the children. Her second son William Hasell, as a tough, blunt speaking veteran of two world wars said, "My mother was a different woman than my father. My mother was very quiet, calm, you know 'cause if she hadn't been, us kids life would have been miserable. I hate to say it, but you've heard that saying too I guess. The English are very strict. You see, my father being English in those days why he was pretty strict. He was strict. I know we got some beatings and boy you'd never forget. My poor mother she saved us many a times."

The few times their mother left home for more than a trip to the village or to church, she would dress up and take little Emma with her to Kirby's Corner to catch the trolley to Port Washington, and from there inland to Mineola, the county seat and a thriving turnpike town. "Our usual mission," my mother recalled, "was to take shoes to the cobbler for repair. For my mother "The trolley was more like our own vehicle than the train." Unlike the train whistle screaming out of the bowels of a boiler, the trolley's bell sounded little different than a dinner bell. When they had returned home from these trips, her mother inevitably laid out an afternoon tea with black and white flat key cakes.

For the first six years of my mother's life, family routines went on as they had before her. The world transforming, booming American industry and invention had already changed Roslyn. In 1901 Clarence Mackay and several other wealthy investors had created the Roslyn Light & Power Company to light their estates and the streets of Roslyn. The first electric street light appeared on West Shore Road just outside the village and not far from where Billy Pickering was working on the Pease estate. Billy and his sons and scores of people from near and far gathered around to marvel and talk about its steady, unflickering gow.

The Pickerings did not connect to those power lines until Emma was old enough to remember electric lights replacing the kerosene lanterns. The Roslyn Water District formed in 1910 to run clean water throughout the village, but again, the Pickerings would wait several years before connecting. In 1907 trolley car service started between Roslyn and the county seat in Mineola six miles south. The fare for this early version of "light rail transit" was fixed at a very affordable five cents (a price that would also doom it as operating costs rose and competition from cars grew). As early as 1902 the American Automobile Club had attracted 23 foreign and American cars to participate in a performance competition in the hills around Roslyn. A giant baby carriage-like vehicle called the Locomobile was touted as stopping in 130 ft. from a speed of 30 mph. By 1908 Billy Pickering was shooting pictures of the Vanderbilt Cup Races whose drivers included Vincenzo Lancia, Louis Chevrolet, and Eddie Rickenbacker who would become a WWI fighter ace and then president of Eastern Airlines. Cars racing on the newly

opened Long Island Motor Parkway (with the odd acronym LIMP) averaged 54 miles per hour. Six cars also undertook a 20,000 mile race from New York west across America and Siberia to Paris. The automobile had become the rich man's toy, and the quite rich Princeton president Woodrow Wilson declared in 1906, "Nothing has spread socialistic feeling in this country more than the use of the automobile, a picture of the arrogance of wealth." He reflected a common American distrust of the noisy, smelly machines, but he exhibited the naivete about American optimism and ambitions that would eventually prove fatal to his political life.

While socialism became an increasingly popular theme, what most Americans wanted was not to ban what they had, but to have what the rich had. Billy Pickering wanted a car to replace the horse that pulled his paper wagon.

As Billy photographed the races and hoped for his own car, the man who would sell Model Ts to socialists was already at work in Detroit. A young mechanic and race car builder named Henry Ford had recovered from near financial disaster with the help of a $28,000 stake from investors, and he had begun to build simple cars for the amazingly low price of $825. In 1908 he opened one of the country's first assembly lines and soon took the radical step of raising his workers' minimum pay to $5 a day and cutting their hours. By 1916 an assembly line worker could buy Ford's Model T for $360 or 3 months' wages. As writer Jim Rasenberger noted in his book *America 1908*, "By the time Wilson became president of the United States in 1912, even socialists would be driving Model Ts."

Billy Pickering the small businessman, however, had already bought a 1910 Jackson car when Emma was three years old in 1914. No more hitching the wagon to pick up and deliver papers. No more feeding the horse and cleaning up after it. Turn the crank on the Jackson and off he went. Driving, however, is a set of hand-leg-and eye movements best learned by the young, and Billy turned over the driving and maintenance to the boys and later to Annie.

Wallace was just old enough to help Ted and Bill as "assistant mechanic" and he reveled in his responsibility for the luxurious machine. Its brass trim shined like gold. He kept its kerosene tail lights filled with fuel. The older boys loaded the running board tank's two compartments with the water and calcium carbide chips. The driver would open a valve that allowed the water to drip on the carbide to make the acetylene gas that burned with a fierce white light in the front headlights. The Jackson, like most cars of its day, required constant maintenance. When Wallace helped brother Bill with the weekly tune up that might include removing the oil pan and filing the ends of piston rods, "He and I often had pieces left over following a repair job, yet the car would run."

In the first ten years of the new century America had become a world class military power by ousting Spain from Cuba and the Philippines, becoming the world's major source of oil, the greatest steel and timber producer, and the creator of Roosevelt's "Great White Fleet" that showed 250,000 tons of American firepower around the world and proved that the mother country, England, had been supplanted as "ruler of the waves" by her offspring. Prosperous farm families and a giant wave of rapidly multiplying immigrants had ballooned the population to 90 million by 1910. The immigrants often led desperately poor lives in linguistic and ethnic ghettoes, but they lived on hope and most also sensed the growing power of their new country and encouraged their children to speak its language. Billy and Emma had added eight children and their business thrived on the new prosperity. Billy had become an American with American optimism. Emma lived most of her life in the house and in the store.

Then as always in American life the average citizen looked to the lives of the rich and famous for clues to the future, for entertainment, for fashion, and to assure themselves that being rich and famous didn't mean being happy. The world of the arts, theater, and high society, then as always, did not fail to educate, entertain, scandalize, inspire, and offer vicarious thrills. This was especially true around Roslyn Village where so many of America's most accomplished and powerful men and women had taken evening, weekend, and summer refuge from city life. Billy and Emma's children would soak up this new world in the making and be as different from their parents as any generation ever had been or ever would be.

Alongside the changes in the American life style, forces were gathering for even bigger changes. As Clarence Mackay busied himself with electricity and telegraph communications, his wife Katherine Duer Mackay hosted the first meeting of the Equal Franchise Society at Harbor Hill on November 2, 1908. Among the prominent men and women working for women's right to vote were Katherine's aunt, the novelist Alice Duer, educator John Dewey, and a board of directors of 21 people. By February 2009 over 300 people had joined. Some members, said the *New York Times*, "engage in active daily work for their bread and butter."

Katherine Mackay didn't work for her bread and butter, but with the time and resources of a wealthy woman she had already set about making changes in Roslyn Village. In 1905 she had become the first woman elected to the school board. On Christmas day that same year her gift to Trinity Church was the promise of a new Parish house, a memorial to her father William Alexander Duer. Its designer would be none other than America's most famous architect—Stanford White. But, no, her mother too, Ellin Travis Duer, must have a memorial, and that would be a new church to replace the board and batten church built in 1862 and in which she worshipped along with the Pickerings and other working people. Katherine Mackay said she would be willing to pay $40,000 for the building and another $5,000 for landscaping (over $1 million in 2007 dollars). In choosing White, she made Roslyn a bit player in one of the world's greatest scandals of the time. Before the foundations of the new church could be laid, White would become victim of his past debaucheries, and his death would sell unprecedented stacks of papers streaming out of Billy Pickering's store.

White, a tall, red-haired, mustachioed and very macho 250 pound brute of a man had led a life full of fast and adventurous women and high living that sealed his fate. On the night of June 25, 1906 Stanford White was having a drink on the rooftop garden of the Madison Square Building he had designed. The chorus of the show "Mamzelle Champagne" was singing its final number and the lines, "I challenge you. I challenge you to a duel, a d-u-e-l." At that moment Harry Thaw, the multi-millionaire heir to a railroad fortune, walked up to White's table, pulled out a pistol, and in front of hundreds of witnesses pumped two bullets into White's head and another after White fell. Thaw then walked back to join his wife.

Earlier that year the shooter, Harry Thaw, had married the famously beautiful showgirl and Gibson girl model Evelyn Nesbit. When she confided in her new husband that she had been seduced or possibly raped by Stanford White before their marriage, Thaw decided the infamous and blustering White should die. The "murder of the century" followed by the "trial of the century" swept newspapers out of Billy Pickering's store to slake the public's thirst for details of the classic love triangle played out in their own backyard. To add to the sensation, Evelyn Nesbit's had risen from the poverty of life in the tenements with a single mother to become a sought after model and at age 17 a dancing girl in the famous musical *Floradora*. During two trials witnesses gave lurid details of Stanford White's love nest with its red velvet swing and Thaw's expulsion from Harvard for "immoral practices" that may have included sexual assaults on other men. In social circles he was often known as "Mad Harry" Thaw. In private, with dozens of women, including Evelyn he was a whip yielding sadist.

Evelyn, however, was no innocent. She had played off Thaw against White, hoping to get White to marry her. After she married Thaw she fired him up with tales of her affair with White and of White's prowess. All this and a press campaign by Thaw's mother to highlight White's debauchery sold newspapers like nothing ever had. In addition the state had to try Thaw twice because his lawyers mounted a novel insanity defense. Thaw, they set out to show, suffered from an insanity peculiar to American men--"dementia Americana". It was not a permanent insanity, but temporary (and so the hope was for a temporary stay in a mental ward).

The lead attorney for the defense was the pint-sized Delphin Delmas, famed in California courts as the "Napoleon of the Western bar." He put the beautiful and supposedly grief stricken Evelyn Nesbit on the stand to describe how White had raped her, then to describe how the fact had driven Thaw temporarily insane. Jurors deadlocked—five for insanity, seven against. In a second trial in January 1908 the jury found him not guilty by reason of insanity, and the judge committed him to the Asylum for the Criminally Insane at Matteawan, New York from which his mother helped him escape in 1915, flee to Canada, and finally return to the US where he was judged once more sane, and being sane, excused for his escape.

Life's typical hybridization of vice and virtue determined that the grossly immoral life of Stanford White should end with the construction of Roslyn's Trinity Church with several windows created by White's friend Louis Tiffany. As arrogant as White was, he had never been able to push around Katherine Mackay. After his death she continued to dominate his firm, insisting that Trinity's design echo the great hall in Harbor Hill. "When I first saw the completed church," she wrote to the firm, "I was horribly shocked to find hideous dark brown rafters . . . Now what I want the firm of McKim, Mead and White to do is this: Correct their error in the color of those rafters and trim at their own expence . . . I want samples submitted to me and I want you to see that this work is started by Monday next."[10]

Katherine Mackay's generosity also brought privilege that suited her assertive personality. With the new church came a new minister, the Reverend Norman O. Hutton whom Mrs. Mackay persuaded, we don't know how, to leave his larger church in Mineola. Perhaps to his chagrin, his choice earned him the widely used epithet, "Mrs. Mackay's rector."[11]

The dedication of the church on March 22, 1907 brought a huge crowd that included almost the entire village as well as visiting dignitaries who arrived in shining new automobiles such as Roslyn had never seen on its dirt streets and in such numbers by railroad that wagons and carriages were borrowed from neighboring towns to transport visitors from the station. Elegantly dressed men and women occupied every seat of a special parlor car from New York City. *The New York Times*, reporting the event noted the range of celebrants. "'Boss, d' y' s'pose dey allows cullud pussons in de church?' asked a venerable negro, whose snow white whiskers and hair framed an earnest face. The aged negro was assured that he would be welcome and he joined the other worshippers in the church, which is to know no color distinction."[12]

African Americans were not the only minority present. Sitting with Katherine Mackay were Mr. and Mrs. Benjamin Stern from the prominent Jewish family who owned Sterns Department Store in Manhattan. The crowd filled every one of the 650 seats in the church and hundreds stood inside and out. Among them were the Pickerings, but whether standing or seated we do not know. Together with the fine music and solemn prayers, Mrs. Mackay's hand-picked thirty year old minister, only two years out of seminary, took over from the Yale educated and recently resigned fifty-year old Rev. Isaac Peck. Peck had opposed Mrs. Mackay's plans for the new church.[13]

Rev. Hutton may have been an inspired choice judging by the reputation he built in his career, but he was not inspired by Trinity or its congregation. Within two years he had answered the call to become minister at the nearly defunct and decrepit St. Chrysostom's in Chicago. It's congregation had dwindled to 28 families and rain was pouring in through the roof tiles. This was the kind of challenge the young clergyman wanted. Later in life he reflected, "I — at 33 — wished for challenge and hard work."[14] In a year he was leading a reborn church with a 30 member Women's Guild, 50 members in the Men's Club, 35 in the Boys' Club and 12 in the Girls' Club. Despite Hutton's later reflection that he wanted more challenge, the Pickerings and others must have been convinced of his great devotion to Trinity when, halfway through his farewell sermon, he was "so overcome with emotion . . . that he had to leave the pulpit."[15] *The New York Times* contributor did not specify what that emotion was or how Hutton expressed it. When the celebration was over, another Mackay reform had been established in Roslyn's social life.

Although Hutton served Roslyn only two years, his new style had served Katherine Mackay's cause well. The controversy had involved not only Peck and Mackay, but many other stalwarts at Trinity, among them some of the wealthiest. Mackay's opposition, when faced with the inevitable, had withdrawn their support in Roslyn and without the usual assent of nearby clergy, they built a new Episcopal church in nearby Westbury.[16]

On November 2, 1907 the Pickerings attended the new Trinity Church's fall fair. At the behest of Katherine Mackay, the Duchess of Marlborough, the former Consuelo Vanderbilt of the Roslyn area, tended the candy booth, helped by Alice Duer Mackay, Mrs. E.R. Thomas and Mrs. E.D. Morgan. Among the 51 guests at the Mackay estate that night were some of Wm Pickering's former employers—Phoenix Ingraham and Lloyd Bryce. Also present the Whitneys, Duer Irving, W.K. Vanderbilt.[17] William Pickering may have been present as photographer. He had already become an avid reader of American history, and he understood he was in the company of families who had made and were still making that history. And Billy was recording it in his camera.

High society has always fascinated Americans, especially when roiled by scandal, murder and mayhem. The forces that were creating the most profound changes in America, however, did not emanate from its own often decadent upper crust, but from its generally booming economy. Despite occasional setbacks, the great masses of Americans were successfully working and fighting their way out of poverty. That success and the jobs created by businesses large and small drew America's greatest wave of immigrants, most of them from central and eastern Europe. Until then, America had been populated largely by Anglo-Saxons, Dutch, and French. Americans were worried enough by these desperately poor and often exotically strange people who could not speak English, that few thought about what they were fleeing back home. The conditions the new immigrants lived in, their illiteracy, and their strangeness frightened even educated Americans like Margaret Sanger, the great proponent of birth control. She called them "...human weeds,' 'reckless breeders,' 'spawning... human beings who never should have been born." She advocated sterilization, abortion, and selective breeding to improve the country. Theodore Roosevelt, along with many progressive intellectuals, worried that America was committing "racial suicide." As for the conditions in Europe that drove these immigrants into the boats, Americans cared little. Until 1914.

On the 28th of July, 1914 Billy Pickering posed the Pickering women—his wife and his daughters Dorothy, Annie and three year old Emma--in front of the store window.

Behind them in the two lower corners of the window are posters from *The New York Herald* that advertised its "authentic news" which was very authentic in one word, "WAR!" His wife is wearing her white apron. Sixteen year old Dorothy is in a white dress with a stylish dark bow on top of her head that suggests two velvet ice cream cones gone soggy. She looks studiously at the camera as does 8 year old Annie in her white dress and what seems to be a school bag hung around her neck. Little Emma, also wearing white, has turned away from her father's camera, trying to coax a scrawny tiger cat not to jump from her arms.

Why did Billy pose his wife and three daughters and none of his sons in front of his store window and the war posters? He almost certainly agreed with his hero Teddy Roosevelt that the war must be fought, and he may have been certain that his native England would soon join France and Belgium on the killing fields. Most Americans, however, still wanted no part of war in Europe.

Nothing in the world's scandals, technological miracles, politics, social evolution, or wars meant much to a girl whose greatest pleasures were a few toys and friends and her dog Jud. Even posed by command in front of the historic headlines, she pleasantly preoccupies herself with a kitten. Her greatest fears were her brothers and her father. Nor could she yet care where her own life was leading or that a baby boy born three weeks before her to a poor Jewish family in a walk up apartment in Manhattan's teeming German neighborhood would one day become her husband. Little Emma stuck close to her mother, her favorite brother Wallace (called Buster), and her hideaway in the closet under the stairs.

On a postcard dated October 11, 1915 Billy wrote to his mother Anne Pickering in England describing the scene on the front of the card. It is a family scene that includes three boys now young men, Tom with soon-to-be-wife Anna. The boys are building something with an Erector Set of metal girders, beams, bolts and nuts as the girls and women watch.

"Dear Mother. Here are some of your biggest grandchildren amusing themselves calling on their mother. Its hard to get them altogether. In this bunch are Ted, Tom, William, Arthur, Annie the 2 Emmas and Mrs. Thos. Pickering. We took a long ride yesterday to the south side of the island all well Love to all. William"

Not all the people mentioned in the message are in this picture or the actual picture on the card. In this picture, the two Emmas, Ted (maybe), Tom, Arthur, Tom's wife, Annie.

When Billy wrote that "its hard to get them altogether," that was the truth, but not the whole truth. The whole truth was that Ted, Tom and Bill had already found work outside and that 19 year old Tom was married. Bill had taken a job as a carpenter with Stair Builders and General Mill, and when he was laid off he had pastor Clifton Brewer of Trinity Church write a reference letter that described him as "clean, straightforward, and worth all the consideration and attention that any may wish to give him." He was soon working in the carpentry shop at Conklin,Tubby & Conklin lumber yard.

His eighteen year old daughter Dorothy had already begun sneaking out of the house at night to meet boys. She, like Annie and Emma after her, was forbidden to go out on a date with a boy. She would soon leave home. The boys, of course, could and did invite out Roslyn girls. Young Emma first saw the effects of love on her brothers when Jack fell in love with a local girl. Since the house had no bathroom, the boys and their father all washed and shaved from a basin in front of a mirror on the door of a hall closet. Many nights little Emma watched brother Jack shaving and singing the plaintive slow waltz of, "Oh What a Pal Is Mary."

Mary o' mine, Mary o' mine,
Grew like a rose in a bower
Bloomed for a day,
Faded away
I lost a beautiful flower.
Sweetheart and friend,
Right to the end;
That's why I miss her sooo.

Oh! what a gal was Mar-y, Oh! what a pal was she,
An an-gel was born on East-er morn, and God sent her down to me.
Heart of my heart was Mar-y, Soul of my soul di-vine,
Though she is gone, love lingers on,
for Mar-y old pal of mine.

The exodus from home and the family business may have moved Billy to sell his routes in Roslyn Heights to Josh Adelstein for $1,450 (about $27,000 in 2006 dollars). Adelstein would establish his own store, much like Billy's, opposite the Roslyn train station. Billy's son Bill had wanted to buy the business that Adelstein got. Bill said, " He didn't think I had the money. I don't know what he got for it" but Bill was angry to lose the opportunity. He bought what he could afford. "I gave them 100 bucks. I had the route that went from here to Glenwood. That's how I got started." (A few years later he would open a small store and real estate office at the Glen head railroad station.)

With a thriving business in both the village store and photography, Billy certainly didn't need the extra money except as capital to invest in his new endeavors—trading in old books and antiques. These items had recently appeared on the new white on black sign that extended over East Broadway from his store. He may have moved into these lines as a result of his estate connections—finding in them either his suppliers or his buyers or both.

Emma and Annie Pickering, about 1921

CHAPTER 9: THE NEW AMERICA

My mother wanted so much to write what was inside her that in her sixties she took the mail order "Famous Writers' Course." Her one published article, in *Mobile Home Journal* did not make her famous. She did make others famous, but only within our family. Like all parents, she told her children stories. They were not the fantasies that Auntie Dot had told in England, but the stories she remembered and wanted to tell became an oral mosaic of how she understood the turning points in her life and what she wanted us to understand about life's risks. Those risks were almost always surprises. Many of them were mini-tragedies.

That same year she began kindergarten at the nearby Neighborhood House and started on the education that promised so much, she also fell victim to the first of several accidents that seemed to her almost part of a plan to thwart her athletic ambitions. Like many the most disappointing events in life, her first tragedy began with great joy. One summer day, perhaps her birthday, her mother gave her a present she had long wanted, a large but thin paper book on whose stiff cover smiled the image of one of the world's most famous and admired girls—Dolly Dimples. Dolly had been invented by one of America's first woman cartoonists, mainline Philadelphia socialite Grace Gebbie (later by marriage Grace Wiederseim, then Drayton). She gave birth to the character Dottie Dimple in 1910 and to Dolly Dimples in 1915. Dolly appeared in newspapers and magazines adventuring into danger and exotic places with her friend Bobby Bounce. Among American girls Dolly Dimples was then as popular as today's Barbie or Dora the

THE MOLE AND MRS. MOUSIE WERE IMPATIENT WITH DOLLY AND BADE HER COME INTO TEA.

THAT NIGHT DOLLY CREPT BACK TO THE MOLE'S HOUSE WHEN ALL WERE ASLEEP AND HID THE LITTLE BIRD IN A LITTLE CAVE BACK OF THE PASSAGE.

Explorer. She seemed about my mother's age, a friend, not an ambition.

Emma immediately wanted to show her prize to her friend Helen Conklin who lived across the road. Clutching her Dolly Dimple book closed the door behind her hoping that Helen would be home. A large horse was coming down East Broadway dutifully pulling its milk cart on the daily rounds. She paused, then sure she had time, she jumped over the stones that formed the "curb" of East Broadway. The tired horse was slow, the milkman daydreaming. She was in a hurry. She stumbled in the dirt road and fell in front of the horse. The horse's big foot and iron shoe came down on her right knee. Maybe her cry saved her from the full weight of the horse. By evening she was recovering nicely. Her mother had wrapped her very swollen knee in cold rags. She and Helen sat on the floor and cut out the doll's elegant clothes and bent the tabs around Dolly to hold the clothes in place. She was too young to know anything about bones and joints. She was sure this hurt would disappear as all of her cuts and bruises had disappeared.

Typical Dolly Dimples doll and clothes

When Emma was not busy with newspapers and washing prints in her father's darkroom, the Conklins who lived across the road became her second family, their large house with its wrap around porch became her second home. At the Conklin's she and some of her brothers and sisters learned that the world offered entertainments, pleasures, knowledge, and culture that were excluded from life regulated by their workaholic father and beleaguered mother in their large immigrant family. For Emma the Conklin house was across the street and a world away, not unlike a certain Wonderland that a certain Alice entered when she had fallen through a hole in her lawn.

Conklin's however, had no frightening Queen or Mad Hatter. Instead of a Mad Hatter it had Jonathan Conklin in his calm 70s with a long white beard and his daughter, the bird-like Auntie Bert (Bertha) who had taken charge of Helen and her younger brother George after their mother's death. Emma had never had a grandfather or any grandparents. Auntie Bert was not old and tired as her own mother usually was. Auntie

Bert had reached her early 40s when she became the lady of the house. She was just old enough to be "Auntie" and young enough to join the games.

Emma, Auntie Bert and Jonathan Conklin
1915

Emma delighted in lunch or supper with the Conklins. Instead of the old wooden table in her mother's kitchen and the rough oilcloth that covered it, the Conklins set their table in a real dining room and covered it with white linen table cloths, and each person had a linen napkin. The Conklins' more modern house also had a kitchen sink where the water came not from a hand pump spouting cold water, but by turning the handle of either a hot or cold faucet. Upstairs they used an indoor bathroom with a porcelain flush toilet and a sink and a long, white, oval tub big enough for a child to lie down in. Auntie Bert often invited Annie and Emma to use the tub into which she could instantly summon enough crystal clear hot water to swim in. At home the girl's had to wait while mother fired the kitchen stove and heated water in the tank at its side, then drained the water into a round zinc tub where they bathed, sitting upright in the middle of the kitchen floor.

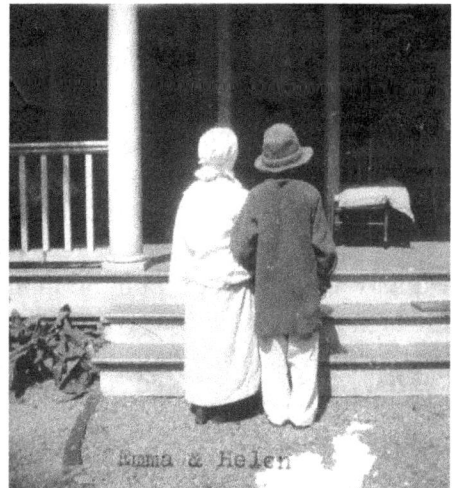

At Conklin's Emma, often with her sister Annie, could enjoy a childhood impossible in their own home. Auntie Bert showed Emma how to find and identify birds' nests and eggs and taught her the names of common wild flowers. Auntie Bert also specialized in children's games and taught them to play checkers, flinch, rook, and Parcheesi. For rainy days a wide covered porch ran around the front and side of the Conklin house and provided a dry playground. If Helen and Emma didn't play on the porch on a rainy day, they were often in the attic going through trunks of old clothes. Emma remembered, "Helen always dressed herself as a man and I dressed as a woman. Yet I was the tomboy and Helen was the delicate child."

In good weather they were often outside in the Conklin yard or in the neighboring swamp which the township was then turning into a park. Their games were games played centuries before them and games still being played a century later despite television and computers. Mr. Conklin who worked in his brother's lumber yard, made stilts and pogo sticks for the girls and their brothers. As long as Emma could stay away from home they might play Mumbly Peg a game in which they faced each other and threw a pocket or kitchen knife into the grass as far from the other's foot as possible. Each in turn had to spread a foot out to reach the other's knife until one could no longer stand. Their favorite was Duck-on-the-Rock, a simple game in which a small rock (the duck) is placed on a big rock. Standing an agreed distance away each tried to tumble the duck. If successful the thrower had to collect her stone and be back in place before the other could replace the duck. With another player or two they played Hopscotch, May-I, hide-and-go-seek, and tag. Something in games that have lasted centuries satisfies an inherent need in children. Anyone who finds a neighborhood without such games or where parents or society discourage or replace them, may have found a sick society or a dangerous experiment.

THE CONKLINS AND PICKERINGS, An Album

The obvious happiness of the days Emma and her sisters and sometimes her brothers spent with the Conklins shows in these pictures. Those hours of happiness in some ten years of Emma's childhood she would frequently summon for strength throughout her life.

Emma, Helen & Elmer

Emma and Helen

Emma Helen George

Emma, Helen, George, Annie

Annie, Helen, George

Dorothy, Emma, George

Conklins, Pickerings and others go for a sleigh ride. Conklin house behind them.

East Broadway's biggest attraction for children large and small was its swamplands, rapidly growing into a public park as Emma herself grew into a girl, then a teenager. Under Aunt Bert's supervision she and Helen waded in icy pools and gathered watercress growing where the waters sprang from the glacial clays and gravels cold and clear. In the spring they roamed the new, semi-wild park gathering violets, dog violets, miniature white violets and Emma's favorites--forget-me-nots. Her brother Bill was still selling muskrat pelts to a local furrier and now making a little extra money from the gloves he made from their pelts.

Playing in the park also left its mark on Emma. Before she was ten she came down with malaria which was then a common disease in the North as well as the South. . For many summers the fever would return, and her mother would sit by her bedside soothing her with a sponge of cool water. Her sister Annie also came down with malaria Although Helen and Elmer never had it, they passed on to Emma measles and chicken pox and a variety of colds and coughs. Her own mother applied the old English cold preventives to all her children. In winters they frequently went to school, on their paper routes, or out to play wearing around their necks a little flannel bag. Inside the bag nested a long block of sharp smelling camphor. For the common cold, their mother spooned into their mouths a mix of sugar, margarine, and lemon juice. A more severe cold called for a little kerosene in the mix to induce sweating.

One winter when Emma came down with a serious cold that left her struggling for breath, a neighbor brought in a little steamer heated by alcohol and poured into the vaporizing container enough creosote to permeate the room. Doctors as well as mothers often used creosote to treat bad colds and the dreaded pneumonia and whooping cough. Whooping cough was then the most frequent cause of death in young children, and a tough disease called forth tough treatment. Most pharmacies sold creosote to be taken by mouth.

Every winter took its expected share of lives from both young and old, as it had taken the life of Robin Pickering in 1902, but winter also offered its own riches for the living, especially the young. The Pickering house had a large supply of long underwear, sweaters, wool coats, hats, scarves, gloves, high top shoes, and winter leggings that buttoned up to the waist. When the youngest children first went to skate on the ponds they started with double iron runners clamped onto the edges of their shoe soles. The older children had clamp-on single runners.

When the snow fell hard, horse drawn plows cleaned some sidewalks, and main roads were cleared by a team of horses drawing a big V-shaped blade. In a day before the automobile became cheaper than horses, however, snow stayed on most roads to be packed down by hundreds of hooves and the sleighs they pulled, bells jingling from the harnesses. Such winter roads often provided a smoother ride than the rutted and potholed roads of spring, summer, and fall, not to mention they were refreshingly free of dust and mud.

The end of school in June blessed the boys and the girls with extra hours beyond their duties in the store, darkroom, and making deliveries. The family garden claimed some of those hours. The Pickering vegetable garden took up the hillside land between the house and the store and some space behind the house. Everyone helped with turning over the soil, planting, fertilizing, weeding, thinning and picking. Grapes from two large arbors had to be picked, washed, mashed and hung in a big cheesecloth bag while the sweet red juice dripped slowly overnight into a big pan. Emma and the girls would add sugar, boil it into sweet jam thickness, pour it into jars and melt a half inch of paraffin on top to seal it. In the park they picked blackberries and raspberries that became pies, roly poly, or jam.

In the fall the big black walnut tree behind the house covered the ground with nuts in their green round husks. The children gathered them by the hundreds, and, wearing gloves, pulled the acrid smelling husks from the nuts and spread the nuts on the roof of the woodshed to dry. The dry nuts defied a nutcracker and had to be broken between a rock and a hammer before the oily meats could be picked painstakingly from their inner crevices. In the ever hungry Pickering family where children and teenagers lusted after the concentrated energy of sweets, everyone in the family knew their jams, jellies, cookies, cakes, pies and steamed puddings from seed to satisfaction.

Herman Melville observed in the first chapter of *Moby Dick* that humans are drawn to water. Given them a day of leisure and, "They must get just as nigh the water as they possibly can without falling in." Adults learn how to moderate or disguise this passion or seem indifferent. Give children half a chance, or give them none, and they want to wade in, splash through it, fall into it or plunge in. In Roslyn they had a full chance. For Emma with her bad knee, the water endowed her with freedom as nothing else did. She became a dedicated swimmer, and when she became an old woman shrunk with arthritis and osteoporosis she would still find water as liberating as the first day she jumped into the brackish waters of Roslyn creek.

Roslyn Harbor began where the swamps and ponds drained out of Silver Lake under the main village street into the "creek." The water slowed and warmed under the sun. In that narrow nipple of the harbor beginning every Pickering child learned to swim. Billy's friend Tom Fearns who had emigrated with him taught the children to swim and how to dive from the bulkheads. Once a young swimmer could solo across the creek and back without water wings, the instructors announced he was on his own. For wider water the swimmers sometimes walked up West Shore Rd. to Hewlett's beach where great sand barges lay off shore receiving the sands mined from the hills and used for construction all over New York City and nearby Long Island. When the McCue family with its children moved onto East Broadway, on weekends Mr. McCue cranked his car and took the swimmers to Bar Beach a mile up the west side of the harbor toward Port Washington. Now and then the way home would be blocked when a heavy rain washed tons of sand out of the mined bluffs onto the road. The McCues also added enough children to make baseball games part of neighborhood recreation.

On occasions rare enough to be well remembered, Billy Pickering accompanied his family to Bar Beach. Once he even acquired a tent for changing. On another well remembered outing he and Emma accepted the invitation of his affluent friends the Olsens for a cruise on their launch. (The Olsens would later leave Roslyn and make a small fortune collecting and reselling horse manure in Chicago.)

Like the rare family outings, the home entertainments themselves were rare enough to be well remembered. They included a stereoscope for visiting exotic places in three dimensions, even if only black and white or sepia. Exotic, of course, meant any place not on Long Island. A beloved music box (its tune not remembered) eventually was joined by the Model T Ford of music—"his master's voice" coming from the big funnel shaped horn of a Victrola. Its famous advertisement showed a dog sitting in front of the horn with its head cocked to one side, listening to "his master's voice." The dog perhaps had a singing master.

Most of the toys in the Pickering family were handmade, often by the boys using a simple coping saw or "jigsaw." Wooden dancing dolls joined their mother's rag dolls sewn from old clothes and socks with buttons for eyes. For outdoors the boys banged together old pieces of wood to make wagons fitted with scrounged wheels from baby carriages or bicycles. The one large purchase for entertainment was the Erector Set that Billy gave to his boys for Christmas. Billy featured on the postcard that he sent to his mother in England in 1915.

The only organized activities for kids were St. Mary's Cadets to prepare boys for military service. Billy Pickering's friend and fellow immigrant Tom Fearns, the veteran of the first Boer War in South Africa, organized and led the group. Using guns, bayonets and swords from the Civil War, he trained them in the basics of marching, riflery, and saber handling. As they acquired instruments, they became an admired fife and drum corps. In 1911 when several of the Pickering boys joined the newly organized Boy Scout Troop #1, the first troop in Nassau County, Fearns' converted his Cadets into Troop #2.

Tradition, of course, organized some activities with minimal instruction. Long work days and weeks made holidays seem like world altering events. May Day or the first of May has never been important in American tradition, but an English family drew on deep wells of rural village history. That history took place in a latitude where the first of May marked a turning point in the weather and all kinds of rural work. The Pickering girls followed a May Day tradition from the south of England where their mother had been born. The first of May had been Garland Day. Children made the rounds of their villages giving bouquets even to strangers and presenting miniature flowered maypoles to neighbors. English history suggests the Maypole originated in the time of Roman occupation to honor the goddess Flora or perhaps in the days of the Druids in the honor of Bel Tein. The tradition flourished in the 13th century when the poet Chaucer wrote:

> Forth goeth all the court, both most and least,
> To fetch the flours fresh, and branch and bloom;
> And namely hawthorn brought both page and groom,
> With fresh garlands partly blue and partly white.
> [Language modernized]

Long before Emma Hasell learned the tradition in England, the English had adapted it to Christianity with such verses as:

> A garland gay I brought you here,
>   And at your door I stand.
> 'Tis nothing but a sprout, but 'tis well budded out,
>   The work of our Lord's hand.

Little Emma with Annie and Dorothy did not know that they were the last in this family to practice this 2000 year old tradition, but as enthusiastically as any courtier in Chaucer's time or village child of their mother's own childhood, they gathered their flowers on the first of May from the hillsides or around the swamps and ponds. They fashioned them into small bouquets and hung them on their neighbors' doors. At church they celebrated with a big May Pole. Annie remembered that, "A large pole was put in the ground on the front lawn with pretty ribbons attached. Each child would dance around the pole following the pretty ribbons, followed by games and refreshments."

The Pickerings also embraced American traditions from Thanksgiving to the 4th of July. On the Fourth, Annie says, "Children would get up early to see which family had the flag up first and set off the first fire cracker." Boy Scout troops would go to Mackays to display their uniforms and skills. Billy sold fireworks from the store, and in the evening he would hand out firecrackers and sparklers to the children while he set off Roman candles and skyrockets that sizzled and smoked their way up into the sky and arched over the new park. For Thanksgiving they gladly accepted the turkey and fine vegetables that some of their rich estate customers sent to merchants. November was also the time when Emma would buy a big piece of suet from butcher Craft, mix it with fruits and do the first of several steamings that would eventually turn it into a Christmas pudding.

Christmas celebrations began the week before Christmas with a short tip beyond the village to the estate of Mr. and Mrs. Benjamin Stern in Wheatley Hills. Benjamin Stern and his brothers, self-made millionaires from a Jewish immigrant family, owned the famous Stern Brothers department store as well as real estate investments in New York City. Their friends from the early days in business used to tell how the older brothers would close the store, sleep on the counters, and open the doors again in the mornings. The Sterns sponsored numerous charities and charitable extravaganzas such as the 1915 drama "Forbidden Fruit" staged by the Washington Square Players in the Stern estate's sunken gardens for the benefit of the Roslyn District Nursing Association. The Sterns also financed a home for abandoned babies on their Scudders Lane farm in adjoining Glenwood Landing. Most of the babies came from New York City where Benjamin's older brother was well known for his support of a Jewish orphanage that provided the best in modern accommodations and education.

Each December the Sterns invited the merchants and business people who supplied their estate to bring their children to a party at Claraben Court, their three story stone mansion with the five story square tower on one side. Approaching the grand front door along the wide garden-flanked drive endowed the beginning of the Christmas season with pomp and circumstance and wonder. To children the mansion seemed big enough to engulf the entire jumble of houses and stores that composed the village itself. Inside they assembled to work their way along a huge buffet of refreshments—meats, cheeses, tiny triangular sandwiches made of white and pink and green things they had never seen before; plus cookies, cakes, pies, cupcakes, and puddings. They piled their plates high, then went through a door to take a seat in another room to watch that newest of all forms of entertainment—a motion picture. Each child left with an elegant gift. Christmas had begun.

What dazzled the children in these homes were not the people but the things and the amount of things—from food to toys. The things that filled the village and its stores and workshops were familiar and largely practical. But these things too could be strange and mysterious to outsiders and new residents. *New Yorker* writer Christopher Morley drew both scenes and characters from the village. He often lingered in Pickering's shop talking to Billy or the children or the other customers. Among Roslyn's characters, many, like Billy Pickering, spent their lives as proprietors of small businesses. By the time Emma began to roam the village her father's status in the business community and in civic life gave her and her brothers and sisters easy access to the larger community— homes, offices, and businesses. In my mother's descriptions of these places and proprietors the notable absence is any ugly or even unpleasant character. In a village every business owner's livelihood depended on the good will of customers. Owners were usually present in the front room rather than operating from the distance of a board room or private office. A sour personality did not survive unless he was sour in a very original way or had no competition.

Across from the school stood Mrs. Horton's store where kids who had an extra coin could buy candy and ice cream. At Craft's butcher shop the Pickering kids scuffled across the floors where sawdust soaked up any slippery blood or fat. They could always count on a free Frankfurter or slice of bologna. A short way up Mill Dam Road (Northern Turnpike) the Hicks family operated a larger grocery and general store whose order and neatness impressed itself on Emma as a contrast to the cramped and crowded store her father ran. At Hicks a shopper could buy groceries, bolts of cloth, ready-made clothes, fishing and hunting gear, or tools for the farm or shop. Hicks piled his dry goods on shelves which reached to the high ceiling. To retrieve the farm tools and implements hanging from ceiling hooks or the boxes of hosiery and underwear on the top shelves, Mr. Hicks pushed a tall sliding step ladder in place and clambered up and down. Along the walls of the grocery area stood open tubs of butter, cookies, flour, and other foods.

For haircuts in good weather the boys often went together for a family trimming on the front porch of the barber shop. For toothaches and cavities the Pickering boys

Ted (bald) and Tom watch Bill's turn

claim to have been clients of the famous "Painless Parker." Edgar Randolph Parker started his flamboyant and controversial career operating, in every sense of the word, from a chair in the back of a horse drawn wagon. As a boy Bill Pickering remembered that "Painless Parker had a dental chair on a small truck, and Parker would park in front of Pickard's Drug Store and do dental work, including pulling teeth." It's the kind of exhibition an eight or nine year old boy would remember, especially since Painless Parker was 50% showman, and 50% dentist. In collaboration with a pharmacist he had developed an anesthetic based on cocaine. To support his guarantee of painless extraction, he sometimes supplemented the act with drum rolls and the blast of an assistant's trumpet at the moment of the final pull. (The noise also masked the patient's cry if the drug was not sufficient.) Parker tirelessly and profitably popularized dentistry and once extracted 357 teeth in a day long Vaudeville stage performance. He also took to wearing a necklace of extracted teeth. Harassed by the state of New York for using an "assumed name" he abandoned his long Island estate and practice for the then freer life of California where he became a multi-millionaire owner of 30 franchises. To protect his trade from the problem he faced in New York, he officially changed his first name to Painless. Although he was an anathema to other dentists, no one did more than Painless Parker to establish preventive dentistry as an affordable routine for working class Americans.

A traveling street dentist may seem exotic today, but in the early 20th Century he was notable mainly because among the many people who carried their businesses around, dentists and doctors were not common. Small town Americans often welcomed traveling businesses as a break from daily routine or for the entertainment value of their slick sales pitches. They were the most creative advertisers of the day and the forerunners of television ads that hold the attention with mini-stories and unexpected bits of information or visual surprises. Some, like the traveling umbrella man, the knife sharpener, and the rag man provided specialized services delivered to the doorstep.

The first six years of any person's life run like a fabulously rich and novel torrent of sensations and events, of joys and fears, a time when almost every day brings wonder or terror. Yet twenty or thirty years after becoming adults, we remember from all this novelty only a few specifics.

As my mother herself looked back on those years through eight decades of experience, dreaming, brooding, and confusion she tried to understand their influence. She found in them all the basic lessons about life—the nature of love, hate, responsibility, fairness, giving, loss, fear, and friendship. She learned the tedium of drudge work and the relief of play and the consolation of nature and the shelter of friendship. She learned what a community is, and she understood that the greatest dangers for the future lay not outside but inside her own family.

As Leo Tolstoy once noted, small children already have enough experience of life and enough imagination to ask all the ultimate questions. My mother lived more than 90 years, but not long enough to answer them.

CHAPTER 10. TED AND BILL GO "OVER THERE"

A new history of the world will be written and it will date, I think, from the beginning of this war. Secretary of War Newton D. Baker.

By 1917 the Billy had bought electric service for their home, and wires from the line down East Broadway now swayed from their pole to the insulators on the side of the house as well as the store. The 1914 purchase of the Jackson motor car had extended the reach of his paper business and served to carry him and his photographic equipment to engagements. To the sign outside the store he had attached a blue and white square plaque advertising the new Bell telephone available to the public. Like almost all Americans, the Pickerings welcomed the new comforts and opportunities. Emma and Billy, however, were also worried about their friends and families in England who were facing the dark side of modern technology.

Most of the spectacular scientific discoveries, new inventions, and big businesses that transformed America and the world in the early twentieth century expressed themselves as machines that concentrated energy to extend human powers. Nothing distilled all of these creations in one event until war broke out in Europe in 1914. A few people had already warned that war between industrialized nations in the 20th Century would dwarf all previous wars in its gruesome and yet unimagined powers of destruction. A single fanatical assassin in the relatively undeveloped Balkan countries of eastern Europe set off a fatal cascade of diplomatic miscalculations when he assassinated Austria's archduke Ferdinand in the cause of independence for Serbia. When Austrian forces brutally punished little Serbia and killed thousands of innocents to teach extremists a lesson, they acted with the rash assurance that Germany would support them if Russia, ethnically and religiously linked to Serbia, threatened to intervene. Russia did threaten. Germany came to Austria's side. That triggered an alliance with France, England and Belgium against Austria and Germany. Germany gambled on a decisive August strike down through Belgium into France. Each country threw its entire industrial and economic power into the fight. For the first time in any large-scale fighting motorized vehicles like tanks and airplanes that had been adapted for bombs and machine guns magnified the killing power formerly reserved for simpler machines, horses, small arms and human muscle. More than a million European soldiers perished in the first year and nearly as many innocent civilians. From its beginning in 1914 Americans had been watching the war with intense interest since 1914. President Woodrow Wilson, a Princeton scholar, had been elected in 1912 as the peace candidate because Teddy Roosevelt had abandoned the Republicans and run as Progressive Party and doomed the Republican nominee.

Along with the news of war came what might be called the culture of war. Americans not only read the news but absorbed the new stereotypes of the Bosch, the Frog and the doughboy. Americans whistled and sang English marching songs like "It's a Long Way to Tipperary" and "Pack Up Your Troubles in Your Old Kit Bag and Smile, Smile, Smile." Although Americans had taken up the songs sung by Allied troops from the war's beginning, they were also singing anti-war songs. At the beginning of the war most Americans opposed any alliance with the warring nations. As late as January 1917 President Wilson declared a policy of "peace without victory." When he proposed arming American merchant ships, Mid-Western congressmen defeated the measure. Among the anti-war songs was 1915's was "I Didn't Raise My Boy to Be a Soldier." The sheet music's cover showed a young man kneeling into the embrace of his seated grey-haired mother.

A 1916 cartoon of a sinking ocean liner with only its bow above the water captures America's transformation. The periscope of a U boat in the foreground looks on and the name of the ship is "U.S. Patience." Early in 1917 a new song hit the charts in America and tumbled off the lips of anyone who enjoyed a jaunty Tin Pan Alley tune. "Let's All Be Americans Now" by a once poverty stricken young Russian immigrant, one of Margaret Sanger's "human weeds" of the tenements of New York City. Irving Berlin's song was printed and performed by the American Quartet even before the official declaration of War. In typical Berlin style the swinging lyrics swept up both emotions and motion. Irving Berlin, however, would not become an American until 1918.

Peace has always been our prayer
Now there's trouble in the air
War is talked of everywhere,
Still in God we trust.
We're not looking for any kind of war,
But if fight we must

It's up to you.
What will you do?
England or France may have your sympathy
Or Germany.
But you'll agree
That now is the time
To fall in line,
You swore you would,
So be true to your view,
Let's all be Americans now.

Lincoln, Grant, and Washington:

They were peaceful men each one.
Still they took the sword and gun
When real trouble came.
And I feel somehow
They're wond'ring now,
    If we'll do the same.

By 1917 President Wilson realized he could no longer maintain neutrality and began to sell the idea that if America went to war, it would fight "a war to make the world safe for democracy." As soon as Congress declared war in April, Wilson issued an order creating the Committee for Public Information. The CPI enlisted more than 75,000 men and women volunteers who fanned out across the country to popularize the war effort. The carrot was also followed by the stick--laws punishing dissent. Popular socialist leader Eugene Debs and union organizer Big Bill Hayward, were thrown in jail for urging Americans to oppose the war.

Among the new weapons of naval warfare, the German submarines were the most feared and had become the key players in the Kaiser's attempt to starve Britain into surrender by naval blockade. The U boats ultimately failed to starve Britain, and the policy of attacking all inbound ships began a decisive swing of American opinion to the Allied forces. The greatest outrage came at 3:10 pm May 7, 1915 when the commander of the German submarine U-20, turning for home with only 3 torpedoes left, spotted Britain's "Greyhound of the Seas" on the final day of its sail from New York to Liverpool. The Lusitania had survived its voyages by relying on its speed of over 20 knots, but on this day she had been slowed by fog. Although she was in waters known to be infested by U boats, her captain had not ordered the zig-zag maneuvers that would have slowed her even more but made her a harder target for a submarine. The U boat's captain recorded the final moments in his journal:

Clear bow shot at 700 m. . . angle of intersection 90 [degrees] estimated speed 22 nautical miles.

Shot struck starboard side close behind the bridge. An extraordinary heavy detonation followed, with a very large cloud of smoke (far above the front funnel). A second explosion must have followed that of the torpedo (boiler or coal or powder?).

The superstructure above the point of impact and the bridge were torn apart; fire broke out; light smoke veiled the high bridge. The ship stopped immediately and quickly listed sharply to starboard, sinking deeper by the head at the same time.[18]

The boat sank within 20 minutes and 138 Americans died with 1,060 others. The horrors of modern warfare that Americans had been reading about almost daily, no longer supported an effective anti-war sentiment. The President now found his views falling behind public opinion. He too had been watching the war in Europe with horror, but remained committed to keeping America out of it. His note to the Kaiser protesting the sinking of the Lusitania concluded,

> The Government and the people of the United States look to the Imperial German Government for just, prompt, and enlightened action in this vital matter with the greater confidence because the United States and Germany are bound together not only for special ties of friendship but also by the explicit stipulations of the treaty of 1828 between the United States and the Kingdom of Prussia.

Germany backed off its declared right to attack all shipping bound for Britain and its allies, and Wilson continued to hope for peace. Britain soon found the key to forcing Wilson's hand. In February it gave the American ambassador a copy of a telegram it had intercepted. The "Zimmerman Telegram" sent by German Foreign Minister Arthur Zimmermann to the German Ambassador to Mexico on January 19, 1917 announced that Germany would resume attacking all ships trading with Britain, and that if it could not keep the US neutral,

> WE PROPOSE ALLIANCE TO MEXICO UPON THE FOLLOWING BASIS: TO MAKE WAR TOGETHER; MAKE PEACE TOGETHER; GENEROUS FINANCIAL SUPPORT; AND AGREEMENT ON OUR PART THAT MEXICO SHALL RECONQUER THE FORMERLY LOST TERRITORY IN TEXAS, NEW MEXICO, ARIZONA.[19]

That winter and spring the Germans also torpedoed four American ships, killing fifteen Americans. Wilson knew he had to ask Congress to declare war, but he told a confidante the night before his request that he feared it would destroy the Constitution. "It would mean that we should lose our heads along with the rest and stop weighing right and wrong. It would mean that a majority of people in this hemisphere would go war-mad, quit thinking, and devote their energies to destruction."[20]

Young Bill Pickering did not quit thinking, as the elitist Princeton scholar predicted of ordinary Americans, but he decided to devote himself to destruction of Germany and the Austro-Hungarian Empire. His older brother Ted would also fight. They would enter the war willingly and apparently as two young men with the same background and similar personalities. They would return home still looking like two peas from the same pod, but soon they would become very different men with surprisingly different futures.

Friday April 6, 1917 on Long Island began as a cloudy day with the temperature right at freezing. A light rain came and went. When the Pickering boys brought the evening papers from the station the headline in every paper informed readers of what they had expected since President Wilson had talked to Congress on Monday: the United States Congress approved a declaration of war against Germany and its allies. Since Monday Congress had debated for 16 hours and sat through more than 100 speeches. Despite often hot debate, a once isolationist Congress and the Americans it represented had decided overwhelmingly that German attacks on US shipping and the offer to give Mexico part of the United States could only be answered by war. The House passed the war resolution on the morning of April 6 by a vote of 373 to 50. Billy Pickering thought his new country had already delayed too long to come to the aid of his native country where his mother and brother, sisters, and cousins still lived. Britain, Belgium, and France had been fighting for 3 years, losing hundreds of thousands of men.

Billy Pickering also knew that Congress intended to pass a law drafting one million young men between the ages of 19 and 25. His sons Ted, William, Tom, and Jack were all eligible.

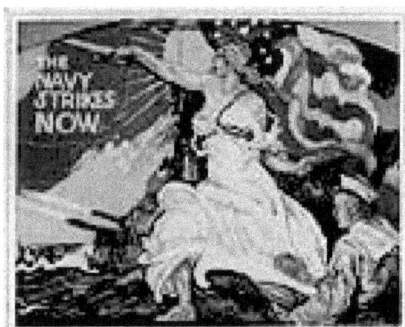

THE NAVY STRIKES NOW.

FOLLOW THE FLAG
FOR
FREEDOM

Your Choice.
NAVAL RESERVE,
COAST GUARD
OR NAVY · ·

The day Congress declared war 22 year old Bill Pickering and his friend Johnny Peel were working at Conklin and Tubby's lumber yard. Bill was as close to Johnny as to any other friend. They had been born the same year, delivered by the same Dr. Bogart. In the evening Bill helped deliver papers with the blazing headlines of war. The next day, inspired by the patriotic calls to defend America's honor and whip the Kaiser, the two young men, each with twenty-five cents in his pocket, met at the Roslyn Clock Tower in the center of the Village and boarded the trolley for Flushing. The trolley bell tolled, the steel wheels rumbled down the steel tracks and they thought they were off to war. Several friends who had gathered to see them off wished them luck. The conductor thought they were on their usual trip to Flower Hill to meet girls. But in Flushing they took the train to Manhattan and disembarked on Columbus Circle where they were directed to go downtown to the recruiting tents on 23rd St. They borrowed the fare and joined a mob of young men eager to be on their way to training camps and off to "beat the Huns."

"There was the Army, Navy and Marine recruiting station," Bill remembered. "If you couldn't get into the Marines (you gotta be good), you went to the Navy. If you didn't get into the Navy, you went to the Army. They took you," Bill said. "Nobody would go to the Army in them days." The Navy was not a reluctant second choice.

Theodore Roosevelt's program of fleet development had endowed the United States with the most modern and powerful fleet in the world, and young men like Bill wanted to share that power. Bill and Johnnie signed up for the Navy and inched forward in line for their physical exam. They were the last two in line.

Johnny went in first for his physical. Bill waited. And waited longer. Bill thought he would never "come out because he always limped a little, nobody knew why." When Johnny did come out, he told Bill he had been rejected, told to "go home and cut out the beer and stuff and eat a lot of bananas to put on weight." Johnny was 25 pounds under weight. When Bill went in the doctor told him, "I don't want to examine any more of you." The doc began packing up and told the boys to go home. Bill said, "Listen chief, we come 25 miles. We said good-bye to a bunch of boys back home and we can't go home now."

"Where'd you come from?" the doctor asked and Bill replied Roslyn.

The recruiters gave them fifty cents and they returned to Roslyn. Bill, however, was soon back at the recruiting station taking his physical. "I don't think I was in there 15 minutes. 'Go home and get your birth certificate,' they told me. My mother and father knew nothing about it." His father found out in a few days when he saw a Navy envelope arrive for Bill and questioned him. Billy Pickering had read all the news of the war and of the German submarines, and he was not pleased his second son would soon be in the north Atlantic chasing them. At the same time, his own mother and brothers and sisters were the subject of the German efforts at conquest by starvation. By the time Bill left for Yorktown, Virginia "all was forgiven." Six months later the doctor would clear Johnny Peel for the Army.

Bill's older brother Ted had left home some months or even a year earlier, and his sister Dorothy had also decamped, both of them in New York City. In an undated letter in mid or late May written from the Stapleton neighborhood of Staten Island, Ted told his mother he regretted the death of family friend Fred Ried. He may have been working in a boatyard since he says, "I was out on the bay Sunday on one of the new little gun boats up here they have just built. There is some class to them and speed to." He says that the city will mount "big guns on the hills up here. Next week they will be 12 inch guns for Home Defense. They were all war Brassy up here in Staten Island." He thought the defensive guns would be a good thing for Roslyn too.

He wrote that he had heard that his brother Bill had gone in the Navy with the first volunteers. "They won't let a German live on Broad street any more if you live [leave] it to some of them up here Mother." Two weeks earlier he had visited his sister Dorothy who told him she was going to join the Red Cross.

He says about the departure of men enlisting to serve, "I am in no hurry till the time comes. Witch I don't hope it will be. I don't think its right to send our men over there so soon they will be nead them here if things keep on the way they are now." If he gets called in the draft, he wrote, he would come home to see her by Decoration Day "if the Boss has no grudge against me. If he has anything to say about me coming home to see you all or any of the family, why I like to no when you write, Mother. I don't want to have any hard feelings when I come home there."

Bill had been gone only a day when he wrote his mother a letter on April 16 from Brooklyn's Navy Young Men's Christian Association that kept a correspondence room for sailors.

> Dear Mother,
> Arrived here for the night.
> We left New York about 1:30 o'clock and there was ten of us that went over hear and had a good time getting here on the subway. Had a good supper. A Navy Speacial Steak and if I got that every day I will be all right.
> This is a kind of Place we shoot Pool and had a good swim all for 15 cents.
> I feel all right now and having a good time.
> We go back to New York tomorrow at 9:30 o'clock and leave for Newport, R.I.
> Will write when I get there.
> We are going to bed now and sleep on a cot as there is so many here. This place is crowed [sic] but all happy.
> Hoping that you are all well I will close.
> Your loving son,
> Bill
> My first night in this Navy.

Two nights later, as promised, Bill again wrote to his mother, this time from Newport, R.I. He was now in Barracks C with company 19. He said he had sent his civilian clothes home and that now

> "we all sleep together in a hammock, get up at 5 o'clock and have a hot and cold bath before eats. Then we Drill from 8 o'clock until 12 o'clock and have a hour for dinner. Then we drill from 10 o'clock until 4 o'clock. Then we have a good time whashing [sic] clothes or anything we like Box, swim, dance, smoke and I sleep. There is a store here but it is only open untill 12 oclock till one.
> It is some crowed that we can not get anything and I had to borrow this paper and write this letter on the Floor. We have a nice rifle range here that we shoot at once a day it is fine here will leave hear about a week. Please send me a Roslyn News. I just bought a paper the first in a week.

Let me know if the clothes arrived home. Tell pop there is one film in the Machine could not take any more as we move too much.

> Address
> Newport Training School
> Newport R.I.
> Barracks C
> 1st night Com 19
>> Your loving son
>> Bill.

Emma wrote back but what she said, does not remain in the family papers. His high school teacher Mrs. Charles Willis had written to him the second week of March. "Mrs. Willis said that all the boys that have left Roslyn Names were read Sunday in church and that it made her proud to think that they all were in her class at once and that she hoped to see us all home safe soon."

One of his father's customers, General George Rathbone Dyer also wrote to Bill in May and Bill reported, "Dyer said that he was pleased to see that I had done my part ant that he would help me all he could." What kind of help that might be Bill didn't say, but Dyer, originally from Rhode Island, had served in the Spanish-American war and on the Mexican border, mustering out in 1916, only to be enlisted again and assigned to active duty with the New York Guard three days after the US declaration of war. A biographical summary in a history of Rhode Island depicts a man, son of a former governor, who was solidly connected to the New England and New York elite:

> His clubs are the Knickerbocker, Union, Piping Rock, Manhattan, Seawanhaka Corinthia Yacht, Fort Orange, Governors Island, New York Press, Beaver Dam Winter Sports and the Bankers' Club of America. With his family he is a member of the St. Paul's Protestant Episcopal Church of Glen Cove, Long Island. General Dyer's fraternal affiliations are with Kane Lodge, No. 454, Free and Accepted Mason, and Lodge No. 1, Benevolent and Protective Order of Elks. He is a member of the Rhode Island Society of the Cincinnati; the Sons of the Revolution; Society of Colonial Wars; Military Order of Foreign Wars of the United States; Naval and Military Order of the Spanish-American War; Manhattan Camp, No. 1, United Spanish War Veterans; Veterans of the Seventh Regiment, National Guard Association of the United States.

A family friend with the C.I. Hudson stock brokerage company wrote to Bill in the 3rd Co. Barracks in Newport, R.I. on May 14:

Dear "Willie".

I was very glad to get your letter.

You must not get discouraged. You will be called upon to do all kinds of duty – some will be pleasant – some will be very unpleasant, but you must perform them all well, and cheerfully. You will be far happier in so doing – and when your services ended and you come home again, you will have the great satisfaction and reward of having done your duty well and faithfully. Write me again & let me know how I can help you.

Your friend,
G.R. D[ugan]

On May 19 Bill wrote that all afternoon some 8000 sailors had been on parade in Newport, a signal that this would be their last day of training. "Went up around the big burgs places and there are some nice places here. We were gone all afternoon and it was some drill." He promised to send postcards of it later. He had had his last Captain's inspection in the morning and last shore leave that evening and expected to ship out, hopefully for Brooklyn.

Two days later he wrote in frustration from Newport that he "had our clothes and all washed up and ready to go this morning" when they had been quarantined for a week in Barracks B because a man had come down with diphtheria. "Will be here a week at the least so don't forget to write a letter soon," he pleaded. He added, "The boys are all getting cake and candy from home. Why not sent me some of those nice little round ones you use to make. They will be all right getting here as it only takes a day to get here."

As soon as his ship did leave Newport, he sent a telegram from on board to his mother saying he hoped he would be home. He had to send it collect because he had only a dollar left in his pocket.

On morning of June 8 his ship headed into New York Harbor and steamed up the East River between Long Island and Manhattan putting the US Navy's might on display. They were greeted enthusiastically on their cruise by Manhattan residents and boat crews but were not allowed shore leave. "All the boats we meet would blow a salute and whistles all the way up and down." The celebration of their imminent entry in the fight against the Germans was celebrated again that afternoon on their departure for Virginia. "When we left you could not hear us talk on account of the noise. They were waving flags from all the windows in sight." He also reported a new part of modern warfare. "We saw the airoplanes up in NY." On the way south they passed three big nets that had been set out to foil submarines. He said he would try to get a furlough for July 4th. As they steamed south toward the Atlantic, passengers on a small boat making the crossing from Long Island to Staten Island stared from the deck at the huge warships slicing through through the gray-green waters, black smoke streaming from their stacks in dark ribbons. One of the passengers was Bill's brother Ted who sent his mother a postcard saying, "Coming over I saw 3 more Big Battle ships and the rest. I wish you could see these forces."

A Wonderful Opportunity For YOU

Ashore, On Leave.

United States Navy

Bill had been assigned to one of the biggest ships in the US Navy, the USS Wyoming, launched in 1911 in the continuation of Teddy Roosevelt's effort to make the US the world's greatest and most invincible naval power. At 562 feet long the ship displaced 26,000 tons. She was the lead ship in the new class of dreadnoughts. Her 12 inch guns had a range of 4.5 miles. With coal fired boilers, she was well adapted to North Sea duty where oil was scarce. She could sail over 5,000 miles without refueling. Her biggest drawback was the placement of powder magazines in an area surrounded by steam pipes, making for rapidly varying and very hot temperatures. That meant different loads of powder performed differently. Bill was one of more than 1,000 men in the crew. He soon began doing his time time in these magazines and gun turrets. He hated the close quarters, the constant heat, the imprecision of the work. He wanted work he knew and did well. He asked for a transfer and wrote his mother that he expected to be assigned to the carpentry shop below deck.

On June 20 he received his second packet of $30 monthly pay, and from aboard the USS Wyoming he sent a letter to his mother saying he enclosed a money order. The English thrift he had learned at hom guided his directions for the money. "Keep the five out and put the rest in the bank for me. I bought a liberty bond here last week. We have to pay five dollars a month for nine more months. It is a $50 one. Most of the boys on board bought one." The letter, however, includes a P.S. saying that he had not been able to send the money order because the post office had closed by the time he went. "Had my money all right when I went to sleep. When I got up in the morning, my pants was gone. I found the pants but the pocket book was gone with about $22. . . . Had to borrow a stamp to send this." The tables had now turned and instead of sending $5 for his mother, he wrote, "Will not get any until next month. So if you want to send some, all right. I will thank you very much."

When he wrote again on July 7, he did not mention receiving money but thanked his mother for a packet of *Roslyn News* papers since he was then working in the carpentry shop and had free time from Friday evening till Monday morning. He was also glad to hear from his brother Tom and wanted to know, "Did the beads get home to Emma and Annie without breaking. I got them out of a candy box. I thought they would like them as they came all that way." He was back in the money, having received $21 a few days earlier which was in his division officer's safe keeping. $5 for his Victory Bond. He said he would keep another $5 for himself and promised to send his mother $10 soon. Four days later he sent his mother $10 with a postcard of American, French and British Flags, the Statue of Liberty and the globe on which he would soon be fighting for what the card called "International Liberty."

He didn't get home in July, but he got homesick. Almost every letter repeats his request for copies of the *Roslyn News*. On July 18 he notes that he has not received any recently so, "Do not forget to send it as it makes me feel good to read it." He also says, "I am sending you some thing that you have asked me for a long time. Will not tell you but I mailed it tonight with this letter."

He wrote to his father once from Newport News, Virginia to say he had received a package with fresh film and was sending three rolls home for his father

to develop and print. He asked his father for six prints of each of the other sailors in the pictures. This might have been asking a lot except that he followed his order with the promise, "I will send you the money in a day or so." He said he expected to be home on leave in a week and signed the short note, "Your son, Bill."

His ship was back in New York in early September, but he wrote to his mother, "Had a bad boil on my face the last week or I would have been home for labor day until 3 o'clock this afternoon. Had some clothes to wash in a bucket when the chief asked me if I wanted to go." Instead of going home, to pass the time he attended church on board on Sunday and spent a lot of time washing his clothes, then sat down to write his letter "to help too." He hoped to be home on leave in a week or two, and meanwhile asked his mother to send the newspapers and, of course, the prints from film he had sent.

In early October he was back in Roslyn on a seven day leave before shipping out for more training and fitting of the ship in Virginia. His father took pictures of him in uniform. In a studio picture set against a tapestry of trees son Bill sits arms on the arm of his mother's chair, arms folded across his broad chest, looking slightly down and boldly at the camera. His mother sits beside him with her hands clasped in the lap of her ankle length heavy skirt. She has a small tight mouth with thin lips, her hair tight on her head, bags under her eyes. In a Sunday dress up photo taken a week before Bill left for the Navy, he is wearing his tall black spit polished shoes. His mother wears her black coat and her broad brimmed black hat. Six year old Emma sits on her mother's knee in a floppy hat, white dress and shoes like her older brother's.

The Roslyn News ran a small social note about his last weekend at home, saying, "he is very proud of his promotion to shipwright. He has some famous sea yarns which delight the youngsters and his mother, but so far he has failed to report the recovery of the Golden wheels of Pharaoh's chariot that were lost in the River Jordan."

It might have been on this leave that Bill frustrated his younger brother Buster's (Wallace) plans to go to sea. Buster had turned 16 on July 7. When America entered the war and his brother Bill enlisted, Buster wrote, "I thought of nothing else but getting in . . . . I knew it was impossible to enlist so thought I might be able to smuggle aboard a troop ship!" He already had practice in running away from home. A couple of years earlier he and the dog Jud whom both Emma and Annie claimed as their own had left home, traveled ten miles and returned by nightfall. A year after that he left and stayed away for a week although he later wrote, "I wanted to

Bill, mother and sister Emma, 1 week before sailing, 1917

return but could not go against my pride. A brother was sent and duly returned me home." Buster tried several more times, each time turning back or being caught in his preparations.

He was not trying to run away from his parents, but trying to run to adventure or opportunity, or at least he thought of it that way. "I could have had no better parents, brothers and sisters," he explained. The urge, he said, "was a trait that was probably inherited from my father. Years later I paid a visit to one of his (father's) brothers who told me that Father was the same when he was a boy."

Not far from Roslyn gangs of laborers busily constructed Army training camps, and on one of those projects Buster met a young man from New England. He confided his dream of travel to this new friend from what seemed like a far part of the nation. In return, he had an invitation to visit Rhode Island. Asking no one's permission, he seized the first opportunity. "A magnificent four-masted schooner arrived at one of the local docks. I lost no time in going down and inspecting her and ascertaining her destination. I paid many visits to this ship in the course of which I would picture myself on her decks in a rolling sea; in the rigging in a storm and even to having been knocked cold with a belaying pin wielded by her Skipper. Said I, 'Here is where I depart from the family fireside for the seven seas.'" As soon as he found out the day and time the ship would depart, he told his brother Ted. "This proved my undoing; he related my story to the folks, so they maintained a close watch over me until my beautiful white schooner departed."

He still did not give up. One day, looking at the stacks of unsold, outdated magazines that his father had stored in the barn, he had an idea. He would take a bundle to nearby Camp Mills to give to the soldiers. "It occurred to me that I might possibly be able to join up with a troop there, smuggle aboard ship with them." The soldiers were glad to get his magazines, but when they would ship out was a military secret.

The day the telegram with final orders arrived, Bill and his father and sisters were cruising Long Island Sound on a launch owned by their friends the Olsens, a family of Swedish descent who would soon move to Chicago and make a small fortune picking up and recycling horse manure. When Bill and his father came home he read the message ordering him to report the next day at the Brooklyn Navy Yard for duty on the USS Wyoming. As he packed his sea bag, his father handed him a gift, the popular and easy-to-use box camera by Kodak, a Brownie Number 2.

Bill's ship left the next day for Lynnhaven Roads near Norfolk, Virginia. Bill stood on deck as the battleship sliced through the choppy waters into The Narrows that separated New York's inner harbor from the open ocean. In the narrows a patrol boat drew close and waving from it was Bill Mahon, the last familiar face he would see for two years.

On October 20 he writes from the ship that he has received his mother's letter, newspapers and a letter "from Mrs. Olsen's friend in the Bronx." The friend was a woman, and Bill says, "Received them both the same time. . . . Of course you know I had to read the girl's first as it was the first one, but they were both nice letters. I will try and write one to Mrs. Olsen and my girl friend today." He wrote the letters from his bunk in the sick bay where he was being treated for a very bad boil on one arm that prevented him from working. Who the girl was he did not say, but her name might have been Ida who appears with him in two or three pictures looking affectionate, and whom he mentioned in later mail.

At the end of October they were still in training or patrolling off the coast of Virginia. By this time German mines had been strung like a deadly necklace from Newfoundland south to the waters off Virginia. When he wrote to his mother October 27th that he had turned down an eight day leave because it was too expensive. The boil on his arm was gone but "was some sore for a while." He asks her to be sure to get prints made from film he has sent, "about 3 or 4 of each" for his friends in those pictures and before signing off he says "Do not forget the Pictures what ever you do." Three days later he sent four more rolls home after he had been roller skating with friends. The ship had taken on its full complement of guns and he had just returned from a full day's target practice. "It is some sight to see. Could not take any pictures as I was in a turret all day." He did take pictures of the old training ships that visited port and he hoped his pictures of "airoplanes" that were in constant flight around the ships came out well.

USS Wyoming (Larry Bonn / USN photo)

On October 22nd the Germans had decided to launch a final naval offensive in the North Sea against the British Grand Fleet. The British had recently reduced its naval strength by retiring five older battleships that had become hopelessly outclassed compared to their German adversaries. The Germans were confident that they could multiply the successful raids on merchant shipping. Those raids had already made the British government afraid it would have to abandon its French and Belgian allies and quit the war effort. The Germans expected a British surrender by the end of the summer of 1918. However, the British admiralty had finally accepted the solution to the terrible toll the German U boats were taking on merchant ships supplying food and raw materials. Previously the idea that scattered individual merchant ships were safer from U boats waiting in the shipping lanes had prevailed over the proposal that they be grouped in large convoys escorted by British destroyers and dreadnoughts. One or two experiments with convoys proved they were far superior and the escorts dramatically reduced shipping losses. The British, however, needed more ships to protect the convoys. To fill the gap, the British invited America to send four of its fourteen dreadnaughts. The US did not send its very best ships, and the British did not want them because, like all the latest ships, they used oil for fuel. The German U boats had cut off much of the British oil supply and it had little to spare. But four fairly recent American ships, including the USS Wyoming, burned coal and British mines were producing rapidly.

On November 24 Bill picked out a card with a flag and a few lines from the Star Spangled Banner and wrote his mother that he had "arrived on board safe and well." During the month Bill and the other seamen camouflaged their dreadnought to look like an old merchant ship. On the 25th of November Bill put his postcard in the mail just before Battleship Division 9, the Wyoming and three other battleships, sailed for England to become part of the 6th Battle Squadron of the British Grand Fleet. All of England knew the Americans were coming. Bill had received a postcard from his grandmother and aunt in Tunbridge Wells dated November 10 sending their address in case, "you should land anywhere in England. We shall be delighted to see you."

On the passage, their first day out off North Carolina's Cape Hatteras, they met the first seas stormy enough to threaten a large ship. Off the coast of Newfoundland they

steamed into a 90 mile per hour gale. Giant waves rolled over the decks and battered the superstructure of the ships. Lifeboats were crushed. "We had gasoline drums and what not on the deck of the ship . . . Linoleum, dishes, everything was gone." In the fury the four ships were reported to the War Department as lost. They were soon found. The rest of the passage could not have been much easier. "How we ever got [to England] the lord only knows," Bill said. "The British finally came out and found us and took us into Scapa Flow." Scapa Flow had become the main base of the British Grand Fleet, a vast quiet water in northern Scotland surrounded by islands, entered only through seven narrow channels and used since the time of the Vikings a thousand years earlier. Now the Grand Fleet rested with little worry in these waters thanks to the added protection of mine fields and hydrophone listening devices. The one German U boat that dared to attempt entry met a grim fate when the hydrophones picked up the noise of its propellers, and listeners on shore threw the switches that triggered the mines. As the American ships sailed in among the British fleet, from Admiral Beatty's flagship Queen Elizabeth rose three great cheers.

During their first month the American ships largely carried out exercises to integrate the two commands into a smoothly run battle fleet. The British officers were dismayed by the inaccuracy of the hastily trained American gunners who had never fired in battle or even in the rough conditions of the North Sea. Bill enjoyed relatively routine naval life through Christmas.

On December 30th he wrote his mother that he had received her packages and letters and also a Red Cross package from "a Miss Morrison who lives at Riverdale-on-the-Hudson." His package had the usual cards, cigarettes, candy, soap and "a lot of good stuff." He listed the ingredients of a four course Christmas dinner served on board, complete with cigars and cigarettes. He saved part for his supper. He missed only one thing. "All it lacked mother, was the plum pudding." While his own ship had not yet seen battle, he had seen the results of battle on his first shore leave in Britain. "I was ashore one day last week and believe me, you see what war is. We had a dinner in a big hotel: no butter, a taste of sugar, a slice of bread only, with the meal, and each person gets one meal here. The men you see are all sober, and as you look around you see they are all injured in some manner." He asked his mother to send more home newspapers as soon as possible. "I enjoy reading them all, especially the Roslyn News. The city papers you sent are the first I have seen since I left home. I read them all, even the advertisements, am so glad to have news from home."

(USS Wyoming sailors, Bill Pickering third from left)

Two weeks later he was still "having a good time" but as always, pleading for more copies of the *Roslyn News*. When he had gone ashore the day before, he became a little homesick watching Scottish children sleigh riding. "They put me in mind of the good time Emma is having home, I expect. We gave them each a penny in American money for a ride. The kids think they are rich when they have a penny. When we first went ashore, all the kids followed us, crazy over American coins." Although his impression of the Orkney Islands was that they were "nothing but peat moss and few natives," he was homesick enough that the acrid smell of the peat that villagers burned in their homes reminded him of the smell of Roslyn Harbor muck that had once been dredged up when he was a boy delivering papers. He and his brother had walked out on the dredge pipeline to the boat to sell papers to the crew. The crew had fed them steaks and pork chops. It was the kind of medley of strong sensual impressions that imprint on a young boy, and the smell of the muck came back to him in the barren Orkneys. He also recalled that the peat "was all that they [the villagers] had."

The few times the ship anchored near a more populated place, enlisted men were not allowed ashore "because if we did there would be a fight between the British and Yankee sailors which there always was the few times we could get together." On some occasions sailors managed their rivalries by throwing bottles from one ship at another. Bill's one extended shore leave in Scotland was sick leave. He had again developed a carbuncle, this one on his arm and seriously infected. Doctors talked of taking off the arm. "I lay in the Edinburgh hospital. They almost cut my arm off. The fleet had gone out . . . . I used to go with the nurses around town, and try to keep the boys from ducking in the back bar rooms. You weren't allowed to go in barrooms . . . ."

In 1918 he did get some shore leave and obviously left an impression. A letter written from the island of Flotta in the Orkneys on Aug. 8 from Miss J. Sutherland is addressed to "Mr. Pickering." The writer says, "Yes, I heard all about you all being at Kirkwall. As you said, I don't think the people there will ever forget it. . . . We shall be very pleased to see you when you come back again as we liked you coming across."

Late in the afternoon of February 6, 1918 as the short northern day gave way to dark, the USS Wyoming and the rest of the Grand Fleet sailed out to guard a convoy of freighters carrying coal that Britain had promised Norway. The North Sea in winter can be one of the roughest seas in the world, and even veteran sailors become sea sick, Bill included. The convoy, however, sailed out upon a quiet sea and suddenly found its ships illuminated by bright dancing curtains of colored lights—the Aurora Borealis. They delivered their convoy of 13 merchant ships to Stavanger without incident, but Bill wrote that they had dodged torpedoes. This probably refers to either the standard changes in course that ships took to throw off submarines, or to the report on the morning of their departure from Stavanger when two other American battleships reported seeing periscopes. None of the British ships saw these, and the British commanders dismissed the reports as whale fins. German naval records record no U boats in the area at this time.

During another escort trip in March American ships again reported seeing periscopes, but again, the experienced British saw none, and Germans records show none on duty near the Grand Fleet. The fact is that the US ships were always deployed in the safest positions, last in the line of escorts. The British felt the crews and officers, untested in battle, would not get in the way if Germans attacked. The last convoy for the Americans came on April 18, again, uneventful except for a gale that scattered the convoy over sixty miles of sea before it reached its destination. The presence of the American dreadnoughts, of course, was one reason the Germans did not risk repeating their strategy of early fall when they sent light cruisers traveling at 34 knots per hour on the attack. They had destroyed nine merchant ships and two British destroyers in the first raid and more in a December raid before the American ships were integrated into the convoy escorts.

Although naval records do not show any significant encounters between American and German ships, Bill said that in the early spring of 1918 the Wyoming suddenly found itself closing with several German ships. "The German ships had up their battle flags," Bill recalled. "You know, *you fire, we fire*." Battle flags, of course, were the naval equivalent of war paint.

He wrote to his brother Tom, "Well, brother, I am still enjoying life as usual 'over here'. Have the usual good time whenever I go ashore. All we see or hear here is war. Getting to be a real job. Some sport chasing the Huns around the North Sea. It is some sea, what I mean. Go to sleep in the night, get up in the morning sea sick. That was my latest experience. I never will forget the North Sea. It is the nearest to H___ that I ever seen and I don't want to go any further."

The American ships had done all of their training in the Atlantic. The Atlantic, of course, has storms and large waves, but is generally a mild ocean, and even its winds are usually predictable in strength and direction, a fact that enabled early explorers, even without the benefit of good weather forecasting, to quickly establish reliable routes that would fill their sails both to and from Europe. The North Sea's almost constant winds that shift with little notice create wave regimes that often produce powerful competing wave trains with sudden giant waves. Many times even the huge dreadnoughts seemed to disappear into an oncoming wave like a submarine with only its conning tower showing. To these hazards the northern climate added the plagues of driving rain, dense fogs, sleet and hail. Bill's general good cheer in this context is typical of his good nature and upbeat character. None of his brothers and sisters came near that positive outlook and easy going manner except his sister Annie and his brother Buster. Annie he would be close to his entire life, but he would soon have an argument his brother Buster (Wallace) that would put unbreakable silence between them for the rest of their lives.

Possibly Bill and Buster were never close. In his letters to his mother he never mentions his brother Buster, but then he doesn't mention Arthur or Dot either. Emma,

Annie, Tom and Ted appear with affection and concern. He asks when Jack will go into service. His mother sends him news of all his brothers and sisters. Buster has already left home at age 17 and Emma says, "I don't bother much to write letters to him. I send a P.C [post card] he said one time he was going to send some money home but have not seen any yet—I should worry as Emma says." In another letter she sent Bill his brother Buster's address in Providence, Rhode Island.

Although Bill had no experience of the war on land, those involved suffered more casualties and misery than most sailors. In early March Bill's Roslyn friend Monroe S. Wood wrote from the 23rd Infantry "somewhere in France" that they had had it "pretty hard" since landing in France. "We haven't had over two or three weeks of sunshine since landing." And he had not yet faced battle. He shared the general confidence and impatience of troops about to be tested. "Gee! I certainly will be glad when we have the Boche [sic] cleaned up and we can get back to the dear old States. We are the boys that can clean them up to. [sic]"

Monroe's reporting show's no trace of his father who was a well known Long Island journalist who had died of tuberculosis in 1913.

Little Emma, of course, had been worrying about brother Bill since he left for the Navy. When her mother signs off on her March 18, 1918 letter to Bill, she writes after her name,

> God bless you and take care of you and thousands more as Cissee
Emma says in her prayer.

> Now I lay me down to sleep
> I pray the Lord my Soul to keep
> God bless my brother gone to war
> Across the sea's in France so far.
> Oh may his fight for liberty
> Save millions more than little me
> From cruel Fate or Ruthless blast
> And bring him safely home at last.

Bill's mother had taught little Emma this prayer from a poster urging citizens to buy the war stamps that could be saved in a book until they were enough to trade for a government bond. On the same letter Emma had also written in the top margin of the last page, "I expect Ted will be going to camp soon. He's in Class A." [top draft category] Bill's brother Buster had also considered enlisting in the Navy, but at the beginning of the war he had been too young to join without his parents' permission. However, he did concoct a scheme of taking some of his father's old magazines to the Army trainees at nearby Camp Mills where he planned to "join up with a troop here, smuggle aboard a ship with them." When he began asking the troops about when they would sail for Europe, he found that they didn't know.

Whether or not the American ships engaged the Germans, something caused the Wyoming to dock in Edinburg for repairs in April. Most of the crew received a week's leave.

Bill immediately booked a ticket to the south of England to visit his grandmother and his aunts and uncles. Bill had been ashore enough to understand the shortages the German blockade had caused and to know how few things the English rationing system allowed ordinary citizens to buy. Maybe he had already heard from his grandmother and his aunts how little they had. Before he left the ship he used his ration card to buy a quarter pound of sugar as a gift. He also knew how men going ashore could go to the chaplain who was also the censor and get him to stamp "Censor" on a plain white piece of paper and seal the seaman's shore bag with it. Inside their sealed and approved bags they carried extra rations.

With his little sack of sugar, on April 26th he and a buddy took the overnight train to London, and he would go on from there south to Tunbridge Wells, the village in the countryside of Kent where his mother had lived and worked until the month she sailed for America and marriage. On his way south Bill rode first class. "We always went first class and didn't have to pay railroad fare," he remembered clearly when he recorded a tape of his life in his late 80s. On the train his buddy met an appealing young girl. He wanted to give the girl his sugar ration but couldn't find it. Bill said, "Here, give her mine," but his buddy said, "I couldn't do that Bill, I know you've saved it for your grandmother." On the train the American sailors spotted a kilted Scotsman standing in the aisle that ran the length of the train outside the compartments. They took turns walking by and "kicking up the kilt on the Scotsman."

Somewhere between Edinburgh and London he had bought a card showing "HIGH LEVEL & SWING BRIDGES, NEWCASTLE-ON-TYNE" and he jotted a note to his mother as he waited in a London Station for the Tunbridge train.

> "Dear Mother:
> Have seven days' leave, passed through this Place yesterday. Will arrive at Grandma's this morning about 11:30. Will write a letter from there.
> Son Bill.

His father's sisters and his grandmother in Tunbridge Wells received him as a welcome lost relative. He would regret for years after that he couldn't find his bag of sugar for his grandmother. Perhaps she didn't need the energy. He says that even at 85, "She walked me off my feet." Those are the only surviving details of his visit on which he met relatives from both sides of the family.

His mother had warned him, "If you ever meet your grandmother, watch your language." It was not his grandmother but one of his aunts who was "awfully religious" and who put him on guard. He survived and wrote to his mother from the train on the way north and again when he re-boarded the ship on May 2nd. Meanwhile, passing through London he visited his mother's sister Eugenie Marie. She was 41, but he says nothing about her.

He obviously did not send enough details of his visit with his father's or his mother's family. His postcard, also May 2nd, to brother Jack said no more than "Had a fine time. It is some place. The only thing that was roung [sic] was we could not get a square meal." He also reported that he had returned with no more problem than fever sores on his lips.

His letters stirred old memories for his mother. She wrote a note (in her often careless or hurried style) and wanted to know, "Did Auntie Dot show you Hamilton Lodge in Tunbridge Wells when I used to live some nice walk to Southborough?" When she had left England a Scottish pastor resided in the lodge and an adjoining building served as a school for small children. As Emma walked by Hamilton Lodge and its school she may have fancied herself there with other children rather than living with her aunt Maria Howard at the mill in Hornchurch or working as a serving girl to families whose children were in the school. Emma wrote to Bill on May 25 asking if her cousin Tom [Thomas Cornell Howard] had come up to Tunbridge from London to see him.

Besides visiting the family, Bill also wrote about his visit to the YMCA "Eagle Hut" in London where a staff of 800 volunteers provided entertainment, beds, meals, tours, lectures, religious services, and a soda fountain to help American servicemen enjoy a vacation from the rigors and horrors of war.

Bill left behind among his relatives the impression of a lively young man with good manners and an outgoing personality. The letters from them after his visit are since, even romantic invitations to return.

On 9 June the daughter of his aunt Mary Anne (Pickering) Norman wrote to him from Tunbridge Wells. Four years earlier she had married Alfred Terry and their first son arrived a year later. At 30, she was eight years older than Bill. She begins even before the greeting with what may be a humorous reference to the very religious Auntie Dot, a Baptist: "would you like a few Tracts?" The letter also implies that some romance may have blossomed between Bill and his cousin the 22-year-old Ada.

> My dear Billy,
> you will think a letter at last. I am sorry I have not written before but I have been busy at needlework as I go to my Husband's home on Thursday for a week or two, so I know you will forgive me. I was very pleased to get your two letters also Photos enclosed, especially one of you. Am I a special favorite that I should have one?

I suppose you have got Ada's letter before now, yes we have a HIM to write to, every other day or so, but you will understand as you are in love yourself.

Glad there was no sermon in Dot's letter, perhaps she does not know which one to write to you or maybe as you say they are "wise" to you now.

The piece where you said about going somewhere was cut out by the Censors, Billy, so I don't know what it is or where it is. I am glad you are a good boy and write to your Ma once a week. I guess you are glad to get news from them all.

Yes Dot was very nosey about that letter you wrote Ada and asked me if I had heard from you, but no we did not let her see it & have not let her see any of your letters, so don't worry. Yes the Raid must have been terrible in London, so you think it won't last very long now Billy well I guess I hope you are right, for I want my boy home again he is expecting getting leave next month. I wish you could come & see him when he does come.

Glad you are feeling alright hope you have got rid of your cold. Yes we had some lovely weather just lately, it must be nice up in Scotland, and I have heard it is a pretty part, my Boy has been to Dumferline. Yes it would be a bit more like home if we were near you, so that you could come & see us when you were ashore. You will just have to write the War Office & see if you cannot be moved nearer England or nearer Tunbridge Wells. How will that do? Well now I don't think I have any more news to tell you. I'll write again soon as I should have more time at Will's. If you do write next week my address will be.

Mrs. A.V. Terry
"Brickworks"
Rowfant
Nr Crawley. Sussex

I shall be glad to hear from you there as it is such a Country place. I live on letters almost. Well now I say goodbye.
Love & x x x x from all of us. Your loving
Cousin Nellie [Ellen Annie "Nellie" Norman, age 31]

Bill wrote back as soon as he received her letter. And she was quick to reply on June 24th. He had written jokingly about finding a widow with "pots of money" but also to confirm that he had written to a girl back home. She wrote from the little country village of Rowfant.

My Dear Cousin Billy

I was glad to get your letter last Friday the 21st & <u>you</u> wrote it on the 12th wasn't it a long time coming?　　　Glad you hear from the "girl you left behind you". You naughty Boy Billy you <u>must not</u> forget her, as you will be glad of her when you go back to the USA won't you? Well I don't know if it <u>is</u> cheaper to get married Billy, anyhow, it is not much being married nowadays with your boy away from you for years. & Yes you do have a chance to see the world if you are single & enjoy yourself but when you are married well, you <u>have</u> to be good. Well I don't know about a widow with pots of money, <u>money</u> is not everything in the world, you know, <u>love</u> is the greatest of all. Don't you think <u>so?</u> Yes, you would have a good time if you had stopped at our house, for we girls are all very proud of Boys, & get on as a rule, very well with them, but of course Grandma & Dot wanted you all on their own, & I don't think wanted <u>us</u> to see you very much at all. Especially wanted you all to herself & did not like you going to Pictures with Ada and I. I feel sure she didn't but after all you are as much to us as you are to her, & <u>why</u> shouldn't we be Chums, but it's her way, and I can tell you,.& I are <u>no Friends</u>. I never get on with her very much. I love Grandma & would do anything I could for her, but I can't stick Dot, so don't let her know when I write or what I say will you please?
Well it is very quiet here. Only a few houses. No Shops at all.
I am going back to Wells on Thursday.
Yes I guess New York folks have got wind up a bit after Germans <u>Subbing</u> them, perhaps things will look up a bit now & we shall soon hear of Peace. Glad all are well at home. I hope we shall have the pleasure of seeing your Brother & <u>you </u>again although I hope the war will soon be over.
My sister in law is coming up to Scotland next month. I don't know what part, she is married though, no family her Boy is a Sailor. Now Billy I don't think I have any more news to tell you. Jim was 3 yrs old Sunday he is a little Tinker I can tell you..
　　　　　Goodbye. lots of love & x x x x x
　　　　　Your loving Cousin Nellie

Another cousin whose signature on the letter is illegible wrote to him on July 31 with news of his grandmother. She asks him to be sure to ask his parents to write to his grandmother. "Have you learned from home lately; we have not heard since the letter we had before you came down to see us; and Grandma get so anxious; when you write home; ask some of them to drop her a line occasionally; as she does so long for news. . . . How nice it would be if you could get another leave; and come down, about that time; and then we could have grandma's 85th birthday party which we hope to have when uncle Ted and aunt Ada are with us."

On August 6 Nellie wrote from Tunbridge Wells. Her little feud with Auntie Dot continues. ""Auntie Dot said she has not heard for a long time, from home I mean. .I hope you will get a leave this month . Dot knows you are coming doesn't she? As last week, when I told her my Boy was coming she said oh, I hope he comes when Billy is here, so I said "is Billy coming then?" (Of course I did not let her know that I knew.) So she said "yes he is coming in August." Did you tell her, as I nor the other girls have mentioned it to her! But still she would love to know this wouldn't she?" Like many wives in England, Nellie's husband had already been away for three years during which millions had died on the mainland. As much as she wanted him home for her birthday on the 21st, she wrote, "still I don't mind when he comes as long as he does come in the end." Bill had asked her whether she had been swimming and whether she had been to the movies and she replies that she hasn't been to the movies since he took them. She also says, "some hopes of me joining up, Billy, but anyhow I'll join the Navy if I do." In fact her sister-in-law had already joined and gone to serve in Scotland.

On Aug 8 his cousin Ada Norman, the 22-year-old daughter of his father's sister Mary Alice, wrote to him from Tunbridge Wells. [punctuation and spelling as written]

> 133 Camden Rd
> Tun Wells
> 4-8-18 [day-month-year in European style]

Dear Billy,

　　　At last I am answering your lovely long letter so sorry I have not done so before. . . Was very pleased indeed to hear you expect to have leave this month. We will have a jolly good time when you come this time, not half. . . . And Ada & uncle Ted are coming down here for the holiday, perhaps they will be here when you are. Thank you very much for the photos & also the books they are very interesting. . . . So you had a good time in the island although it was not very big. . . . We had some excitement here. We are having a big baseball match here next week, the Americans & Canadians. We often have them here on the Commons. . . . I received your card from Kirkwall & thank you for it. I read Nellie's letter she had from you last week. I don't know if she has answered it yet. Alice's husband was home for the weekend. Bessie's boy expects to come to England next month for two months on tour with the band & then he will have 10 days leave only wish it was my boy but still I must wait I suppose. I have not seen Auntie Dot & Grandma since I went for my holiday, but most likely I shall be going up there this week. How are they all at home quite well I hope. I guess you would just like to be going home to see them all & also your young lady, & my wouldn't she be

152

pleased to. . . . We must enjoy ourselves while we have the chance we are only young once. Glad to say we are all well at home. Several of them had the Flu, but are better now. Hope you are keeping well, & looking forward to seeing you very soon. Well Goodbye with heaps of love & kisses.

Your loving cousin
Ada
X X X X X

Bill apparently did get another leave and got at least as far as London. This much and more is implied in a letter from his cousin Nellie who wrote to him again on Saturday September 14, this time from the southern coastal city of Brighton. The letter is warm verging on steamy. Although she is married, she leaves no doubt that she had fallen in love with Bill.

My Dear Billy,

I am sorry r did not get a chance to write to you yesterday, but as it is pouring with rain today well, here goes.

I hope you got back on Ship alright [sic] & that you were a good Boy in London. also going down in the train. poor old Kid I guess you feel a bit dumpy don't you? I wish some of us girls were up there with you but it is no more than I miss you Kid & wish you were here with me. it's wet but still we could go to pictures or Theatre & sit & hold hands couldn't we? but guess it's no use wishing all this nice things would happen we just have to put up with it don't we? & we did have a nice time together didn't we Billy although we are only cousins.

I wonder if you saw Dot, & did you get the Bus alright & your train Kid? please write & tell me all about it won't you?

Bessie was down at the Station to meet me when I got here. we went & had some dinner & then on to the Beach. but it kept raining so we came home as soon as we had some tea. & I was tired out, so sat still & just thought of the happy time we had with you & wondering where you were. I never thanked you Billy for giving me such a good time. I ought to have done so. I was going to the morning I came away, but did not seem to get a chance as I could only thank you with love & kisses, but you know I was thankful don't you Billy? & you must take my thanks now although I would like to have done it in a way you (& 1) would have liked better, but you understand don't you Kid? Oh dear, how I wish you were here to look after me & love me & don't you wish you were here with me Kid? it would have been nice to have had a day or two down here, but I would have liked it to have been just us two wouldn't you Kid?

Well now I can't think of any more to write. please write to me
soon & tell me if you miss me. you can write to me here, Kid can't you? I
hope you get this Tuesday and then you will write back as soon as you
can.

Now Goodbye. lots of love & xxxxx
from your loving
Cousin Nell.

While Bill's duty was mostly routine and he had enjoyed two long shore leaves
living it up in England, his brother Ted had reached the front lines where hundreds of
thousands of men fought almost daily and steady streams of the wounded, dying and dead
were leaving the field and fresh men replacing them. Although the Americans had
entered the war only a year earlier with great confidence and enthusiasm, the grim
realities of trench warfare quickly took their toll. Germany was pouring in hundreds of
thousands of troops freed up from its eastern front when Russia surrendered. In the early
months of 1918 they had advanced far enough toward Paris that they began bombarding
the city with the giant Krupp guns sometimes called Big Berthas. These guns had to be
hauled to their firing positions in pieces and assembled on concrete firing pads, but once
in place they had a range of 75 miles. They had already reduced some of the best French
forts to heaps of rubble.

The initial German advances in early 1918 were stopped by the Allies with the aid
of hundreds of thousands of American soldiers arriving on convoys that the German U
boats had not been able to penetrate. The first 14,000 Americans had arrived in June
1917 and on July 4th the American Army staged a symbolic march through Paris to lay
wreaths on the grave of Marquis de LaFayette, the Frenchman who had come to the aid
of George Washington. The first battles to engage American troops occurred in October
1917, but American troops played little more than a supporting role for the French and
British. Until the spring of 1918 most would be still training in bases General Pershing
had established throughout France. When the first large force of Americans faced the
Germans in April of 1918 over 1 million American men were in France and more were
soon to follow. The Americans were then under the independent command of American
officers.

In spring of 1918 Bill's brother Ted felt the time had come for him to join the war
effort. He had tried to enlist four times. Four times the recruiters turned him down for
reasons unrecorded. Possibly, like Bill, he had tried for the preferred Marines or the
Navy and could not qualify. In April, however, he received a notice that he had been
drafted into the Army, and on April 27 at nine in the evening he reported to Camp Mills
in nearby Mineola. By 4 in the morning he had his papers, and his uniform. After basic
orientation he was sent to join the new contingent of 15,000 draftees at Camp Upton near
Yaphank in the eastern Long Island pine barrens where one day Brookhaven National

Laboratory would replace it. There he was assigned to the 149 man Company A of the 324th Ammunition Train, part of New York's "Fighting 69th" infantry regiment. Camp Upton had become a small military city with almost everything a man could need, except women. An entire division of 50,000 men had already trained and departed from the camp.

Ted found himself in that small city not far from Roslyn answering the call of the bugle every morning at 5 a.m. Many of the other recruits had recently immigrated to the US and few of them were happy about the idea of going back to Europe to fight. One of these draftees who had left just before Ted's arrival had been a Russian Jewish immigrant named Israel Baline or Belice who had become an American citizen only on February 6, 1918. That same day he became eligible for the draft. He had come to America as a young boy in 1893, and in his early teens he had become an orphan scrounging for money on the Lower East Side of Manhattan, eventually becoming a singing waiter. By 1918 he had become famous as the composer of Alexander's Ragtime Band and more than 100 other tunes. He was making the fabulous sum of nearly $100,000 a year in royalties and had changed his name to Irving Berlin. Nevertheless, he took his $30 a month salary, and he trained at Camp Upton like every other draftee—learning to use the bayonet, take apart and reassemble a rifle, crawl under barbed wire, march in close order drill, how to throw hand grenades, and fight hand to hand and do KP (kitchen patrol). War-hardened European officers taught them how to dig trenches and "go over the top" of a trench to attack or die as millions of Europeans foot soldiers had already done on the largest killing fields ever known.

Berlin did not have to go to Europe, but he may have hated training more than others because he had lost more. Berlin later said, "I found out quickly I wasn't much of a soldier. There were a lot of things about army life I didn't like, and the thing I didn't like most of all was reveille. I hated it. I hated it so much that I used to lie awake nights thinking about how much I hated it." In New York City Berlin had become used to staying up until two or three in the morning composing.

Before being drafted he had tried to support the war effort by writing patriotic songs, but none of them worked with the public. With real army experience he found he could write a new kind of song. His first tune he dedicated to the man in the next bunk who also hated the 5 a.m. bugle. The song instantly caught on in camp, "Oh! How I Hate To Get Up in the Morning."

"Oh! How I Hate To Get Up In The Morning,
Oh! How I'd love to remain in bed
For the hardest blow of all is to hear the bugler call:
'You've got to get up, you've got to get up,
You've got to get up this morning!'"

Someday I'm going to murder the bugler
Someday they're going to find him dead
I'll amputate his reveille and stomp upon it heavily
And spend the rest of my life in bed!

That song would soon be followed by several more, and Berlin received permission from the camp brass to put them together in a musical that would be performed by 350 of his fellow soldiers. Among the songs he composed was one he dropped from the show because he considered it too serious, and a bit too much like other patriotic songs other composers had published. That one, which would be performed years later by Kate Smith, was "God Bless America."

Ted Pickering was one of the boys who enjoyed singing along with "Oh! How I Hate to Get Up in the Morning," but he would depart for Europe before the show, "Yip, Yip, Yaphank" was first staged in August. Ted seemed to take camp life and routines in good humor. On May 15 he sent a card with a picture of recruits labeled "Double Time" to his mother:

Double Time

A few lines to let you and the rest no I am well and getting a long nicely. Recived the Roslyn News. Have not much time to write a letter just jet. We are on the go most of the time. Will try and see you all next month if I am still in Camp Upton.
Pvt Eddie

He did come back home on June 24 on a 48 hour pass to say good-bye. On the 26th he and his regiment boarded the converted ocean liner Cretic and tried out their bunks with the boat still at anchor. The 16 year old ship had been painted "dazzle" camouflage to make her harder for U Boats to target. Over 2,000 soldiers crowded into the ship built for no more than 1,500 passengers. Ted rotated sleeping in a "hot bunk" with another soldier.

USS Cretic of the British White Star Line

Some previous passengers had begun to call the ship the "Creeping Cretic" and on July 4th Ted found himself in mid ocean. However, despite the masses of men eating in three shifts at every meal, Ted would always remember the British jam served at mess. Two weeks after boarding Ted walked down the gangplank in Liverpool. Within a few hours his regiment had been packed on trains headed south to the historic cathedral city of Winchester where they spent the night before going on to the rest camp of Winnel Downs near Aldershot. The rest was not long. The next night they embarked for France on the channel boat King Edward. In homage to the royal name, Ted and almost every other soldier on board got royally seasick during the stormy voyage to Cherbourg. They no sooner landed than they had to walk three miles in a driving rain to eat a one o'clock lunch at a rest camp. "Gold fish and cheese," he reported, but also "some of the real English jam we all liked so well on the boat." Their rest consisted of baths, early lights out, and the bugle sounding reveille at 5 the next morning. They formed up in columns and hiked back to Cherbourg.

In Cherbourg they found the infamous "side car Pullmans" waiting for them. These were the French box cars that served as troop transports. They rode for several days, sleeping on the floor, eating hard tack and corned beef. After a brief stop for hot coffee in Tours they climbed back into the boxcars and resumed their southward rattling until they reached the famous wine region of Bordeaux.

A post war recreation of the French "side car Pullman"
The "40/8" means 40 men or 8 horses per car.

They disembarked a short distance from the city, shouldered their packs with their bedrolls draped over the top, and began a ten mile march to a place Ted called Vigson, a mile and a half beyond the present village of Eysines. The summer sun beat down steadily through a humid, breezeless summer air. The men were soaked with sweat in their heavy uniforms. The sandy, cultivated lands had few trees. One at a time, then in groups, the men began to fall out, too exhausted to march on. "I was one of them to fall out only ¾ of a mile from Vigson," Ted wrote.

At that camp they drilled for two weeks and received their overseas caps marking them as a ready part of the American Expeditionary Force. On July 22nd Ted, who signed most of his letters to his mother as "Private Eddie," received his stripe for Private First Class. He also began to sign his letters "Ted."

On August 8th they left for the American artillery training range 7 miles south at Camp DeSouge. The camp had previously been abandoned by both the French and English as uninhabitable. The land was soft and sandy, covered with scrub, plagued by flies. Ted must have thought of the tent behind his home in Roslyn where the boys slept in summer, and the mosquitoes that now seemed friendly compared to the French biting flies. As they neared the camp the incessant gunfire gave the impression they were approaching the warfront, but it was just another day of learning to use the big French artillery pieces.

Ted's experience at Camp DeSouge could not have been much different from another American soldier, Albert Willard, who penned these lines:

Well we scarcely had landed in France above three days or more
When we received the orders to our disappointment sore
To board the stock cars for camp DeSouge where there's nothing to be found
But sandy swamps and soldiers, but with these it does abound.

So we finally did reach Bordeaux, and 'twas there we spent one night
For when the morn did finally dawn, our bunch they looked a fright.
Our faces were a horrid sight, our backs were like a bow.
I never will forget that night we spent there in Bordeaux.

At noon we landed at DeSouge and looked us up some shacks
For which we might stretch out there in and ease our aching backs.
So after our schooling all was o'er having so long to stay
We decided we'd make some souvenirs to pass the time away.

We went out on the target range; it was covered with low brush
And many different kind of things were collected there by us
While some were pounding out the bands, others were spoiling cash
But we were always at the kitchen when they were dipping out the hash.[21]

Meanwhile, Bill Pickering sailing the stormy North Sea, knew that the daily life of a foot soldier was misery and that trench warfare had been a slaughterhouse. In August he wrote home and asked his brother Tom if he had heard from Ted. "Sometimes you never hear from the boys in the trenches for months. I did not hear from Monroe Woods for two months when I first wrote him. I have not heard from him since."

Ted was still far from the fighting, of course. His duties seem to have been transporting, cooking and serving meals and coffee. He wrote home about a trip south to Camp Hunt where the 314th division gathered and prepared artillery pieces for a trip to the front. "We were gone 2 days and 2 nights helping to feed the boys. All of us in the kitchen had no sleep at all on this trip. So it's some life when you had a taste of it. Made the boys hot coffee to go with the corn beef."

His time in Camp DeSouge, however, was more routine and he had a pass to go to the local towns. His favorite was St. Medard. France, of course, had millions of young men in the army and had lost over a million killed and several more million wounded. French cities and towns had a large surplus of women, but Ted's letters to his mother say nothing of them.

Ted's description of marching in the rain and heat reflect thousands of years of the tedium and discomforts that soldiers had endured. He would also participate in one of the great revolutions in military tactics. Like all foot soldiers in that war, his short service would span both the ancient past and the future of warfare. As the weather cooled in the first week of September trucks, ambulances, and wagons by the hundreds assembled for the trip to the front 500 hundred miles northeast toward the German border. World War I marked the first the use of motor vehicles as the main transport for armies and their supplies. It also marked the replacement of mounted cavalry with the much more devastating tank. The full importance of both innovations would not sink in until the beginning of WWII when the Nazis used them to race across Europe before their victims could mount effective opposition, making the French Maginot Line of giant concrete fortresses as useless as trees in a footrace.

The men at Camp DeSouge had another 500 miles to go before they would see battle. The 324th Ammunition Train was now one of the many regiments from across America that composed the famous 42nd Rainbow Division of the U.S. First Army. Its leader was Brigadier General Douglas McArthur who was also the man who conceived the idea of uniting the National Guard units from across America into a single huge division. The advance of Ted's unit was part of a massive advance of Allied troops pushing north and northeast toward Belgium and Germany. They passed through towns and villages devastated by four years of fighting. In some places the local people swarmed joyously around them, the first American troops they had seen and a sure sign that war in that village was over.

Ted says they left DeSouge on September 4th or 5th . Despite the motorized transportation, they seldom made more than 70 miles a day. After ten days they arrived in Toul a few miles behind the front lines where the Americans had taken a key German stronghold, St. Mihiel in a five day battle that lasted from September 12 to September 16. Ted's unit must have received the news as they approached Toul, and the news was historic. The American commanders had disagreed whether the heavily fortified St. Mihiel was a necessary part of the strategy to drive the German lines back. The Germans had held it for 4 years and had built up elaborate fortifications on a tongue of high ground fifteen miles wide and twenty-five miles long that commanded the Meuse Valley below—front line concrete pill boxes, barbed wire lines, trenches and gun emplacement. However, the salient was not big enough to allow the Germans to use it for staging attacks. In the end the Americans agreed to attack St. Mihiel, but insisted that the attack would be planned and commanded solely by American commanders. This was their first go at fighting a big battle entirely in the American way.

German intelligence noted the 300,000 American troops and 110,000 French gathering for battle, and the buzz of reconnaissance aircraft may have alerted them to the fact that this would be the biggest air assault of the war and one that would validate Col. Billy Mitchell's sometimes derided notion that future wars might be won only by a nation with a powerful air force. Mitchell employed almost 1,500 aircraft in support of the St. Mihiel offensive. Motorized transport, tanks, modern explosives, and an air force were all new and awesome to everyone who saw them in coordinated action. These new powers dwarfed individual men as never before. To a greater extent than ever before soldiers existed to service and operate the machinery of war. Each had a life to live or to lose, a life that meant more to him than almost anything in the world. At the same time that life was more expendable than at any time in history. Ted Pickering from Roslyn commanded no men, made no plans for battles, didn't even command one of the machines that could project his power into the enemy lines. He may have been thankful that he was not one of the hundreds of thousands of men "going over the top" into the storm of bursting shells and machine gun fire, or he may have felt left out. The only record he left were a few observations and a sense that he was lucky to live.

World War I. An Album

Women's Home Service of WWI on parade by Pickering store, East Broadway

Women's Home Service, Neighborhood House, Roslyn Village, 1918. Emma pickering front right corner.

Ted Pickering front rwo end; rear row: ??, Dr. Jessup, Albertson Hicks, William Gay
WWI Officers and men on Willow St., Roslyn Village

CHAPTER 11. BUSTER BLACK SHEEP

The friend Buster had met at Camp Mills continued to write to him and renewed the invitation to come to Rhode Island. Buster's schemes to join the military had failed, but in the summer of 1917 at age sixteen, he did run away, this time for good with the help of a new suit of clothes. He had outgrown his summer suit and his mother decided the time had come for a suit with long pants. "I accompanied her to a local dry-goods store where she paid $12 for my new suit. It took her a long time to part with that $12 for it was much money to her." A few days later his mother told him, "Put on your new suit, take these tickets and you and sister [Dot] go to the church's Ladies Aid Society. And come directly home." When he returned from the charity dinner, he changed clothes in the tent behind the house where the boys slept from May till November instead of in their hot and crowded attic room. He packed his new suit carefully. Like his father, Buster had ambitions, and he was not going to run away from home in well-worn, every day, work clothes like a hobo.

After the dinner Dot went into the house and Buster went into the tent to wait for his opportunity. "If there was no light in the hall window we knew the folks had turned in; if a light was there we knew they were still awake. This had often been our guide; when the folks turned in we turned out for a few hours fun. This night the light remained on until about 11 p.m. which was unusually late. I departed as soon as the light was extinguished and went to the house of a friend where I related my plan. The father of this friend thought he could dissuade me by putting me up for the night. In the morning he found it was useless for I made an early start toward New York. My parents would not miss me until about 6:30 A. M. which gave me a good start."

He was up and out of his friend's house while everyone slept. He boarded an electric trolley car, and in the cool of the morning, wearing his new suit and feeling himself a man of the world, he rode to the end of the line in Flushing. He paid for a shoe shine and asked where he would get the train for New York City. There he knew a boat was making ready to sail for Rhode Island. The rest of the day he moved in a dream, and dreams, we all know are quickly forgotten. No more than ten years later he would write, "I have a complete lapse of Memory from the time of getting my shoes shined in Flushing up to the time of sailing which was 5 pm. It seems curious to me that such an exciting, for it must have been exciting, event in a boy's life would be a total blank. I have often endeavored to retrace this route but always in vain."

His ticket for the overnight trip to Rhode Island did not include a stateroom, but he was wide awake when he disembarked in Newport and boarded the train for Providence.

From Providence he wrote to his mother. She was glad to know where he was, but his departure left her and Billy with a labor force of three girls and 14 year old Arthur.

Among Buster's lifelong ambitions, he wanted to be a writer. Like most young writers, his first subject was himself. Like most young writers, even those who finished high school and studied creative writing in college, Buster needed an editor. He never found either editor or publisher. He wrote well, however, and the story that follows is what he wrote, lightly edited for the modern reader.

The first day in Providence I spent taking in the sights on the seat of an oil truck driven by my friend. That night, Saturday, we went to a rooming house which was operated by an elderly couple he knew. I engaged a room for the sum of two dollars per week. I soon learned that this house had regular customers and inmates and served liquor. The customers, however, were never disorderly. This would be my home for the next year. The old couple and I would continue to be good friends for a number of years.

The following Monday, while walking down the main street, I procured a job as "pearl diver". I noticed a sign in a restaurant window which read: "dishwasher wanted". I didn't do like the "movie boy" who confidently enters, pulls the sign out of the window and asks for his first task. I stared at the sign for a while, stepped in quietly, and asked for the job. My compensation was three meals per day and $7 per week. The hours were long and split up. I reported for work at 11 A. M. and worked until 2 P.M washing dishes, floors, stairs and toilets. I returned again at 8 pm and worked until 3 AM.

Since my arrival in the city I had been living at a level where "the cops" punctuated many conversations. My first encounter with "the cops" was about 3 A. M. one night when I noticed the counter man looking untypically befuddled and nervous as he talked to two men and the night manager. He untied his apron and tossed it on the counter, one man on either side. Then he put on his coat and walked out with the two strangers. The night manager assumed the duties of the missing counter man. He explained to me, "He has been appropriating the night's proceeds to his own use instead of depositing them in the firm's cash register." His son had been doing the same thing in another of this firm's restaurants. '

Life was commencing to unfold itself to me. In the dawn hours customers were mostly young people who frequented the cabarets--street walkers, dopies and prostitutes. I became quite adept at identifying the numerous characters of life. Their favorite drink was "coffee royal." This was made by adding whisky to plain black coffee.

I thought it would be great to drop in and eat on the house when off duty. One afternoon I walked up to the big husky counter man, said a friendly greeting followed by, "I'll have a cup of coffee and apple pie."

His reply, "You don't eat on the house at random, boy. You have your meals while working and that's all you get." I then and there listed him as one of the meanest men in the world. These counter men (all restaurant help for that matter) are continually changing places of employment. Whenever I ate in the restaurant where this man was working, I always ordered my food in the meanest way I knew how. This happened often for years following.

Two weeks at this job and I thought I could get along without eating so I quit. Two days later I discovered that it was necessary to eat and to eat I had to have money. Again I encountered a sign proclaiming "dishwasher wanted." I applied and when I showed up to work the manager told me this was only a relief or "spare man job." The first day I worked and I ate. The second day I was not needed and I did not eat. A tough break but I continued to exist. Two partners ran this concern, one of whom shortly engaged me for a permanent job with him.

The firm rented a tumbledown building and called it their bakery. It was one of the filthiest places I have ever seen in my life. It was their favorite advertisement to say that their pastry came from a modern bakery. The only sanitary law violation that he ever worried about was his continued smoking of a corn-cob pipe while working. I am firmly convinced that most health inspectors are afflicted with blindness.

My boss "D" was one of the proprietors who supervised and did much of the baking. He thought a coat of paint would make the place look cleaner. (It never occurred to him to put a torch to this dump.) I applied the paint--one coat at least one half inch thick did the job. I was complimented for having done such good painting. I did not admire D's ability for appraising painting jobs. That was the first and last time I ever handled a paint brush.

He promoted me from painter, at $7 per week, to kitchen helper at $9 per week with meals. I was supposed to report for duty daily at 3 AM. Most of the time one of my fellow workers had to phone for me. The phone, of course, was not mine. The landlady owned it. She was unhappy when her phone rang at this hour. I usually worked until 4 or 5 in the evening. My fellow workers were a Frenchman (one that another Frenchman would not be proud to know), two Greeks, the boss the Irishman and another Irishman. The boss was a splendid man, a good advisor and teacher and an employer who had an equal interest in his firm and employees.

Making corn-muffins, doughnuts and other pastries came easily to me. Frying doughnuts did not. The grease continually burned my arms until I acquired the knack of turning the doughnuts without splashing. Then I became fond of this job. I also cleaned two dozen chickens each day. The cook put these chickens in every dish except clam-chowder. D taught me how to make excellent "Field's Point clam chowder." I acquired the fine art of baking "palatable beans." I had no talent for art so did not fare so well in the frosting of cakes. I lost a cheap signet ring in a mixture of pie filling I was making. I guess some patron got it.

After a few months here had a hot argument with the Frenchman. I quit, although I don't doubt the argument was only an excuse for getting out of there. I look back now and think what a chump I was for getting out of a business I was learning from the bottom up.

However, greener pastures beckoned. Rumor was abroad that men were receiving $2 per hour for 8 hours a day and 7 days per week. First I tried again to enlist in the Navy. The Navy refused me. I took the job filling hand grenades with "TNT" at the Gorham Manufacturing Company. (Until that year Gorham had made only fine silverware. Gorham prided itself on craftsmanship and patriotism. The patriotism was useful in complying with government demands. American soldiers appreciated the craftsmanship.) Gorham became the only company to build grenades from beginning to finished product ready to ship overseas. America eventually shipped more than 21 million improved grenades.

The labor of loading hand grenades all day was tedious drudge work, but on this job I met my second love, the first being a home town girl, who had ignored me. I resigned from this job through having had an argument with one of the foremen. I was not the only one whom he succeeded in getting out.

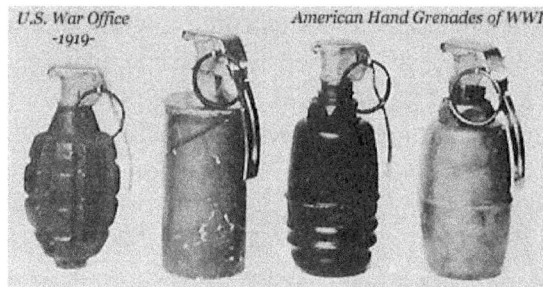

U.S. War Office -1919-   American Hand Grenades of WWI

"Some man has been calling several times a day for you," said my landlady. This happened about one week after I had left the hand grenade factory. At last I happened to be at home when he called. He did not make his mission or identity known to me over the phone so I began to think that my family had made a determined effort to return me to the family fireside. I said I would meet him. I thought this man was the person to return me to my home. Frankly, I would have been pleased at returning.

We had no sooner shook hands than he identified himself as a representative of the U. S. Department of Justice. He questioned me closely about my employment at the hand grenade factory. Without reservation I answered his questions. He was kind enough to explain his visit to me. He described a certain fellow-worker of mine whom I knew quite well. I then remembered some of his actions which at the time had not impressed me. No doubt this fellow was in the employ of the government of Germany. His duties were to stir up unrest among factory workers in this country. This was my first and only encounter with a spy or secret agent. How many seventeen year old kids can boast of this!

Gorham Manufacturing, Providence, RI

We leave Buster's memoir for a moment to note that his life in Providence wasn't all work and looking for work. In a postcard written sometime in 1918 to brother Jack he said, "I have been out in a Winston Six Roadster all day and part of yesterday and we sure did have some time. I feel like a spring chicken. I weigh 142. Bro. WGP" In typical Pickering style, he added a note across the top: "How is your little dizy[sic] Helen? (Helen Nalevaiko, who would soon be Jack's wife.) Why don't you write once and a while. How's my Sarah John O.K.?"

[His memoir continues.]

I shortly procured a job in a rain coat factory which supplied U. S. Army contracts. Here whites and blacks (these blacks were Bravos, natives of the West Indies) worked side by side. I was assigned to a foot press which pressed eyelets in the arm pits of the coats. It was not a hard task. Once I inserted one of my fingers where the coat should have been. My finger was not impressed permanently in the armpit of the coat, but for sure it could not work for many months. For want of a finger a job was lost.

A few doors beyond this factory stood a rubber goods factory, my next place of employment. I did not work here long. The heavy smell of hot rubber made me sick. I was soon without funds and in debt to the landlady. This shame greatly injured my pride.

I resorted to the art of pearl diving as spare man in a Y. M. C. A. restaurant (operated by the firm who owned the bakery I had worked in). I had washed dishes only a few days when I procured a job greasing bread tins for a large nationally known baking concern. This was the worst job I have ever had before or since this time. I was escorted to the locker room by a Negro porter. In there ran roaches as large as turtles. I was shown how to grease pans with a brush. I never saw so many bread tins in my life. There must have been five thousand in the greasing room. I learned that first night that the foreman could ascertain whether I had properly greased the tins. He chewed me out several times.

After I had finished my greasing task I toured the factory. I stared in amazement at machines without operators doing so many operations, even to the wrapping. I wondered why some one had not invented a way of greasing bread tins with machinery. Each loaf of dough passed thru the right hand of a man. This was to ascertain the weight was correct. This fellow was so adept at this that he rarely ever made a mistake.

After two weeks of bread tin greasing, I ventured into the office of time keeper for a construction company. This firm was erecting a dam at the outlet of a river on which many factories depended for their water supply. My salary was fifteen dollars per week. This proved to be the best school thus far. I learned some mathematics, rigging, the operation of hoisting engines and derricks. The moving of a seventy foot derrick was a challenge but well done by our chief rigger. Walking a 2x4 was simple. I met my Waterloo on one of these. At the end of each day I set about my routine of determining the amount of coal and water used by each boiler (of which we had five). One cold February day to cross over to the engineer to inquire about the day's consumption of coal and water I stepped upon a 2x4 to cross a canal. I had accomplished this crossing many times. On the day in question this timber had been un-nailed, so immediately upon putting my foot upon it, I was thrown into the cold water. To make matters worse this spot was near the sluiceway where the water ran fast and deep. The location retarded my rescue. The completion of the dam severed my connections with the construction business. This was a disappointment to me for I was engrossed in this line of work.

A week later I secured a job as pressman in a plant which was manufacturing six inch cannon shells for the U.S. Navy. My particular job was to set discs of brass on a solid steel cylinder, then release a powerful hydraulic press which would descend on the disk and mold it around the cylinder in the shape of a shell.

CHAPTER 12. HOME FRONT

Music may not really "tame the savage beast," but the best music is a welcome life raft to a soul in the troubled waters of worry or depression. Once Emma Pickering's sons Ted and Bill had gone to war she frequently sang a song composed in her home country to brace the spirits of its fighting men and their families. The song tells the simple story of Private Perks "lov'd by the privates and commanders for his smile his funny smile" that never fades as he goes into a war whose mechanized killing was rapidly demoralizing both the troops and their loved ones back home. Private Perks "came back from Bosche-shooting with his smile his funny smile" and recruited more men to fight. The little pep talk of a story didn't inspire or console as much as the chorus verse that is still sung today.

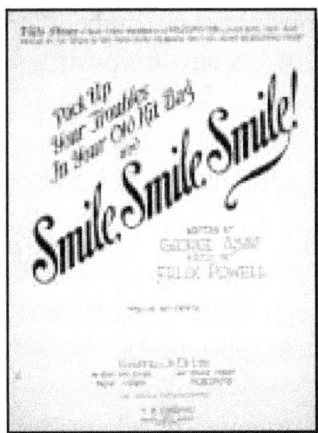

Chorus (sung twice after each verse)
Pack up your troubles in your old kit-bag,
And smile, smile, smile,
While you've a Lucifer to light your fag,
Smile, boys, that's the style.
What's the use of worrying?
It never was worthwhile, so
Pack up your troubles in your old kit-bag,
And smile, smile, smile.

"Smile, Smile, Smile" had become an instant hit in Britain in 1915 and quickly jumped the Atlantic to America. Emma learned it by heart. She would still be singing it to her grandchildren many years later. In the 1930s she taught it to her granddaughter Eleanor who said, "Whenever I was unhappy I would sing it to myself." Little Emma also learned it and taught it to her own children.

Emma also sang "It's a Long Way to Tipperary" a 1912 comic song about a simple young Irishman visiting London and longing for his girlfriend in Tipperary. Its brisk, upbeat rhythm and nostalgic lyrics won it a place as a preferred marching tune for British troops in 1914. Her son Ted knew the song before he left, and maybe before he set foot in France he had learned the refrain added by lusty young soldiers:

That's the wrong way to tickle Mary,
That's the wrong way to kiss!

Don't you know that over here, lad,
They like it best like this!
Hooray *pour le Francais*!
Farewell, *Angleterre*!
We didn't know the way to tickle Mary,
But we learned how, over there!

If television and radio journalists had been reporting from the French and German trenches before 1917, America might never have entered the war. The American public has come to think of a war that grinds on for more than a couple of years as a "quagmire," and a few thousand deaths shown in full color brings home individual pain and suffering in a personal way that has a profound impact on public opinion despite the fact that the toll of war on soldiers has decreased enormously.

In the early 20th Century even the first three years of black and white newsprint and fuzzy photos of what was then called "The Great War" did not convey the mechanical slaughter of millions and the inability of either side to capture and hold large pieces of territory once the fronts had been established. The result was that only when Germany attacked individual US ships and promised Mexico part of US territory, war fever swept like an irresistible tide across the country.

Most Americans soon found something to do for their country long before President Jack Kennedy famously demanded, "Ask not what your country can do for you, but ask what you can do for your country." The effort to sell the war created a wave of enlistments and citizen support. Bill and Ted Pickering had volunteered. Brother Buster had tried to lie his way into service at 17. Art and Jack were ready but too young. Tom had married and his first son, had been born Nov. 6, 1916. (Tom and Anna christened their first born with his father's name, including his grandmother's maiden name-- Thomas Vickers Pickering, Jr.)

Those who could not fight "over there" enlisted in civilian organizations here. Emma and Billy and Roslyn joined the effort. Emma became part of the Red Cross supply chain working out of The Neighborhood House on East Broadway where little Emma attended kindergarten during the day. The Neighborhood House became the center of the community's war effort. To prepare men for fighting in France, musician Albert Monestel taught French lessons. In the Neighborhood House annex thirteen year old Annie Pickering hung an apron over her dress, donned a Red Cross cap and stood with dozens of women operating a canning kitchen where they preserved fruits and vegetables for delivery to poorer citizens. These kitchens helped alleviate food shortages by salvaging badly packed fruits and vegetables from the warehouses and docks and canning them for sale or distribution at big discounts. (Perhaps in that kitchen, wearing that cap and apron, Annie began her lifelong dedication to nursing whose work she would continue into her nineties.)

Seated: Eva Henry, Emma Pickering, Kitty Darby O'Leary
Standing: Connie Charlick Terrell, Lillian Nelson Rinas, Annie Pickering

In the nearby paper mill building other women made bandages for the Red Cross to take to France. Annie also remembered that Mrs. Eugene Conklin led a group of ladies and girls who knitted scarves and gloves for men in service.

In Glenwood landing the Fire Company formed a Home Defense League to help in maintaining and possibly defending the home front. The flagpole, was presented by James Fyfe, and dedicated in April, 1918. It was a mast from a large sailing ship which raced in the International Yacht races. Fifty-two year old Billy Pickering, still talking with a strong English accent, his hair thinning and a little paunch rounding his waist, joined his local defense unit, the Roslyn Highlands Hose Company. He drilled with them on the landing grounds on Hempstead Harbor.

His children scratched metal foil from candy and food wrappers and packed them into balls to be donated to the war effort. For a certain size ball the donor received a 25 cent Thrift or War Saving Stamp. Annie, Emma, and Arthur all pitched in to earn the money to buy their 25 cent Thrift Stamps. Annie and Emma were delivering papers during the war and when they delivered to Henry Eastman's law office, the lawyer would give them a stamp and advise them to save up for a Liberty Bond. For a book of 16 stamps they received a $4 War Saving Stamp or certificate which the post office would register in their names. That was their loan to the government to pay for the war. In return the government guaranteed a 4% return by 1923. The Pickerings and many others in Roslyn became part of a movement that brought over $1 billion into the US treasury.

As soon as Bill and Ted had volunteered for service and left home, the family business was short on labor. Tom had a wife. Buster had run off to New England to search for a life. Billy had drafted six year old Emma for service in the newspaper and photography business. "He made me set aside my small teddy bear and fill my arms with newspapers," Emma remembered. Her first remembered duty was to sit beside the big green box emblazoned with an advertisement for the *Brooklyn Daily Eagle* and displaying various magazines and papers. "In back of me hanging in the store windows were two white flags with red borders, each with a blue star in the center. I was proud of them as it told the passer-by that my brothers were in service."

Soon, however, she found herself suffering through the "countless afternoons he ordered me into his darkroom where I spent the hours until supper time washing photographs." The only light in the darkroom's little annex to the store filled the space with a dim red glow to which films and print paper were not sensitive. A few feet away, her father stood loading film plates into a large square box of developing chemicals or printed pictures. His chemicals filled the room with a mildly acid and metallic vapor. Negatives held by wooden pegs to overhead strings overhead dried and awaited printing. Emma's job was to rock long enamel trays full of prints for twenty minutes per batch to clear the prints of the hypo solution that fixed the images on the prints. As she carefully laid each finished batch on clean blotter paper, her father loaded a fresh batch into her tray. Tray after tray made the afternoons seem endless and supper

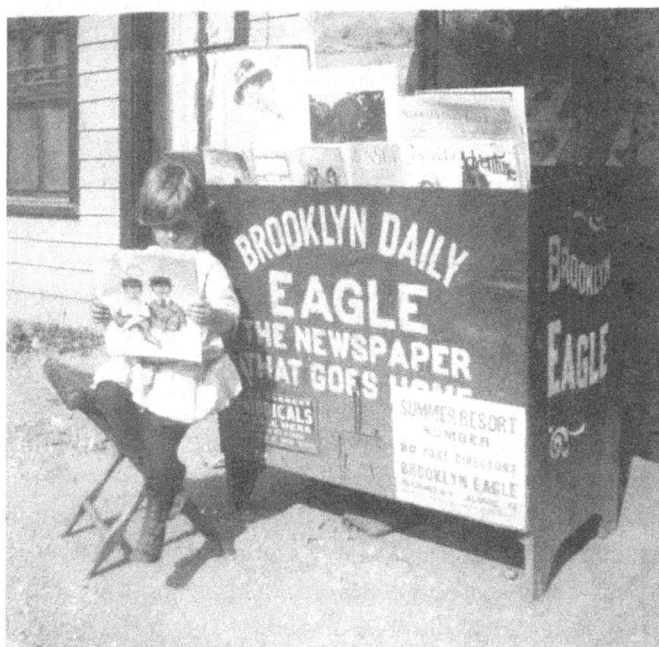

Emma Pickering Tending the rack, about 1916

delicious, as much for its food as for the relief from the limbo of red light. Her first sales duty required her to sit next to the green board sign advertising *The Brooklyn Eagle* and sell papers.

Her father, however, was not all task master. A phrase in one of his letters at this time indicates that when they were not working together, Emma sought his attention as any child does of a parent she loves. One afternoon as Emma came in from the park singing while he was writing to son Bill, he concluded, "I can't write while she is around." He turned that letter over to little Emma for a note. In full it said, "Dear Billy. Pop bought me a moving picture show." Both Emma and Annie also remember outings

Emma and Jud, 1917

with their father to Bar Beach or traveling with him to New York City when he had business there.

In the store Emma learned to read the names of the papers and set them aside for their subscribers. Her responsibilities here too made her part of the family enterprise. "If one of [the expensive subscription only papers like *The Racing* Form or *The* Telegraph] was missing from its stack, I bore the blame." Her father also sent her out on the street to sell newspapers. In the summer of 1918 her mother wrote to her son Bill, "Emma is getting to be quite a paper girl. Sells 12 & 14 papers down the street some nights." Sometimes she had help. After little Emma's moving picture show remark, her father continued his letter, "She's gone to sell papers now Laurence takes her down in his hack [cab], to the PO. He thinks the world of her and waits for her every day." Little Emma also learned to deal with adults on their own terms. "I learned to cope with the rich and the poor, the nice people and the crabby people both in the store and on my paper delivery route. On that route I first met old men with indecent ideas in their heads and their hands."

The family dog Jud, who delighted in wrestling Emma for rags or pulling her on the wooden sled with its wooden runners shod in iron, had grown into formidable size. He added to his role of playmate, the role of companion and protector. He behaved as well as Emma herself. "Shopkeepers did not hesitate when I brought him into their stores. He never stuck his nose into the large tubs of butter or the barrels of cookies. He was not a thoroughbred but to me he was royalty."

In the store and dark room and on the paper route, she understood that while she suffered, she was following in her turn the line of brothers and sisters who had been the laborer force for the family enterprise. She also understood that even the least interesting and most common photos were often the most profitable. Every chauffeur, for instance, had to have several ID photos, and they or their employers paid a dollar a dozen. That was the equivalent of almost a half-day's work for a common laborer.

As soon as Emma became a contributor and her father's co-worker, she began to think and feel differently. "After that I no longer feared the 'Bellman', the knife sharpener," she recalled. She also missed the security of being a little girl with adult brothers, and sharp details of that loss engraved themselves in her memory.

Few years made as deep an impact on little Emma's character and view of life as those two years of World War I. She would always remember the day President Wilson declared war and called for American troops to aid the British and French. She did not understand the causes of the war, but she understood the excitement that war news caused in her customers. The store would sometimes be crowded with immigrants—English, Irish, Germans, and Poles reading and talking about the war news from their homelands. She learned that lurking beneath the big ocean were deadly U boats. She remembered the *New York Times* announcement that the Germans had moved their super-cannon named Big Bertha to a position where it could use its 75 mile range to bring Paris under artillery fire for the first time since the war began.

Emma and Jud, 1916

She not only became a working girl, but she started kindergarten in the old Neighborhood House on East Broadway. The Neighborhood House also provided English classes for the growing number of immigrants in Roslyn who worked on estates and in the trades. With so many men at war, immigrants who were not yet citizens had become an increasingly important source of labor.

Emma began kindergarten with much more enthusiasm than she started work. Accompanied by one or more of her brothers or sisters, she walked from the house down East Broadway, past the Connolly brothers' blacksmith shop and its clanging of hammers, iron and anvils, to The Neighborhood House.

In a simple classroom the soft spoken and reassuring young woman they addressed as Miss Monestel taught more than twenty children their first letters, how to sew stitches from dot to dot, and eventually how to spell their names. School and education became an alternative to home, danger and work. Its windows on the wider world kindled ambition. Emma would never have the grand ambitions of fame or power, but her ambitions were often enduring. Such was the goal to write the story of her life and her family.

Emma who played the man when she and her friend Helen Conklin dressed up, became a tomboy in grade school, maybe even a bully at times. "I enjoyed beating up the village sissy," she said. Teachers gave them a chance to study adults close up for long periods. "One of our teachers, Mrs. Parsley, wore purple bloomers which amused us. We were innocent of sex and seldom saw anyone's underclothing. Those purple bloomers were a great source of amusement to us." She liked her teachers, or most of them, but she joined the pack in that universal willingness of students to seek out a teacher's weakness and exploit it. "In my day we abused teachers mentally. I recall Mrs. Ramsey leaving the classroom to cry outside the door."

For students, then and now, pranks on teachers, challenging authority in a pack, allows them a power over adult authority most never have at home, and so it was in the 1920s and for centuries before and undoubtedly for centuries to come. Certainly for Emma school was a refuge from home with her strict parents and nothing but older brothers and sisters who had an authority of their own. She attended the large two story frame school in the village which had recently absorbed the black children. Until 1917 Roslyn's black children attended a one room k-8 school across from the Clock Tower. Emma had counted some black students among her friends and playmates since her tomboy days in grade school.

Her first grade report card shows she got off to a good start. The third quarter grades slumped, possibly as a result of 27 absences. Even then her grades were no lower than 80, except for "writing" which was weak all year. She ended first grade with a 100% test score in math, 90 in English and 88 in spelling.

Emma could not imagine the distance between her and her brothers. She expected any day to see Bill or Ted guiding the horse and buggy up the hill toward the railroad station to pick up the bales of papers. Friday was still the day when Bill might come home from Conklin's lumber mill with a package of Hydrox black and white cookies for her, paid for from his pay envelope. "No one gave me copper pennies to put in the monkey's hat when the organ grinder came." The man who used to come with his dancing bear also vanished.

Ted, Dot, Bill, and Tom and bear man

The greatest absence, of course, were her oldest brothers Bill and Ted. Their absence was not the normal and nearby absence of young adults leaving home for their own lives, but a disappearance into unimaginable places obscured in an atmosphere of national emergency that made itself concrete in small and large ways. At age 7 "Instead of white sugar, we now had brown sugar. We heard the news shouted by newsboys with cries like, '*Extra, Extra, Read all about it: Allies invade France.*' Instead of the monkey man and the dancing bear coming to the Park for amusement, we had war rallies, we hung the Kaiser in effigy, and gathered to sing patriotic songs." A letter from her father to his son Bill described her: "Heres [sic] that young Emma coming bothering now singing away, she is getting quite a singer . . . singing the Star Spangled Banner You'd think she was a whole Choir Herself."

The war became the central fact of her childhood. It permeated adult talk. Her parents sent papers and letters to Bill and Ted and waited for answers. A letter from "the front" always brought the family together to hear the news. *The Roslyn News* printed some of them. The village government sponsored victory rallies in the park. These rallies entertained as they roused patriotic sentiment and solicited investments in war bonds. At one rally that newest of all fighting machines, the tank, demonstrated its prowess by crawling into and out of swampier parts of Roslyn Park. On the mill pond a bemused boatman poled his skiff decked out like an Italian gondola while a rotund little opera singer sang to the audience on shore. People hung rag effigies of the German Kaiser. Suspicion of German immigrants began to spread as the government warned of spies and saboteurs.

The Pickering kids joined the enthusiasm for supporting the troops and the war effort. On April 10, 1918 their mother wrote to her son Bill. In the letter Annie took dictation for her little sister Emma. [spelling and punctuation as written] "I am wirting to you for Emma. She is telling me what to wirte as she can't wirte good enough.

I am selling papers at the _____ post office every night so the polelock can not beat me. And every Sat. I get a thrift stamp. I have one already. Annie has five and a big 5 dollar one. Annie got hers by selling papers. Mr. Eastman gave her 4 for Christmas. Then she got that book full then on her birthday she got 4 herself and Elner [Elmer Conklin, the boy across the street] gave her one. So that make 5. On apr. 5, 1918.

From

Emma

A.P. [Annie Pickering writing for Emma]

Their mother let Emma paste a row of American flags across the paper.

Opera singer at
Roslyn Paper mill Pond

PHOTO BY
W. H. PICKERING
ROSLYN, N. Y.

CHAPTER 13. BUSINESS TROUBLES

It's a truism in business education that "success breeds competition, and competition breeds ruinous competition." In other words, Billy was bound to have competitors in the news business, and sooner or later one or more dealers would fail. News did not yet travel by radio, and telegraph was not a means of mass communication, and certainly not of entertainment. When the big distributors in New York City began selling papers to new competitors, Billy was among the many established dealers who protested that they had exclusive rights to certain territories in the city or on the island. The Long Island dealers had formed their own association, and on May 23, 1917 they elected the feisty Billy Pickering President of the National Association of Newsdealers and Stationers on Long Island.

The Association also gave the dealers bargaining power with the papers and their distributors. *The New York Times* and other big papers had combined in what would now be an illegal price fixing scheme. Phil Ochs of the *Times* and Wm. Randolph Hearst with his chain of papers agreed to charge one cent per weekday copy. They agreed to give the dealers 40% of that or 40 cents per hundred copies. The dealers paid the papers in advance for all the papers they took, regardless of what they sold. Those terms made a secure territory and predictable number of sales important.

That one penny for a paper didn't pay the cost of materials, buildings, machinery and reporters. Advertising did that. When the war forced up the costs of materials and labor, the papers again arranged a fixed price—100% higher or 2 cents a copy. They told dealers they too would benefit. They would now receive 60 cents per 100, a 50% increase. Ochs and Hearst thought the dealers would be delighted, but they didn't understand economics. The dealers protested because now they had to front 100% more money for their supply of papers, and they would lose more on unsold papers. They also understood that if you raise the price, demand is likely to fall.

The Long Island association joined the New York News Dealers' and Stationers' Protective Association strike in January 1918 and refused to sell many big name papers and magazines including *The New York Times*. The mayor of New York all but threatened the dealers, and city police cited kiosks for being a few inches out of place. *The New York Times* began its own deliveries to apartment buildings. Distributors hastily organized the United Newspaper Delivery Company which began putting up its own newsstands around the city.

On Long Island Billy's customers began looking for other places to buy their papers. Young Bill would soon go into the business himself and learn the inside politics and scheming of the newspaper world.

"It was dirty politics too. It was a nasty game. There was what they call the Rockaway News Company. This is a true story. You may not believe it. They were going to throw me out of the 8 or 10 story old World Telegram building in New York right opposite the city hall because I was like my father. I was always fighting. He fought the newspaper people too. Oh he really fought 'em. There was an Irishman who was the czar of this racket. He was the person who was going to throw me out the ten story window. Well I tell you. This newspaper racket before the Rockaway Newspaper company took it over wasn't too bad. You got your newspapers from the railway station. Somebody had to go get them, you had to pay somebody like my daddy to bring 'em down town, or one of us kids go up and bring them down.

This was a Jewish fella who was like myself or my father. He started in Rockaway, a little small newspaper business. In the meantime trucks became involved. The Long Island Railroad was sick of the newspapers. They couldn't see this coming either. See they used to bring them on the train like on Sunday morning, had them at the door. That's when they stopped making bundles. Like even with cement a man couldn't lift only so much weight. They just throwed them over on the street, in the snow and everything else. And you had to fix them, pick them up, and what have you. And this Rockaway, this Samiat, was the name, he got the idea, same as United Parcel . . .
So he goes to the newspapers. Here's how it works. You go to New York and you buy your newspapers at what they call a city rate. Then they come out here and sell them at the country rate. And this was all done for nothing first. . . .

Bill tells of an incident when he was in the business where a new dealer, Ike Raff, in nearby Sea Cliff started delivering to part of what Bill considered his territory. The Irish czar overseeing distribution,

. . . he summons me and this Jewish fellow who started up in Sea Cliff. Here we are you see. When they got me in there they made a fool out of this little Jewish boy. That's how smart they were. This is the Irishman too. So he said I got in and he said, where's your friend? I said, "I dunno know." But he finally come in. So they got after him. He was clay right in their hands, see. "But where you been? When you get a summons, aw you know, . . " Well he was late the poor guy, so the Irishman says, "Okay, sit down here." They had warned me beforehand, "Now, don't you say nuttin' Pickering."
I said, "If I have to I will."

They said, "Okay, you keep quiet."

He gets in, they says to the boy, "Now listen, who told you to do this? What kind of business were you in before you came out from New York City?"

He says, "In the kiddy clothes business."

Right away he knew the kid didn't know nothing about the newspaper racket, get the story? So this is how it all winds up. The Irishman told him—and I'm just sitting there—"You give Pickering a thousand dollars or else if you want that route." Which it was worth, more than that at the time, the town is building up all the time. . . .But that's how the story was. They would go around and threaten these people see. . . .

The storekeeper dealers and kiosk owners and newsboys with routes had very little power to bargain with the publishers and distributors. The strike begun in January 1918 began to peter out before the month ended. More and more dealers left the strike until it was officially called off on February 8.

Most of the action had taken place in the city, but Billy found himself also under assault. Someone had begun to spread rumors that he was going out of business, obviously hoping this premature notice of his business failure would force him to give up or would inspire competitors or would simply punish him for his leadership in the strike. On February 14 Billy felt he had to reassure his clients that he would be a reliable dealer. He wrote and distributed this notice:

WILLIAM PICKERING

News Dealer and Stationer

Roslyn, N. Y., Feb. 14, 1918

TO OUR PATRONS

Some malicious person has been circulating the report that we have sold our newspaper business, and that we were no longer carrying on that business. This was false and was evidently done with the intention of injuring us. While we were conducting the recent strike of newsdealers in New York and adjacent territory we felt morally bound not to carry any papers that we considered unfair to the newsdealers. But, we still carried the other papers.

Matters having been settled between the Publishers and the Newsdealers, we have commenced to carry all the newspapers again.

Thanking our friends and patrons for their very kind support, and sympathy, during our troubles,

   We are sincerely yours,
   WM. H. PICKERING & FAMILY.

The writing as well as the content deserves a note. He doesn't write 'we've begun to carry' but 'commenced to carry.' Billy no longer uses the language of the British or the American working class. Finally, he wrote this in the 'we' form. That's common in old business communication or in the editorial *royal we* that the queen or king would use to signify the royal role as voice of the nation, but here, supported by a few other communications, the royal we and the signature indicate Billy now believes he owns the business *with* his family. His reading and maybe his changing sense of his place in the community had changed his language.   His native phrasing, however, still appears in 'Thanking our friends.' Many working class English merchants and laborers still say instead of 'Thank you,' the phrase 'Thanking you.'

The strike left a hole in family finances. Also Billy had begun to spend on his addictions. He disguised as expanding business his ever growing collection of old books, antiques, and Indian artifacts, but he bought much more often than he was willing to sell. As one antiquarian friend, the educated and wealthy Raymond Newton Hyde, said, "The history of Long Island seemed to fascinate him. When he was living with his family on $20 a week he started collecting old books, manuscripts and historical matter. He was indefatigable in collecting details of things that happened 200 years ago." Books began accumulating in the store and in the room above the store.

Once again he had to borrow money. This time he did not have to use the house or the store as collateral since his friend Simon Replogle, the Glenwood postmaster, signed as guarantor.

The signs on the storefront over the years tell the story of his interests and growing collection. In the earliest picture, sometime before 1908, the store and its little wood shingled studio sit side by side.   The only sign is a long painted board nailed to the wall above the windows and awning.

WILLIAM PICKERING, GENERAL PHOTOGRAPHER,
KODAK DEVELOPING & PRINTING - SODA.   CIGARS AND SOUVENIRS

Emma with Ted to her left, Bill to her right, Arthur standing
Seated Jack, Buster, Tom, Dorothy. About 1905

By 1910 he had replaced this simple sign with a large white sign that stood out horizontally from the second story of the building. His name, "W. Pickering" arched over his skills and wares:

PHOTOGRAPHER
& NEWSDEALER
OLD AND RARE BOOKS
CIGARS CANDY AND STATIONERY
PHOTO SUPPLIES
DEVELOPING AND PRINTING
SOUVENIR POST CARDS

Sticking out even farther from the edge of the sign was a metal Bell Telephone sign. Within a few years the local power company would bring electric lights.

In 1918 or shortly afterward Billy replaced his white sign with a black sign bearing white letters. His name still arched over the top but the mix and typography had changed. "Photographer" now assumed equal size with news dealer.

**PHOTOGRAPHER
& NEWSDEALER**
CIRCULATING LIBRARY
OLD AND RARE BOOKS
CIGARS &CANDY PHOTO SUPPLIES
DEVELOPING AND PRINTING
LAUNDRY AGENCY

Annie, Emma, and daughter Emma

The telephone sign again stuck out from the edge of the sign. The laundry agency was a business he had started ten years earlier, but its announcement had moved from a sign on the ground below the window to the bottom edge of the hanging sign.

Within a few years this black sign with white lettering would be replaced or repainted. The final sign on the building hung above the newly paved and curbed East Broadway:

PICKERING'S STUDIO
PHOTOGRAPHER
NEWSDEALER
PRINTING AND DEVELOPING
CIGARS CANDY STATIONARY
BOOKS AND ANTIQUES
BOUGHT AND SOLD ON
COMISSION

His spelling of stationery had been correct on the white sign, but he had never been a good speller, and on this final sign 'commission' is spelled incorrectly. The telephone sign was moved to the power pole. As if in afterthought he regretted the smaller lettering on books and antiques, he hung from the lower street corner of the sign a smaller sign saying ANTIQUES AND RARE BOOKS.

He did not appreciate the main street grocer Charlie Masini who began selling papers along with vegetables while Billy was on strike with the newsdealers. In March, a month after the end of the strike, Emma wrote to her son Bill in the Navy and said, "We still have our opposition with the paper in the village but I don't think he is doing much. I think he is about tired of his business because most all of the people are coming here, of course he has some and some we don't want to have—the most of the big people are not back yet." She went on later in the letter to say "Masini thought we would never get the paper back but we did but at present he has got them too but most of our people are back to us." She goes on to list some of their old customers and notes, "The dead heads of course he [Masini] will have."

Billy may have honored the strike more in appearance than practice. A family friend who also had a store in town had supplied Billy's customers during the time he was on strike. Emma wrote, "He was very good to keep them supplied and then turned them back to us. The bills were the same as if they were getting the paper at the store. Sunday Masini customers don't amount to a lot because he figures on people going to his store. I guess he will get left out of course he was a louse."

On May 4 Billy took out a piece of the letterhead he had for his position as President of the National Association of Newsdealers and Stationers on Long Island and rolled it carefully into his typewriter. With both Ted and Bill in service, he wrote one of his rare family letters. He banged out a page and a half. Once again money was on his mind, and he was straight forward about and matter-of-fact about asking his son for help.

> Dear Bill.
> Would it be possible for you to make your allotment you send home, fifteen dollars instead of ten, we find that we cannot get any bonus from the Government unless this is made that amount, we are in very much in need of the money as the business is not enough for our living, besides having to take care of your Grandmother, and they are suffering very much over there, I have had to borrow three hundred dollars in the past two months, and we dont want to mortgage our home again.
> I wish you would write to Mr Replogle, Glenwood PO. And thank him for endorsing the note for me so that we did not have to get a mortgage, it is very kind of him, he would appreciate it, he is building a fine boat now and has it nearly completed.

> Business is very slow this season, so many of the boys gone away, Roggie Dugan went this week, our Ted last week, the Village seems deserted,
>
> . . .

He was also keeping a wary eye on their competitor with the vegetable store.

> We are hanging on to your business alright, and run the whole thing with the Ford, Masini hurts us a little in Roslyn, but he hurts his own business more, how he's going to make out I dont know, his order is 180 Sunday papers, and he does'nt sell over 60 and he has to pay for all of them, he has three stacks of papers up to the ceiling, and he never sent in a return since he started, he gets 6 Heralds a day and sells one or two, and the rest of the papers the same way, hes either a damned fool or he's Crazy.

He returns to the allotment:

> Mrs Brewer has already made out our allotment papers for us and wants us to sign them but we thought it better to write you first, lots of the rich people around here are getting it and she says we are entitled to it, as now that we are not getting the nine dollars a week we used to get from you it hits us very hard, I am not able to work like I used to or I could make more outside than I make in the business, I had to see Dr Hock a few days ago, he fixed me up pretty good but did'nt say what was the matter with me; Mother is very well but gets so tired; Buster wanted to get in the Navy, but his boss asked him to stay on, he must have a pretty good job.

Whatever was wrong with him, apparently he had to go out of town to see a specialist since Hock was not a Roslyn doctor. As he would always be, he did not dwell on his personal problems, and he was sure business would improve.

> Phin Seaman, the Sherrif says he thinks they are going to start on the prisoners again [taking photos], the Grand Jury has recommended it again, I hope they do as that will be a big help to me although the criminals are pretty well weeded out now you bums are all away.

Billy worried not only about his own family but about his mother in England who was then 86 years old.

Did you send money home to Grandmother," he asked. "She needed it very much as 31 dollars I sent her before Christmas went to the bottom and we never heard any more of it, I sent her 10 dollars last month that was al [sic] I could spare. You don't need to send her any more when you increase the allotment as we will be able to send it regular. We are going to get Ted to send us some too, as he will never save a nickel otherwise.

He apologized for being so blunt. "Mom says it is about time I took my turn at writing but I tell her that it is her letters you want, she didn't know how to explain this allotment business so I had to do it." He added a note about Arthur that may be deliberately ironic in its description of his success as a salesman and the reward. "[Mom] is the same old mother always bothering her brains about her young ones, jawing young Arthur, he told me just now that he had sold over 2,000 dollars worth of Liberty Bonds and gets a gold medal, he's a lucky guy he sold 250 dollars worth of war saving stamps, and he gets another medal for that." The irony in what he then says about paying his two daughters is not intentional. "Emma &Annie are the great paper girls, they get a war saving stamp every Saturday evening, they are in the Park now picking flowers." He ended his part of the letter and Emma added a note in her own hand with her usual disregard for punctuation and capitalization:

> Dear Bill you see I've got your Pop to write after all. I had just sent one letter off to you when Mrs. Brewer came in to see about Ted she thought like more people around here we were getting something from the government. She says we should get it so will wait now and see what you do we are entitled to it as well as some of the rest. Dont you think Jeff as done well today is the last day. Busters address if you want to write is
> 12 Broad St.
> Providence RI
> I dont think I have any more news this time so good bye old Boy. Send your picture along in your uniform.
> Your Loving Mother
> EP

All through the summer the financial problems continued to weigh on the family. Emma noted in another letter to Bill that Buster (Wallace) "is in Providence. I got a letter from him I don't bother much to write letters to him. Once in a while I write. I send a P.C [post card] he said one time he was going to send some money home but have not seen any yet—I should worry as Emma says."

She was worrying, of course. The war effort had created scarcities and inflation as the government printed money to finance the military. Between 1917 and 1918 prices rose 126% at the same time as the paper business struggled to recover. Emma economized everywhere she could. In the same letter to Bill she wrote that she was glad to have a "load of slab wood from the lumber yard." She was also glad that Jack "is working at Last—drives a bus for Stapleton at Camp Mills. 21$ a week."

From Jack's earnings he could now pay his share of food at home and Emma wrote, "his board money will come in handy." She thought maybe she could get another woman to help with the washing. "My old Lady wanted me to pay 2.50." Emma had to say no. She could send out the laundry, but "[I] could not afford pay a boy to fetch and leave off."

As tight as the budget was, the departure of so many of the boys had forced them to hire help. As Emma tended the store on the slow Sunday afternoon of July 7, she wrote to Bill, "Tom no doubt will be telling you he's not helping with the papers any more don't worry we have somebody in his place. You know how he gets offended. Jack has a job with Hamilton so he has to work Sunday. Tom got paid $2.00 every Sunday so don't think he will gain much 8 or 10$ a month is quite a bit."

On September 4th Emma sent Bill a letter with news of home and Roslyn that she concluded with the uncommon joint signature, "Your loving Mother & Father, E Pickering." In it she says, "Thank you for letting us use some of your money[.] we may need it. Business is very quiet just now. Father says if he can get a light job he will take it, myself and the girls can see to the papers week days, of course he's not able to do anything hard it's to bad he should have to think of it, but he has had to borrow money as you know already this year. There is another paper trouble in New York something like a strike but don't affect us. Father has nothing to do with it I am glad of it. Lost enough by the other one if we would only get the allotment money for both you and Ted that would help but I am like Mr. Bond don't think so altho some are getting it but he has not as yet."

The financial trouble had to be serious if Billy was willing to do manual labor after 16 years of independence as a self-made businessman. On September 13th the financial struggle moved Billy to send another of his infrequent notes to absent family to say things were all right. To his son Bill serving on the USS Wyoming as it escorted war convoys in the North Sea he sent a card whose picture shows Emma with a small baby cradled in her arms. Billy wrote, Things are OK here now and look more promising. I think we'll be on top before long, after a lot of worry. Mom didn't want to send this card so I'm sending it on the QT. Pop

It isn't her baby, don't worry."

191

Whether Emma objected to the photo or to the idea that "things are OK" we don't know. Things were not OK. Billy had come to America as a vigorous and ambitious young man who worked long hours in construction and managing horses before he became an entrepreneur. As a photographer he often hauled his big camera, tripod, glass plates and other equipment wherever he was needed or wanted to go. Now, at 53 he had survived a mysterious illness inside him that sapped his physical energy. He would never be entirely well again. Emma had born ten children, lost one at two years old and raised nine very different and independent children, six of them boys who often rebelled against their father's strict regime and sought her as shelter and mediator. Her hair had gone gray, her skin had thickened and wrinkled, her legs and ankles protested if she walked too far or stood too long. Even if most of their newspaper customers had returned, the loss of free family labor and Billy's growing addiction to book and antique collecting and the support they sent to his mother in England kept them living from day to day with no reserves. Emma seldom complained, at least not within hearing of her children.

CHAPTER 14. VICTORY

The American troops that included Ted Pickering and many other Roslyn boys changed the course of the war when they began arriving in 1917. On the seas, the convoy system and the Grand Fleet all but penned up the German fleet and prevented the U boats from starving Britain. On the ground, since August 1914 the Allied and German forces had fought from the trenches on their respective sides, killing hundreds of thousands of men but changing nothing. The attack on St. Mihiel that Ted Pickering witnessed changed everything. The Germans had begun to withdraw on September 12 when Pershing attacked. In the first three days the Americans lost 7,000 men wounded or killed, but they had captured 15,000 Germans and liberated 200 square miles of France. The job was finished by the time the sun set on September 16.

The next phase of the war, The Grand Offensive, would begin almost immediately with the allied armies launching nearly simultaneous attacks September 26th on Germany's Hindenburg Line of trenches and forts. The Germans had built the line of forts and firepower after the bloody Battle of the Somme in 1916. They successfully created a line stretching from the North Sea to northeastern France where Ted's regiment arrived to support the final battles. From this fortified line named for General Ludendorff who had conceived it, the Germans had been resupplying their armies in France, while armies under dangerous attack could withdraw to the line and regroup. For some two miles or more in front of the Hindenburg line the Germans deliberately destroyed any road, forest, town, house, or hovel that might possibly shelter or aid an Allied attack. Then they sowed the land with mines. This was the famous No Man's Land.

Here in this strip of devastated, barren, cratered moonscape of mud and dust and blasted trees Company A of the 314th Ammunition Train set up camp. Ted's unit was now part of the Meuse-Argonne Offensive or Battle of Argonne Forest, and that in turn was part of the final offensive of the war lasting until the November 11 armistice. In this battle the Germans would kill more than half of all the Americans who died in action in the entire war. Among the reasons why over 26,000 soldiers would die are not only the German defenses, but Pershing's insistence that the first assault waves penetrate into this deep system farther than any other troops had been able to do. The men he chose to do it were largely inexperienced and poorly trained. They were men like Ted who had been thrown together in large units and hurried through a very basic training regime, then immediately sent overseas. Nevertheless, their numbers and courage convinced Ludendorff his defense line was doomed.

Within days of the first attacks, Ludendorff had begged the Kaiser to seek an armistice because defeat was inevitable. The coordinated Allied attacks had made it impossible for Germany to shift its troops from one place to another as it had done when the Allies had attacked in sequence. One of the great tragedies of the war was that the Germans, even while admitting defeat among themselves were fighting fiercely, taking tens of thousands of lives and sacrificing even more of their own men.

The 314th Ammunition Train's job was to bring across No Man's Land the division's artillery, supplies and heavy guns to provide to support to the hordes of infantry troops attacking the German line. They had only 4 roads to use, and those were often under heavy fire. Yet within two days they had achieved their mission with the help of military engineers. They lived in No Man's Land throughout the slowly progressing offensive. By the end of October when the Argonne Forest had been cleared, American forces had advanced only ten miles.

Ted's work was as intense as the battle itself, although instead of machine guns, the greatest dangers they faced were artillery shells and an occasional German plane from which the pilot or his assistant could drop a bomb or strafe. General Pershing describes the intensity of the fighting:

> The demands of incessant battle which had been maintained day by day for more than a month had compelled our divisions to fight to the limit of their capacity. Combat troops were held in line and pushed to the attack until deemed incapable of further effort because of casualties or exhaustion; artillery once engaged was seldom withdrawn and many batteries fought until practically all the animals were casualties and the guns were towed out of line by motor trucks.

> The American soldier had shown unrivalled fortitude in this continuous fighting during most inclement weather and under many disadvantages of position.

> Every member of the American Expeditionary Forces, from the front line to the base ports, was straining every nerve. Magnificent efforts were exerted by the entire Services of Supply to meet the enormous demands made on it. Obstacles which seemed insurmountable were overcome daily in expediting the movements of replacements, ammunition and supplies to the front, and of sick and wounded to the rear.[22]

Once the Allied forces had broken the Hindenburg Line, they advanced with relative ease to the one rail line that had been key to supplying the German forces. The seizure of that rail line broke the last hope the Germans had of resisting. The fighting, however, continued until the moment of armistice on November 11. Ted noted the constant activity of the German fighter planes and several observation balloons he saw shot down in late October. Several came down in flames with the observers hanging on still alive. Ted himself injured his leg but doesn't say how. He noted only that on October 29, "Coming through Thercourt [Thiaucourt, near the Hindenburg Line] had the ride of my life with a bad leg, not able to move. The Huns was sending them over and dropping them from airplanes at us. The driver and the rest of us thought it was our last ride in No Man's Land that night."

This was the same day that the war had all but ended in the North Sea where his brother Bill was serving on the USS Wyoming. German sailors on several ships mutinied when they heard that their commanders were planning to send them into a suicidal final assault on the Grand Fleet--for the sake of German honor.

The land war was blessed with no similar good fortune. German troops fought on. Ted notes that on November 4 "Our doughboys go over the top at 5 in the morning; gain 10 kil. [6.25 miles]" This same day one of Britain's most brilliant young poets, Wilfred Owen, took part in an attack on a bridge, and a German bullet aimed for no one in particular, but for killing in general, chose his life to destroy. His most famous lines, at the end of a poem about a mustard gas attack, are:

> If you could hear, at every jolt, the blood
> Come gargling from the froth-corrupted lungs,
> Obscene as cancer, bitter as the cud
> Of vile, incurable sores on innocent tongues,---
> my friend, you would not tell with such high zest
> To children ardent for some desperate glory,
> The old Lie: *Dulce et decorum est* [sweet and honorable it is]
> *Pro patria mori.* [to die for one's country]

On November 5 Ted records, "American balloon shot at by Huns--three planes came right over us from the clouds. 2 men in the balloon jump to safety at the same time the balloon was all on fire and the Huns firing at our boys. But both came down safe. One Hun on the back was shot down from his last ride. The other one got away."

When the armistice took effect on November 11 the killing had taken the lives of 9.7 million soldiers, sailors, and airmen and almost 10 million civilians. Almost two of every ten citizens of the United Kingdom had been killed. The Kaiser had sacrificed three out of every ten of his citizens. The United States, fighting for only one year had lost 117,000 soldiers, sailors and airmen, almost one out of every ten who served in the war zone. Twice as many had been wounded. In 1918, in addition to the fighting, thousands of men were stricken and killed by an influenza plague. It was especially hard on men living in the dirty and fatiguing conditions of combat zones. In the Rainbow Division 2,000 men died, and over half the division suffered battle wounds. Ted Pickering saw murder, mayhem, suffering and death all around him but reported no injuries or sickness himself except "a bad leg" that kept him off his feet for a few days.

His own note when the guns ceased was, "War ended the 11 month, 11 day and 11 hr. All was happy to me." His younger brother Jack had come of age that fall and on the day the representatives of the warring nations signed an armistice he was in Mineola, the county seat, with his enlistment papers signed and ready to board a troop train. Ted went on with the American troops into Belgium and defeated Germany.

Early in 1919 his little sister Emma received a postcard written in pencil and addressed to "Miss Emma Pickering, Roslyn, Long Island, New York."

In the North Sea the fighting also had stopped on November 11, but the formal surrender did not take place until the 21st. When the Armistice came, the Grand Fleet moved its base south to the Firth of Forth where the city of Edinburg offered greater access to supplies and the comforts of land. On the evening of November 20th Operation ZZ began when hundreds of boats from the great dreadnaughts to small trawlers sailed slowly through the misty night toward the open sea. About 2 a.m. on the 21st the lead ship of the American dreadnaughts raised anchor and turned toward the sea to lead the Sixth Battle Squadron that included Bill Pickering's ship the Wyoming. Lt. Francis Hunter on the New York called that hour the beginning of "the day of a thousand dreams."

Almost four hundred ships and boats sailed out before dawn to meet the German fleet and witness its surrender. Admiral Beatty, commanding the entire operation, had planned every small detail, including the commandment that German guns would face fore and aft and the guns of the Grand Fleet would point broadside at the German ships so there could be no treacherous last attack.

When the sun rose in a red sky Bill Pickering could look over the sea from the Wyoming's deck and see two long lines of boats two miles apart, running east and west. The Wyoming and other American ships were in the northern line. Just after 8 bells sounded and the ships had passed the Isle of May in the mouth of the Firth of Forth, the top lookouts spotted black smoke on the horizon. Then they made out a kite balloon and below it the small British light cruiser Cardiff. Behind its tiny form came the German battle cruiser Seydlitz, and behind her in single file almost all the ships of the German fleet. Again, Lt. Hunter's summary captures the moment.

> It is the sight of our dreams - a sight for kings! Those long, low, sleek-looking monsters, which we had pictured ablaze with spouting flame and fury, steaming like peaceful merchantmen on a calm sea. Then the long line of battleships, led by *Friedrich der Gross,...Konig Albert, Kaiser, Kronprinz Wilhelm, Kaiserin, Bayern, Markgraf, Prinz Regent Luitpold,* and *Grosser Kurfurst...*powerful to look at, dangerous in battle, pitiful in surrender...This, then, is the end for which the Kaiser has lavished his millions on his "incomparable" navy...[23]

Ten days later the American ships said good-bye to the British fleet and sailed out of the Firth of Forth for the last time with the four British super-dreadnaughts and a flotilla of destroyers escorting them. In the past year the Americans had often brawled with their British counterparts. The Brits had often resented the Americans' late entry, their country cousin manners, and their smug confidence. On parting, however, the British sailors played music from their decks and cheered the Americans on their way to the Isle of May, then gave one long loud cheer as their ships turned back to their home port and the Americans began their way home. The last Bill Pickering and his shipmates saw of the Grand Fleet was a banner flying from the masthead of the HMS Barham spelling out,

G-O-O-D B-Y-E-E-E-E."

Bill Pickering's photo of the British dreadnaught Queen Elizabeth bidding farewell to the departing Americans after the German surrender

Bill's departure ended his English escapades and romance. His relatives were sad to know he would not be with them again soon. On November 24 his Aunt Ada, or Big Aunt Ada the wife of his Uncle Ted wrote to "Dear Billy Boy."

Well I suppose we shall not see you for Xmas now; as you will be going home, I expect. Well dear Boy for your Mother's and Father's sake we hope it will be so; though for our sakes we would rather have you with us for Xmas; but you've done your bit for the old country, and with the rest of our Sailors; we must say thank you to you, for your part – so well done for the old country; . . . Grandma says she does wish she could see and hear you all; she would like to come over your ship, and see you all on board, isn't it good to think she has been spared to hear the piece bells rang again? She is so delighted to think there will be no more fighting; have you heard from Ted lately? We have not heard from him; when you write ask him if he got any letters or not? I sent him a parcel with one. What do you think those sisters of yours would like best from Tun Wells. If you let me know what they like, I'll get it and send it to you and you can take it to them when you go, as it would be nice for them to have something from the old town, where their Dad lived as a boy. I expect you recognize that the place on the postcard I sent you; it is where Grandma took you for a walk when you were with us first time you came. Little felicity has gone back to Eastbourne, but I'm still busy making clothes for her. Her daddy has sailed from Turkey and will soon be home now. She & her mother are getting very excited at the prospect of seeing him after 4 years. Thanks so much for the money dear boy; it comes quite regularly now; and it makes life so much easier for Grandma and I.
. . . Grandma sends her love and says "God bless her dear boy, and take him safe back to his Father and Mother".
From Your Ever loving Aunt:
DA

Bill and Nellie had continued their warm and regular correspondence. He had written to her about a shore leave just before Thanksgiving. On December 10th she wrote her fairwell.

My Dear Billy,
I was *very* glad to get your letter this afternoon & know you had got back on Ship alright [sic]. I hope you got my letter I wrote on Sunday. I am writing this hoping you will get it before you leave on Thursday. Are you going straight home Kid or to France. I suppose you don't know yet although by the papers I think you must be going to France with the

President Did you get your thanksgiving dinner on Sunday Billy? or weren't you back in time. Don't forget to answer my letters will you Billy? You had some place to sleep in on Saturday night Kid, but still it was better then [sic] you having to pay an hotel Billy & [guess you slept just as well there as
in a proper bed. it was very good of them. Thanks for picture of it Kid I wish you were on it though.
I wish Portland was not quite so far away. Billy I would come down & go on board your Ship. I wonder which I should like to see most Kid the Ship or <u>you</u> of course I should be interested to see the Ship but I should be more pleased to see you again don't you think so dear? & no work to do. I hope you don't get falling in love with all the young ladies who come Kid but there that's only my fun I know you don't.
No I had not seen in the papers about the Wyoming being the flag Ship. No doubt we shall be seeing some picture of it sometime. Well now Kid that is about all there is in your letter to answer. There are no news to tell you. Hope I shall soon get another letter from you. write when you can won't you dear?
Lots of love & XXX from All.
        Your loving Cousin
        Nell XXXXXX

After leaving Scotland, the Wyoming sailed south to the French coast and became part of the honor escort for President Wilson as he made his way to the peace conference. On December 14 she picked up 381 bags of mail in England, then turned west into the Atlantic and sailed for home. On Christmas day 1918 Bill saw the Statue of Liberty sliding by as they steamed into the mouth of the Hudson River. When he finally returned to Roslyn he learned that out of 135 young men from Roslyn who had served nine had died. Bill's friend Johnny Peel who had tried to enlist in the Navy with him did return, missing his left arm. At the La Vale River on July 23, 1918 German machine gunners devastated most of John's infantry company and left his squad stranded in a railroad cut. Commanded by the courageous Captain George U. Harvey, born and educated in Ireland, the eight man squad stood their ground against enemy troops hidden in a nearby forest. Soon the machine gunners found the squad and poured fire on them. Eight bullets tore through John's left arm, but he survived. In the months and years that followed, whenever anyone said to Johnny how sorry they were for his loss, Johnny replied, "I shot the Hun."

For the Pickerings in Roslyn 1918 ended much better than it had begun. On November 11 Germany accepted the offer of an armistice, not the official end of the war with a peace agreement and treaty, but a decisive end of fighting and the surrender of all German forces. Americans, whose boys had entered the war only a year and a half earlier when the fighting was stalemated in miserable trench warfare, gave themselves credit for the victory and celebrated with typical American patriotism and abandon. The festivities that erupted in Roslyn in honor of American success engraved themselves on the memory of 12 year old Annie Pickering. "War ended at 11 a.m. People went to the churches to thank God for peace. Bells at the churches, firehouses and school were ringing; lumber yard and other whistles were blowing; people banged on tin pans. Rescue fire truck had a big wooden cross with a straw-stuffed Kaiser on it in the big parade—they had crucified the Kaiser. School children and adults paraded. It was a joyful holiday. There were also some firecrackers. Dances and parties were held." Annie would grow into a life of service not only in 70 years of nursing but as a patriot and a dedicated member of the American Legion Auxiliary.

Bill's mother Emma wrote to him on December 11 when she heard his ship was going to meet President Wilson and escort him to France. She knew that meant he wouldn't be home for Christmas even though many of his friends from Roslyn have returned home.

Well the ships are bringing the boys home by the load now. Your friend John Peel was or is at Camp Upton and was in Roslyn Sat & Sun I believe Annie was talking to him down the street he has his left arm gone. . . . I hear Joe Less [? Unclear] is Wounded I don't know if it is so. Well the boys I must say one and all deserve the praise and credit from the nation both in the U.S and England and to think so many got away from it and were what we call slackers and some of them feel ___ to. I think the boys who did go can have the laugh at those kind lots of men working at camp Mills who went on strike the other day because they no longer get paid 11$ for transportation and something else some have been making___of money during the war what with overtime & Sunday work. I bet some were sorry the war came to an and so quick. It certainly came like a thunderbolt at the and no one could help but rejoice.

Ted was also writing regularly but she says his mail did not arrive regularly like Bill's. "I guess I got 8 letters all at once next day got another one . . ."

The sons of nine Roslyn families were buried in France or came home in coffins. Bill's friend George Griffith did not have Bill's luck. He was one of 118 men on the cutter USS Tampa off the coast of England September 26 when his boat roamed too far ahead of the convoy it was guarding. Just after dark a U Boat struck and the ship sank quickly with everyone on board. William Tilley served in France with Ted, but German shells or gunfire tore up his machine gun nest, and he died while medics were dressing his wounds. He was laid to rest with thousands of others in the famous cemetery of Flanders Field. Ted Pickering would serve a few more months as American troops went into defeated Germany. Bill's ship escorted President Wilson's ship to France, but 1919 had hardly started before both Bill and Ted were home again. They and other young veterans sat as guests of honor when Roslyn gave a welcome home dinner at the Neighborhood House on July 9. Their mother had her favorite sons back again. Bill would always be her most attentive, claiming to forsake even marriage to care for her. Little Emma, who had always considered her older brothers her heroes, now had her brothers home again.

PHOTO BY
W. H. PICKERING
ROSLYN, N.Y.

"As I listened to those songs of the glee club, in memory's eye I could see those staggering columns of the First World War, bending under soggy packs on many a weary march, from dripping dusk to drizzling dawn, slogging ankle deep through mire of shell-pocked roads; to form grimly for the attack, blue-lipped, covered with sludge and mud, chilled by the wind and rain, driving home to their objective, and for many, to the judgment seat of God." General Douglas McArthur's farewell speech at West Point. May 12, 1962

After World War I (Willowsly)
Northern Blvd. Roslyn

PHOTO BY
W. H. PICKERING
ROSLYN, N.Y.

EPILOGUE: BILL'S ENGLISH FRIENDS

After returning to the States and to civilian life, Bill continued to write to his friend from Scotland, I. Powell. He had written to her in June while still in the Navy, but received no answer. And she had written to him in May and received no answer. He wrote again in July On August 4, 1919 she answered as soon as she received the letter. "Well, as you didn't get [my letter] I'll have to tell you all the news again. I got married on Feby 6th. My husband belongs to Tunbridge Wells and got demobilized about two months ago and went home there, so I'm left alone. I think I'll be going down there about the end of this month. . . . Have you got a girl there yet. You should get married to if you find a nice girl. It's so nice besides being single." She tells him her name is now Mrs. A.J. Powell.

In November she answered a recent letter and said that she had moved south to the village of Frant, just two miles from Tunbridge Wells. If he would tell his cousins that she was in the area, she said she'd be glad to meet them. She was glad to be in the south. "There's plenty of fruit here, what we didn't have at home. Things are still rationed here. Everything is so unsettled yet with all these strikes." She signs off saying, "Alec & I* both send our best wishes, & hope to see you some day."

His cousin Nellie also wrote to him in August. She tells him her husband is now home and is "still having treatment from the doctor but he is very much better than he was when he first came out of the Army." She says he will soon be looking for work, but with hundreds of unemployed men around and high food prices times are very difficult. Then she asks him, how are you getting along with the girls Billy? Any sign of getting married just yet Kid? Be sure and let me know what you?"

About Auntie Dot she writes, "She comes in here quite often but I don't like her anymore than I used to. But I have to be civil to her for grandma's sake. But she does annoy me sometimes with her silly talk. She made me laugh the other day she got on about the Macaullife's and how fond they were of you etc. etc. she is often yarning about it. It goes in one ear and out the other."

Finally, as if to say things are over between her and Bill but fondly remembered, she writes, "my will has just come in & and said who are you writing to? So I said 'oh only my other Boy.' It's a good job he is not jealous." She signs off as she always had, "lots of love & xxxxx to you dear." Then under her signature as "your loving cousin" she writes another row of eleven Xs.

Late in his life Bill told an interviewer that he met several very nice women while serving overseas and could have gotten married, but "I told this girl she was very nice but I said nope. They had a lot of nice girls over there – they were all refined, very nice girls but so, nope, I couldn't give them as good a home as they had."

Who was the girlfriend that Bill had at home that he had told some of his relatives about? A few pictures and family notes say she was Ida Bartley Burket. She was apparently still single when Bill returned and left the Navy. His mother was very fond of her. "She would come and stay over the weekend, like a daughter. My mother loved her." When he was building the new house for his mother, her friends thought this might be the signal that Bill was getting ready to marry Ida. They teased her, "You're going to lose your boy Bill." Maybe Ida gave up on Bill. Ida went her own way but where that led we don't know.

When he gave an oral historian and interview in his eighties Bill gave two reasons why he never got married. By that time, however, he had become an almost nonstop talker but also almost incoherent, one non sequitur following the other. His mind jumped from one subject and memory to a completely different one. One time when the interviewer asked why he didn't get married, he said, "the English are very strict, and that's why I never got married." A little later he seems to pick up the same thread. "If it hadn't been for both of them, I'd have been married long ago. Johnny Peel and I both would have been married over here in Flower Hill to a farmer's daughters. They was nice too. They was German. We went to say good-bye, boy, and (whistle) we just had to go." During the interview he laughed to hear himself saying this. Was he saying that he was afraid of sex or a romantic commitment? A second time the interviewer asked, he replied, "Well I told you. I think a lot of it was mother love, if I have to say it." This he followed by noting that the second world war was coming and his mother was all alone as if he had to choose between marriage and his mother. Certainly in Ida's case this doesn't make sense since his mother loved Ida. When he was 93 he congratulated his sister Emma on her three boys success as adults and said, "Maybe I was too smart to think of getting married. I always said I would take care of mother. Even Ida, the girl that used to come stay over for a weekend, wanted to get married. I said not when Mother was alive. She quite agreed with me." Ida came to his mother's funeral and that was the last time they met.

On September 9 he sailed for Europe on the Cunard line's R.M.S. Scythia on an American Legion veterans trip to France and Italy. He said of Luzern, Switzerland, "it is the most beautiful city we have stayed in as yet. When we awoke this morning and opened the window, we could see the snow caped [sic] montains [sic]. It was the most wonderful sight I have ever seen. The city was so clean and the buildings etc. It really does look a lot like Roslyn. It is down in a hollow surrounded with the Swiss Alps and beautiful lakes. It is just the kind of place I would like to live for about a year." When he reached England he sent his mother a postcard from London. It says, "Just arrived London. On to Edinburgh tonight." He makes no mention of trying to visit anyone in the family. All the women his age were now married.

Bill Pickering and Ida Bartley Burket

CHAPTER 15. CROSS BURNING, CLASS AND KLAN

My father used to tell people, "You gonna sit around and criticize, you'll never get anywhere."

Bill Pickering, from an oral history in the Bryant Memorial Library, Roslyn

Roslyn embraced the harbor but had no beach. The little southern nipple of Hempstead Harbor that ended at Roslyn Village had once been a muddy outlet of the big mill pond. The mill, boat yards, and the Conklin and Tubby lumber yard embraced it with docks and bulkheads. On both sides as the harbor widened private estates ran to the water. Roslyn people who wanted a sandy beach went up the west side a mile or so to Bar Beach where the bluffs came down to the water and spread a soft carpet of sand along the water.

Billy Pickering and his allies against private claims and sand miners had won their case in 1908 because they cited historical evidence that this beach had been used by the public for more than a century. The advocates of public ownership put on the stand Stephen Speedling who recalled the years 1849-51 when he and several others had lived on the beach and netted fish for a living. Jacob Van Vicklen testified that he worked as an errand boy in the 1850s for a fishing crew living on the beach. Charles Dodge of Port Washington unrolled a map from 1703 showing Cow Neck as public land. In 1912 the appellate court reaffirmed the lower court's opinion that the public owned the beach. Billy and his family felt they were part owners of this valuable and beautiful asset.

With public rights secure, the town clerk began to sell permits for people to put up a tent for changing and camping and partying. The town also built a small pavilion where people could dance. This led to riotous and often drunken parties. But they were not the only members of the public who wanted to enjoy the beach. A lot of the party goers and heavy drinkers were Irish. In the early 1920s Billy's older boys had their own tent on the beach and they didn't care for their rowdy neighbors. They were now young men whose newly formed manhood and identities were easily insulted.

Bill Pickering recalled the situation when he recorded an oral history for the Bryant Library. He and his brother Ted looked to the Ku Klux Klan for the model of how to intimidate people they didn't like. After WWI the Klan became established on Long Island as a law and order group and a supporter of Prohibition. Klan supporters saw the biggest threats to order and sobriety, not in the relatively small black population (about 2%), but in the rapidly growing number of immigrants and in Jews. Historians estimate Long Island membership at over 20,000 out of some 200,000 in New York

State. For most members their affiliation was no secret, and when they marched in robes and hoods they did not cover their faces. Public officials often marched with them.

Bill Pickering told his interviewer, "This was the time the Ku Klux was in power, see, and Glenwood was known as a Ku Klux town, you know what I mean? . . . There was four of us in this tent, four young fellows see. I would come down around dinner time, around 1 o'clock. So we got this idea, 'Let's burn a cross there." Was he a Klan member, he was asked. "No sir! My brother [Ted] was," he laughed. They collected some cotton batting and the wood and they set to work in an empty tent near theirs that was used only on weekends. "We're making it. People walking by never said nothing, was never the wiser. . . . So we had planned this all up. And there was a certain girl down there with another party in Roslyn in a tent and they always had these parties. All night long they would go on. They were either drunk here or drunk there. That's what ruined the tenting thing. Got too bad. No more tents. So we figured here, we'd go out on the end of the beach, dig a hole, put [the cross] in, this was about midnight, when everybody might be asleep. It had pretty well quieted down, so we did. We planted it. We set it afire." The flames roared up the cross and lit up the night and the light shone through the cloth walls of the tents. "This girl, is all upset and comes out and hollers. They [all] went out on the beach. Too late to catch the cross burners.

They had had the foresight to set up their getaway. "We figured we'd get Mr. Craft's boat. He had a boat out on the water. We knew where the oars were, right alongside the tent. He wouldn't know this, see." They were already on the water when the crowd on the beach started yelling insults, "They called the Glenwood people, up on that hill them Ku Kluxers, every name you could think of." Bill knew everyone in Glenwood from his paper business, and they rowed for Jack Whalen's tavern and bait shop but Whalen refused to get out of bed. "We couldn't get back to the beach. We had to row over and get over to Keratsonyis." Keratsonyis was a big resort hotel and a beach just north of Whalen's. "So we stayed over there till almost morning till we finally made our way back. To this day I don't think anybody knew who it really was. But that was the way they used to do anybody."

Bill saw the Klan as the working class wing doing the work of prominent citizens who didn't want to get their hands or reputations dirty. "Around here they [the Klu Kluxers] didn't do much. This is just my opinion, but maybe somebody that hears this won't like it. The Masons would only take in certain, uh, they wouldn't take in what was known as trash them days, like myself, the Pickerings, or the Tilleys or all this riffraff in Roslyn.' Asked who were the prominent people or big shots, Bill said, "Well, a doctor, dentist or some high up. The middle class people you might call them. The story as I got it, they more or less created this Ku Klux Klan. And they [the Klan] would do the dirty work and then the Masons, of course, now you know, you again talking about politics, maybe I'm wrong, little confused. Same with Al Smith when he ran for governor, uh, ran for president. You couldn't elect a Catholic, president. The Masons would take care of this. But do you know, I've taken Legion trips, I've taken about 50 of them, and you go in Italy and they take their [Masons] buttons right off. Because in Italy if you're a Mason, it's your neck. It's politics again, see."

For Bill and his brothers the Klan was an integral part of the politics of his time. America was still very much divided not only racially, but along ethnic and religious fault lines. Just as the Irish came to dominate Boston politics and the Kennedy family accumulated its first fortune through bootlegging and political connections, so too in other places Protestant masons and Ku Klux Klan members tried to control political power.

Ted Pickering and sons at Klan rally

CHAPTER 16. THE COLLECTOR

Just as Billy had adopted a variety of civic organizations and projects, his business interests also continued to expand. In 1922 he led to his home several strong men who carefully carried up the steps and into the living room an elegant little French spinet piano. Little Emma immediately fell in love with both the soft luster of its wood, the candle stick holders each side of the keyboard, and the bright music of its keys. Her father agreed to let her take piano lessons and engaged a Mr. Brand to teach her once a week. Soon the school principal selected Emma and a friend to sit together at the piano and play Sousa marches when the school doors opened and the students came streaming in.

The piano and lessons are signs of a mellowing Billy Pickering. By the time his sons Ted and Bill had returned home from the war in the spring of 1919 fifty-four year old Billy Pickering had established himself as a respected businessman and community activist, a local character, and a failure. The failure was not general and catastrophic kind of failure made obvious by scandal, bankruptcy, foreclosure, or suicide. Billy never called himself a failure, nor did anyone else, but in business, in personal ambitions, and in his family he had failed in ways he never expected. His daughter Emma looked back many years later and wrote what she had often told her own children, "I say my dad was a failure as a father. He was so strict that we all rebelled and lied to avoid his wrath."

The Pickering girls might have played with the Mackay children when they were young, but everything they and their brothers knew about society and things like theater and the growing popularity of cabarets they learned from the newspapers and from certain magazines in the store that they were forbidden to read. They had no burning desire to be part of high society, but they were well aware that the world beyond their home and their puritanical father and his twelve-hour-a-day, seven-day-a-week business. That world offered a freedom they craved.

By 1920, except for sixteen year-old Arthur, the budding teenager Annie and young Emma, the children had all left. Buster had run away to Providence. Tom was married and had his first child. Bill had come home from the Navy to work for the up and coming Curtiss Airplane Company that had built a factory to produce prototypes of new planes. That factory in Garden City had the nation's largest wind tunnel and produced the first sea plane and the first plane to cross the Atlantic.

Arthur was never as confident or as tough as his older brothers, and without the strength of their numbers, he feared his father. What his father considered a boy's work, now fell entirely on him. He complained bitterly about being treated unfairly. Even though he and Annie and Emma had some growing up left, as a family the end was very near.

In June of 1921 Billy again had to borrow $1000 from Glenwood postmaster Simon Replogle who had loaned him money during the war. This time Billy pledged his home as security for the loan and promised to repay in twice yearly installments of $50 minimum at 6%. How he used the money is not recorded.

Buster came home now and then mainly to visit his mother, but he was already being caught up in his new career as a nurse. In his mother's little English book of 30 illustrated prayer-poems, *For the Master's Sake*, a note dated April 29, 1922 in a handwriting that is almost certainly his says, "This was the last one we read together." He would see her again, but things had changed. That same day in England her mother Ann Vickers Pickering died. She was three months short of her 88th birthday. Given the content of the verse if word had not come by telegraph, the other possibility is telepathy.

Billy and Emma knew Jack had been seeing Helen Nalevaiko, a Catholic girl from Glen Cove who he met at a carnival. She worked at a hospital in Mineola. Emma wanted the boys to marry in order of age, the younger ones staying to help with the business when they could. Besides, neither Emma nor Billy were keen on having one of their boys marry a Catholic. Helen's parents were equally, if not more, set against it. With opposition from both sides, Jack and Helen decided the matter themselves. On October 7, 1922 they eloped to Oyster Bay. Faced with a done deed, Billy bullied Jack into signing a paper that made his mother and father beneficiaries of his insurance policy.

The boys, of course, were expected to be more independent than the girls, and Jack's elopement didn't seem to create hard feeling. Not so when Billy and Emma's oldest daughter Dot, a good looking, slim, young woman with long flowing hair, ran off to New York City where she found both work and young men. Dorothy had grown tired of making her own clothes and hanging her finest long dresses on steam pipes in the room that served for both living room and dining room. Her mother forbade her to use makeup. "It will only ruin your skin," she declared, and although her mother was a gentle and soft spoken woman, her word was final. Dorothy rouged her cheeks with beet juice. She left home at sixteen. Dorothy found work as a nurse in a Catholic children's hospital and renounced the Anglican church of her parents and became a Catholic like her fiancé. Her parents disowned her. The estrangement lasted no longer than the few months required for her baby girl Gloria to be born on November 11, 1922. Her mother offered her support. Dot's husband soon abandoned her. When baby Gloria became seriously ill the next summer, Dot's mother and her brother Tom came and took her to a specialist in a hospital outside of New York. Billy and Emma paid the funeral and burial expenses for their granddaughter.

Dorothy and Gloria at far right in 1923.
From left: Anna and Tom with Hazel and Betty, Helen in back of Emma H, Emma S., Thomas Jr, _____?, Dot and Gloria

Dorothy Pickering Clarkson and Gloria

Helen Nalevaiko Pickering and son Jack

Billy and Emma's children had left home with a variety of motives, but to say the least, their father provided no reason for staying. Family word of mouth, letters, and notes preserve very few warm memories of him, but many of Emma. Almost every personal record of William Henry Pickering as a father is a record of fear or resentment. In more than 100 family pictures that run from the 1890s to his death, very few show him laughing and having a good time, no less in fond embrace of any child except a baby. When a smile does appear on his face, it seems tentative, hesitant, may be proud. No photograph shows a warm and welcoming smile. His character would continue to scar his family years after his death, although the evidence to implicate him directly in any single misfortune could only be circumstantial.

Billy, of course, had been supporting his mother, and it's possible that her death and having few mouths to feed at home more than offset the loss of free labor. In mid October he and Emma had bought a few small lots between Glen Cove Road and Red Ground Road from Alice W., Mary and Georgina Titus, sisters in an old Quaker family. Alice, known locally as Miss Alice, ran the Roslyn Tea Room in the old mill building. This time only Emma signed the note to Alice Titus for $500—half the purchase price.

About the same time Billy rented a store in a building near the Tea Room with The Creek and a drive to Waldbridge's boathouse between them. He moved his business into those larger quarters. An apartment upstairs over the store would soon become home to his son Jack and his new wife Helen. The East Broadway building he kept for his photography, antiques and books. He almost doubled its size by adding a two story section alongside the old store. The ground floor of the addition served as a garage and a real estate office, the second story for antiques and books.

Billy was sharing a new American optimism and prosperity and it suited his nature. After America had absorbed its returning veterans, the 1920s were becoming a period of extraordinary change and prosperity. Across the street the Conklins, prospering from the lumber business, had for some years awed the Pickering kids, especially little Emma, with their indoor bath and toilet, hot and cold water and fine china. But even before the war, Billy and Emma had electricity, indoor plumbing, steam heat, and a telephone. They had installed these great conveniences a little earlier than most, but they were part of the general revolution in household technology. In 1907 only 8 of 100 houses had electricity. By 1930 70 out of 100 would enjoy electric lights and plugs for things like toasters, washing machines and electric mixers.

The Jackson car Billy had purchased before the war had cost more than an average man's wages for two years. From the Ford Motor Company's new assembly lines in Michigan cars were rolling out of the great factories at the rate of one reliable car every 10 seconds. They were rapidly replacing the handcrafted carriage. The Ford Billy purchased in the 1920s cost about three months wages.

Banks saw their opportunity to finance all this new technology and a new era of consumer credit was born. Billy did not hesitate to take advantage of his good reputation and assets to borrow the money he wanted to expand his business, or at least finance his passions and hobbies, although he continued to borrow from friends.

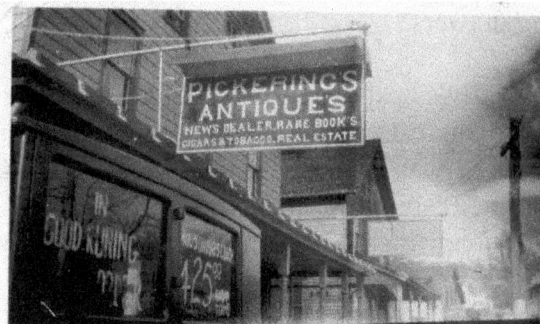

Left, the Old Store on E. Broadway; Right above, The new store on Willow Ave.

His business may have been an economic failure, but at the same time he may have buried any regret about financial problems in his personal satisfaction with being a free man pursuing his many interests. Those interests included reading, collecting rare books, antiques, and Indian artifacts, and saving Roslyn and Hempstead Harbor from politicians, miners, patricians, and the Irish.

A *New York Times* reporter's description of the store is also a description by proxy of its owner.

> [The shop] nestles at the foot of Harbor Hill, the estate of Clarence Mackay. There is scarcely room between the Hill and the road for the shop, which is so full of old furniture, old books, old prints, old glass and everything else that much of a hardier stock over flows on the curb. There in the sunshine and rain have remained, until sold, such Americana as a colored boy hitching post in the high styles of the elegant' 80s, old iron firebacks, brass fenders, stone fountains, marble birdbaths and iron grill work.
>
> The shop door is flanked by two windows. The window display is a conglomeration of the accumulations over 20 years of an antic where, who, perhaps, was keener about buying things for their own sake, then moving them out snappily in the New York manner. Anyway, the stock jams the shop, which reeks of Long Island tradition and sentiment. Not the Long Island of country clubs, aviation fields, traffic congestion, subdivisions and roadhouses, but the Long Island of widely separated villages, real farms, Quaker settlements and a leisurely rural life. Here are candle molds, samplers, hook rugs, Civil War muskets, "presentation" swords, spy glasses that watched for homecoming fishermen, hourglasses, corner cupboards, stacks on stacks of Currier and Ives prints, old maps, candlesticks, Staffordshire figures , tables, commodes, desks and chests of drawers.[24]

Billy's business never provided a comfortable living or a legacy for even his wife. He could not resist the temptation, however, to branch out into new businesses that were more hobby than business, although he maintained the trappings of a business. He did buy and sell rare books and antiques, but his daughter Emma, who passed her teenage years at home after WWI, often said he could never bear to part with his best finds. His reluctance to part with things he loved endowed his daughter with one of her great joys, that spinet piano. Five years later that passion and the business failure it led to would take away Emma's beloved piano.

Billy had his prejudices against the usual social scapegoats, but the names were an unfortunate but common shorthand to summarize behavior he didn't like, that behavior being more common in one group than others. His stereotypes were generalizations that never interfered with his judgement of individuals he knew in friendship, politics, or in business. Nothing he wrote in private or anything he published or said in a public meeting demeaned any individual's race, religion or origins. The one exception were the rich who he often named as the villains in grabbing public lands and foisting on the public treasury frivolous or unnecessary monuments.

In 1916 he had sold his Roslyn Heights newspaper territory to a Jewish news dealer from Brooklyn, Max Adelstein. He had become friends with a local Jewish antique dealer named Zeifman. The two of them scouted Long Island. By 1923 he was spending less and less time in his store and more and more time traveling on Long Island and foraging north of New York City for antiques and books. To find books and antiques he began to travel on longer and longer forays. He had bought a car, but after an accident as he was learning to drive, he left all the driving to his sons or to friends. To his wife's dismay, he often went off on trips to upstate New York with a Mrs. Ludlam (or possibly Ledden)[25] who knew antiques and their values. With Mrs. Ludlam his book and antique scouting took him to both upstate New York and New England. Little Emma, of course, would stay at home with her mother. After her father had climbed into the car next to Mrs. Ludlam and driven off, on more than one occasion little Emma heard very strong words from her mother. "When he would drive with her to upstate New York and surrounding areas, my mother, who never cursed, came close to it."

Billy, however, was no longer a trim, muscular little man. Although in pictures of little Emma and her father before WWI he still has his high cheekbones and square jaw and trim figure, after the war he aged rapidly. He is imprinted on his daughter Emma's earliest memories of him as "a short chubby person with yellowed teeth," who always wore a vest with a watch in one of its pockets, its chain swaying down to its anchor on his belt. Watches, especially large pocket watches, fascinate children, and Emma recalled that her father seemed to be constantly pulling out his watch, consulting it, and returning it to its vest pocket. His other habit that impressed her was "squeezing his nose in both hands as he bent over and blew snot onto the ground, then wiping his nose on a clean white handkerchief."

He did not cut a romantic figure, but most of Roslyn's residents respected him, and some loved him for his populist politics and independence. What Mrs. Ludlam saw in him we don't know, but what his wife Emma saw in her was a threat and a competitor.

Emma also had aged rapidly under the burdens of children and housework. In 1920 she had marked her 54th birthday. In a picture taken with son Bill during the war she looks older than her years, older than her husband. Whatever she might have said to Billy about his collecting and his companion changed nothing.

The stock in Billy's store grew into a clutter. Yet his sales were never enough to cover his debts or to pay off the mortgage he had taken out on his home. He could certainly have made a modest living off the expanded news-candy-photography store in its new location if he had not continually spent the profits on his other "businesses." In 1926 he and Emma sold the lots they had bought in Old Westbury's Red Ground neighborhood, and if they made any profit, that too went into the business. Billy could have had a thriving photography business if he had concentrated on marketing and keeping up with the latest technology. The 1920s, however, endowed Americans with a new sense of both optimism and personal freedom, and Billy was set on having a good time even if his pride in his Protestant work ethic and belief in thrift made him justify his indulgences as business.

The store on East Broadway had become one of the village's de facto community gathering places. Billy enjoyed talking, and people from every walk of life enjoyed talking to him. Among the writers who came often were popular humorist and *New Yorker* steady, Christopher Morley. Frances Hodgson Burnett, best known for *Little Lord Fauntleroy* and *The Secret Garden* also visited. Like Billy, she had had a childhood of poverty and and had suffered the early death of her father in the English midlands before emigrating.

When little Emma, my mother, spoke of her childhood in the 1920s she often called herself "the baby of the family" because she had been the last and the youngest by six years, born in 1911 when her mother was already 44 and her closest sibling, Annie, six. She was not only aware of her place in number, but she would be the last to wear the dresses, blouses and skirts her mother kept to pass on from one girl to the next.

By the time Emma became a teenager, Annie was an attractive young woman with a ready laugh and a teasing smile. She began sneaking out to see boys. Her brother Arthur, already having problems with alcohol, tried to exert himself as Annie's overseer but so ineptly that their little sister Emma recalls him causing such a row outside the house that police came and clubbed him into submission.

Arthur had his own romance. He was a short, trim young man with curly hair and small features. When Emma was 12 he was the last boy to leave home. In 1923 at age 20 he married Helen Biggers from Sea Cliff. His mother's failure to note the marriage in her Birthday Book almost guarantees it was another quick and small wedding without parents present. Arthur had little love for his father and felt he had been treated very unfairly at home. His mother, however, never failed to record her new grandchildren and on January 15, 1924 she notes the birth of Artie and Helen's first child, Virginia.

When Emma could escape from work and school, she found ready friends, although her parents did not approve of all of them. The Conklins across the street were fine, but her father forbid her to play with Bea the saloon owner's daughter. They played in spite of him. One Saturday in October, riding downhill on the back of Bea's tricycle when they were ten resulted in the bicycle flipping backwards, its seat crashing against the knee that had been hurt four years earlier when the milk wagon's horse stepped on her. When a man carried her home, she lied to her parents and said she had fallen. In her mother's "birthday book" where family events were recorded, the record says, "Emma fell off bycle [sic] and hurt her knee 1921." Emma developed water on the knee and lay in bed for a month. A week before her accident her mother had written on Saturday October 5th, "Jack_____Burnt his hands." Jack had been working as a trucker when he tried to put out a fire in the engine and burned both hands. Nevertheless, his sister

Emma would always remember how he attended her as she lay in bed and lifted her onto her bed pan.

Rebelliousness in a family usually begins with a slowly crafted cocoon of independence followed by a sudden emergence. For the girls that cocoon and later rebelliousness may have been unconsciously energized by the new intensity that the 1920s gave to the movement for women's rights and freedoms. That movement, like most social revolutions, was led by the affluent and the wealthy. They had the time, resources, personal confidence, and economic armor to disrupt tradition. At the sprawling 600 acre Harbor Hill estate on the bluff above the Pickering store and home Katherine Duer Mackay and her daughter Ellin became champions of social change. Their lead left an indelible impression on the restless Pickering girls, much of it in ways they might not have been unaware of.

Katherine Mackay imparted to her daughter Ellin a passion for women's rights and a sense of personal freedom from the restraints of tradition and class that would not reappear again in America until after the Great Depression, World War II, and recovery had passed and the affluent 'Baby Boomers' born in the 1950s and went to college. The 1920s was a dress rehearsal.

In 1924 at age 19 Ellin Mackay, a year older than Annie Pickering, was a beautiful debutante in New York City, known for her sharp "Irish sense of humor" as she called it. She had not yet set out in open rebellion, but she had become a favorite at elegant Long Island dinner parties given by her parents' friends. In that society she broke the mold.

At a New York dinner party on the evening of May 23,1924 she hit it off with a man fourteen years older than she was. He had been invited at the spur of the moment to fill in for someone else. He had come to America from Russia, the youngest of the eight children of the Jewish cantor Moses Baline and his wife Leah. Moses and his wife had fled the Cossack pogroms against the Jews, but had not lasted long in America's slums. Israel "Izzy" Baline's parents had died when he was a boy. He sold papers on the city streets when he was eight. He was a saloon piano player at 14. With another waiter at Mike Salter's Chinatown café he wrote a song, "Marie from Sunny Italy," and signed it "I. Berlin."

Irving Berlin had exploded into the American music scene and assured his own wealth by 1911, the year William Pickering's last child, Emma, was born. That was the year of "Alexander's Ragtime Band." By the time he met Ellin, successful theater people had become part of the New York social scene. Despite the fact that Clarence Mackay had close Jewish business friends and associates, he was determined that a Jew, even the most successful composer in America, would not become part of his family. To Clarence Mackay, who moved among clubs that excluded Jews, Irving Berlin was still as theatre magnate George M. Cohan once introduced him, "a Jew boy that had named himself after an English actor and a German city." For a rich second generation Irish Catholic having his daughter marry an immigrant Jew from the slums, even a rich one, was a serious social mistake. The gossip and news filled the more sensational papers in Pickering's store with the social story that had recently come to be called "ballyhoo." In June 1925 *Variety* magazine published the rumor that Berlin and Ellin Mackay were betrothed. Her father declared, "only over my dead body." Month after month the paparazzi and society reporters financed by the new national chain newspapers published true as well as invented details of the Irish golden girl and the Jewish immigrant.

While Ellin Mackay continued to deny she loved the dapper little Jewish song writer, her sometime childhood playmate, Annie Pickering, eloped the day after Christmas of 1925 with a tall, handsome policeman named Bill Buck. They married in St. Paul's Church five miles away from Roslyn in Glen Cove. Annie's friend Anna Peterson and one of Bill's best friends accompanied them as witnesses. (Ellin Mackay waited until 1926 before joining Irving Berlin before a justice of peace at City Hall to say, "I do.")

Annie's marriage left fifteen year old Emma at home with her parents and her brother Bill, then thirty, in those few hours when he was home from work and still awake. With little but work for her at home, Emma treasured her friends at school and especially the attention of boys who may have offered her simple and clear male affection that was in very short supply from her father. (Annie and Dot may have left home and eloped for the same reason. Bill, on the other hand, claimed that he never married because of "the mother thing." He and his brothers all seemed to return to their mother the abundant love and care she gave them.)

In Emma's first "puppy love affairs," as she called them, she doted on Duncan Leckie and Fred Erickson. Soon, however, she started spending time with boys after school and on weekends. Alarms went off at home. Her brothers, when they were at home or in town, added to their roles as teases and heroes, the role of spy, informer, and chaperone. Emma began to sneak away from home to see boys. Her sister Annie and Dot had done the same, before they had run away from home to marry. Her brothers and her parents knew the pattern. They tried the wrong cure, if any cure existed that could undo what had been done. As soon someone noticed one of Emma's absences, Bill or one of her other brothers, if available, was sent out to find her and bring her home.

In high school high school Emma was glad to leave behind ancient history and other non-vocational courses so she could concentrate on business courses. She did take public speaking, a course she enjoyed, unlike art which she had "hated."

Her freshman year in high school her grades were at the lower end of average:

English I	81
Biology	73 and 73 in Regents exam
El. Algebra	82 and 82 in Regents exam
Civics	92 and 81 in Regents exam
Bus. History	73

| Econ. Geog. | 68 and 65 in Regents exam |
| Public Speaking | 90 |

In her sophomore year she took all commercial courses except English and public speaking.

English II	80
Bookkeeping I	80
Com'l Arith	80 and 80 in Regents exam
Typewriting	75 and 75 in Regents exam
Public Speaking	80

For a girl who got up at 6 a.m. to deliver papers and who came home from school to deliver more papers, these are not shameful grades. Emma enjoyed school and for the rest of her life she would be her own teacher and occasionally take a correspondence course.

She envied the other girls who could stay after school for clubs and athletics. She also had ambitions in gymnastics and track. However, the knee first injured by the milk wagon and again in a bicycle accident at age 10 gave out on her at unpredictable moments and that ended her sports ambitions except in swimming and skating. In the cold winters of the 1920s she joined the skating on the mill pond whenever she could. Here, if her knee held up, she could show herself off. The skating she had learned as a child on double runners on icy sidewalks had become smooth and graceful. She would wear her wool turtle neck sweater and the many pleated dark blue skirt. She knew how to turn to make that skirt spread up and out to show off her legs. When her knee did give out on the pond and the graceful skater collapsed in pain, "it was sweet to have young men carry me off the ice." She never gave up but was back to skating within a week, taking her place in a line for crack the whip or again trying figures that would display her grace and her legs.

What she could not do in the gym, on the track or on the ice, she did in the water. Roslyn village kids learned to swim in the "creek" just beyond the great water wheel of the grist mill. She learned to dive from the seawall. As kids grew older they swam farther out or hiked or rode along the west side of the harbor to Bar Beach. She began to win competitions. At age 16 she took home several medals from the end of season races at Bar Beach. Both her triumphs and the freedom she enjoyed in the water made swimming or just being in the water the great physical joy of her life.

In the late winter or spring of Emma's junior year, 1929, her father had begun to grow weaker and suffer from stomach pains. These were the pains he referred to as *Lucifer*. To help in the business and at home, Emma dropped out of school. In fact, neither of her parents were very well. As early as 1922 when Emma was only 11, Annie had written to her brother Buster that their mother had been sick and unable to get up. When their mother received a card from Buster, she sent back her own postcard, a picture of Annie and Emma. She wrote, "Annie says she wrote and told you I was sick well I am up again I guess I was played out could not stand on my legs for a few days I can get around now again had a couple of sticks first day or so don't feel like writing much today." In her birthday book among the many entries of births, deaths, marriages, and illnesses, she never once records an illness of her own.

Billy Pickering grew sicker, and the pain grew stronger until he was forced to go to the hospital in Mineola on May 7, 1929. The record from the birthday book says, "Dad went to Mineola Hospital operated on 21/29". Between the 7th and his operation on the 21st, Billy made light of his problems, or at least tried to hide them behind his interest in Roslyn and his friends. On Sunday, May 12th, Mother's Day, he wrote a long letter to the *Roslyn News*. He lay in Nassau Hospital on Long Island, a few months from his death by cancer, but on that day he welcomed his remaining life. He summarized his good cheer for his worried friends in his hometown of Roslyn. He even proposed a new civic project.

Well, here we are; Roslyn's bad boy and trouble hunter laid on his back at last in far-famed Mineola Hospital, where an attempt is being made to remake him from the head down to the feet and at the same time gradually wash hell out of his insides by frequent baths of soap suds, glycerin and other condiments; results so far being that Lucifer is still there, but, with a strange bedfellow (no other than the angel of health), God bless her we find her here in all disguises from the "can of soap suds," to the chubby X-ray operator (whose finger we were cheerfully amputating, free of charge, and, incidentally the first real meat diet we had tasted in three weeks and which that husky could well afford to lose).

Also in disguise of the jolly little sweepers, the handsome nurses, the pretty nurses, the sedate and thoughtful—all performing the behests of the 'Angel of Health.' Strange Bedfellows; let them lie together. Old Lucifer has given us many a good time, and we still hope to have a few bouts with him, as we don't feel ready yet to sing "When This Cruel Life Is Over." It is still sweet to us and we feel the best part is yet to come— "The Mellow Years of Old Age," with my ever sweet and ever him and him beautiful old dame, and husky boys and girls.

Suffer (Mother's Day). Yes, we have suffered; nights of pain, filled with horrid dreams; days of oblivion, but what are our little pains compared with our fellow sufferers! Listen to those horrible screams coming from a distant ward, night and day (even now on this "Blessed Sabbath Morn" they are still with us). They are the cries of a poor burned girl, suffering tortures far worse than those picture by Dore in 'Dante's Inferno'. Hear the groans of our crushed and broken boys in Ward 1.

No: we are in Paradise, especially when good 'Doc' Galione assists us to a night's rest; and instead of horrid dreams we are floating on air with a pretty nurse, or the Spanish senorita of the kitchen staff, and the boys of the James Lyons Post, God bless the work of the Women's Auxiliary, American Legion, and thanks for their very beautiful bouquets. But what a mess we make of them. Here comes that cheery nurse from Ward No. 1 with a hard luck story of how her boys, racked and broken, seldom had flowers, and snip, the beautiful bouquets are scattered and re-arranged to make the boys in No. 1 happy.

Flowers are, incidentally a thought for the exchange Club. Why not a hospital visiting committee, especially for our boys and men and the little kiddies. Let's mother them by collecting flowers, magazines and, incidentally, a little entertainment; it seems our boys and men are sometimes forgotten in the rush.

Mother's Day. May 12, 1929, Mineola Hospital. – And this is Mother's Day. Let's devote it to the Mothers of Roslyn and the good work of the various organizations of our community are doing (none finer in the county), not forgetting the magnificent work of the District Nursing Association and our incomparable nurse, Mother Riley, a true daughter of the 'Mother of us all,' and while we reflect on Mothers let us thank God that some of our Mothers, Wives and Daughters do other things besides bridge, discussions on birth control, divorce and scandal (instead of educating our boys and girls to propagate healthy families). We have had our disagreements but they are bye-gones. You are doing wonderful work and we have long since given up the hunt for the chimera perfection. There is no such thing in this here old world and it should never have been put in the dictionary.

Dear Mother Riley, never shall we forget when you took us back to our baby days, when I was so helpless that little act of kindness cemented the friendship of a short acquaintance into a lifetime, and you and the DNA qualifications as a magnificent beggar will not be laced so much in the future, when those fine Irish eyes and the little lilt of the tongue appeals for some poor being in distress will find hearty response in this member of the Community Relief Committee. God bless you, offspring of the sturdy, fighting Irish, knowing no creed, color or station on your visits of mercy, ready to meet all emergencies even to castigation of cruel parents if necessary, and with tender hands soothing the sick and welcoming some tiny mite to this world and closing the eyes of the departing. God bless you and through you, the members of your association, and we beg the people of our community to assist you nobly; you have stood the test.

Who can say how much, if any, he exaggerated the hospital's pre-operation treatments. The purpose seems to be to clean out his intestinal tract and pinpoint his ailment problems with X rays. What they saw convinced doctors to operate on him two weeks after his admission.

A few days after the operation and what appears to have been a slow emerging from pain and pain killers, he re-connected with Roslyn, writing another letter to the paper. The paper printed its own introduction.

No Jokes Just Yet says "Bill" In Hospital
Cheerful Word From
Bill Pickering in Mineola Hospital

From the recesses of the Mineola Hospital comes the characteristically brave and cheerful word from our good friend "Bill" Pickering. His many friends in Roslyn have been deeply affected by the suffering "Bill" had been through but as readers can see there is nothing in his latest word to us but good cheer and a brave outlook.

The Editor of the Roslyn News:
Dear Dan:
  "This is my first day back to normal after nights of horror and sleeplessness interspersed with a few hours sleep produced by the

ministrations of good Dr. Galione, when we floated among the palaces and playgrounds of our childhood.

Our experience from the time of the preparation for the operation until after we had the wonderful awakening is almost indescriable[sic]. To be told that you have come back to life, to God's green earth, when like so many poor creatures, we might have been at rest on the cold slab in the little house we so well remembered from our experiences when doing work for the Sheriff and the District Attorney. [as police photographer]

The joy, the ecstasy and thankfulness to God, when at last we realized what our nurse told us was true, that it was all over, and two of my stalwart sons grasped my hands to reassure me. We have had thrills of all kinds from being knocked off a horse, to jumping a speeding hand car at the approach of a fast train or being a loose sheet on the deck of a ship on a stormy night, giving you a game of hop skip and jump across a slippery deck–narrow escapes all–but nothing like this.

Then the aftermath which we would rather overlook as too horrible to write about. And now this morning we are back to normal, still in bed, sore enough with our tight bandages and back aches, but the weakness fast disappearing, again clothed in our right mind and able to greet visitors from Roslyn with somethin [sic] of our old smile, but no jokes or laughs, please, since we are still a little sore for that. But it was great to see old Pat Breen, Tom Fearns, Dr. Tommy Fearns, Harry Eastman, Mr. Pickard (from the Exchange Club) Butcher Herbert, John Hogan, Jim McCue, Nathan Ziefman, Counsellor[sic] Dugan with his jolly laugh and smile. (We asked him one day if there was anything doing, and he replied plenty of time to talk about those things when you come home. But we should worry, we are back on good old Long Island and we will ...

Thus ends prematurely the only copy of that letter that we have. Billy came home on June 5 after almost a month in Mineola Hospital. As soon as he was in his own bed he took up pen and paper and again to Dan at *The Roslyn News* who had kept readers informed about his struggle.

Dear Dan:
We arrived home today and while we are far from recovered, we are well on our way to get away with one of Nosaki's generous meals at the Exchange Club dinner, altho the surgeons have left only half of our storage capacity and we doubt if we can get away with it all.

Before we forget, we want to thank our most recent visitors as far as we can remember them, and also for their generous gifts of flowers, fruit, etc. They will pardon us for dividing some of these gifts with the

crippled boys in No. 1 ward, and others, and this morning before we left
we put some on the desk of that sweet little lady, the presiding genius of
the Annex (where we were located), Miss Loew.

Miss Loew exemplifies my ideal of a nurse; well she is boss of her
department, there is no task too menial, or unpleasant, but, when her
nurses are too busy (as they usually were) she would jump right in to aid
the helpless, with such a quick smile. God bless you, sweet lady, and may
he spare you for many more years of usefulness to Mineola hospital.

He goes on to thank several visitors by name, each with a phrase of characterization:
"Mrs. Jack Morrisons of those wonderful smiling eyes and pleasant ways, she brought
my old lady along for chaperone, I guess." Then it's time for a little highly opinionated
political activism.

We wish now to speak a word for the hospital and those of the staff with
whom we got acquainted. We have heard at various times so many
confusing reports regarding the management and conduct of the institution
and like a number more we got lax in our support of the same, although
personally we were unable to contribute but a small mite as we are of the
class of small businessmen who many consider well off financially, but, in
reality are worse off than the mechanic with his 10 or \$12 a day, and eight
hours work, while we put in any way from 12 to 16 hours. We are done
for everything that comes along, and as Poor Fred the Stock used to say a
till full of tickets you never use and no money; not only that, but some
busybodies who are usually very generous not with their own money, but
undertake the wheedling of money for some cause or other, criticize the
poor businessman because his donations might not be as large as they are
expected; we and many more like us resent that such tactics and refused
for some time to donate to several organizations.

Well, as far as the hospital is concerned, and from what personal
observation we have made, it is O.K. We have only one criticism to make
and that is they can't make a good cup of tea, but there is always a good
glass of milk for the asking.

He did not get "back on his feet" as *The Roslyn News* had predicted earlier. Either Billy,
Emma or friends were convinced he needed professional supervision in a convalescent
home. His pain continued. He was pale and weak, but his spirits remained strong. While
he was at home he wrote a letter to his friends at the Exchange Club of Roslyn. *The
Roslyn News* published it on June 21.

Letter Sent Exchange By Pickering

Thanks Roslyn Exchnge [sic]
Members for Recent Kindnesses

The following was the letter sent to the Exchange Club of Roslyn by "Bill" Pickering, Sr., lately released from the Mineola Hospital, which this paper was able to secure for publication.

Secretary of the Roslyn . Exchange Club:

Dear Fred:

Please convey to the President and members of the Club my appreciation of the interest they have shown in my condition during my illness. We also wish to thank Brother Westermayr for his very kindly letters received, while in the Hospital: A number of the members of· the Club. visited me and jolly Dan Winters spent Friday afternoon with me. Brother Harry Eastman made several visits, but we missed the jovial face of Butcher Gus although I thought after the surgeons got through with me that I would not want to see any more butchers for a while and as for smiling Henry, maybe he's disappointed that he didn't have a nice smiling corpse to perform the last rites on as we promised him the job some time ago. Tell him not to worry tho, there is still hopes for the job if he lives long enough.

Well boys, it's no use thinking that you can vamp those nurses, as my room looked like a harem and I was the sultan. For young and old alike my room was the rendezvous, and any excuse being good enough to gain entry from a cup of good tea to a glass of that cough medicine with a kick or an offer to rub my back with alcohol and powder. (I wish one were here now for it certainly does ache).

It would take too long to try to tell you about the Hospital, but we do say that if people would go there and remember that they are in a hospital and not at home, they would find that it is by no means the worst place in the world.

One item of news and then we will quit and rest up for a while. Mrs. Tabarteo Pickering, true to the traditions of the family, gave birth to triplets. Of course the pile of hook rugs upstairs (her usual bed) seemed the logical place to have them, but the door being barred to her, the next best place, the flivver, was selected. Evidently the boys took the family for a ride in the approved styel [sic] and only one escaped. This one the poor Ma was determined by some means to put in its proper surroundings of antique and rare books. She marched in with the said kitten in her mouth to the astonishment of the customers and placed that mite in my case of choice first editions of Lawrence Stern, Dean Swift, Ben Johnson, etc. The poor thing was tightly wedged in between "Sterns Sentimental Journies" and Dean Swift's "Instructions to Servants."

If it happens to be a Tom cat it will not hurt his morals for they are proverbially bad, but imagine what the effect will be on her future if it happens to be a young she. Now you litteatures and Bibliophiles can enlighten your Brothers on just what that cat slept on.

Please inform the Brothers that we are at home until Friday or Saturday when we go away again to vamp our nurses—probably to Brentwood for about six weeks.

So long,
Billy.
P.S. Now that that is off our chests we will go to sleep.

Billy had mentioned Brentwood because that town in Suffolk County was then a quiet rural place where a grand estate had been converted at the turn of the century into a nursing and convalescent home. Maybe Brentwood cost too much. Instead of that nearby facility, he went north of New York City to another estate-turned-convalescent home—the Convalescent Institute of the Burke Foundation. The facilities emphasized rehabilitation through crafts and other activities, and it served both the physically and mentally ill. Patients not only performed services for the institution but made small items which were sold to pay part of the facility's bills. Billy stayed there from June 21st to July 6. On his arrival he sent a foldout postcard to his daughter Annie whose two year old toddler, Anne Claire, he had come to love. He first addressed it to "Miss Annie Pickering," then crossed out Pickering and wrote Buck without changing Miss.

June 21/29
Dear Annie,

      This is a beautiful place, but not quite used to it yet. There are 220 patients.

      There are no visitors allowed and only one permit a week to go out.

                  Love to Anne Clare
                  Pop

A week later he wrote another card to Annie. Despite the no visitor rule, he did have one visitor, the most wily and sophisticated of his children, Buster.

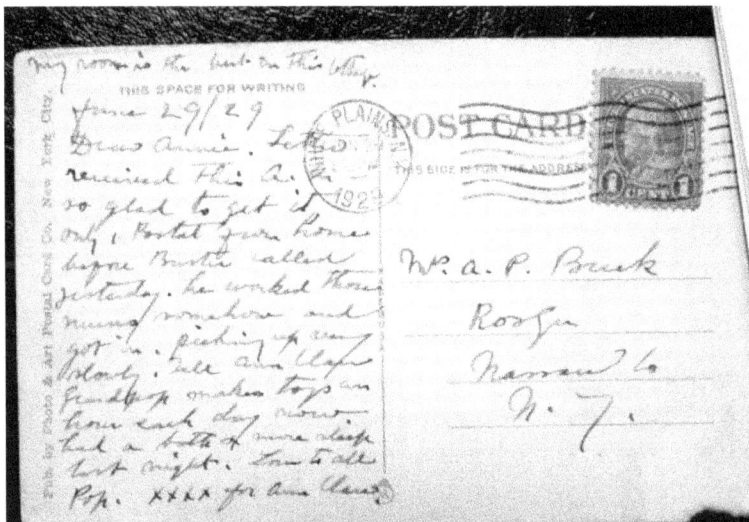

My room is the best in this cottage.
June 29/29
Dear Annie. Letter received this A.M. So glad to get it only 1 postal from home before Buster called yesterday. He worked those nurses somehow and got in. Picking up very slowly. Tell Anne Claire Grandpop makes toys an hour each day now. Had a bath & more sleep last night. Love to all.
Pop. x x x x for Anne Claire.

His son Buster had come in to visit as soon as he had returned to America from accompanying Frank Doubleday on a cruise to England. Buster, of course, had always been a dapper flirt, and perhaps his nursing credentials made his visit acceptable.

No doubt many of Billy's friends knew that his letters were a last good-bye. No sooner had Billy returned from the Burke Foundation than he and Emma began to make business arrangements for his death. They sent out a notice that their son Jack would take over the store. It was also a cordial thank-you and good-bye:

NOTICE

Commencing next Monday July 15, our son, John Pickering, will take over the management of our entire Newspaper, Magazine, Stationery, and Cigar business. This will all be transferred to our Willow Avenue store (Mill Dam) Roslyn.

We were obliged to give up this part of our business owing to our serious illness, which compels us to retire.

After the 15th (Monday), all bills must be paid to John Pickering who assumes all debts connected with that business contracted after that date. Previous to the 15th, all outstanding accounts should be made payable to William Pickering Sr.

We thank our patrons for their loyalty and support during the many years we have conducted the business; we have endeavored to give our people the best service possible in spite of many obstacles, and we know that our boy who has lived all his life among you will do credit to the old name and give you as good and better service than his Dad has given you.

All we ask is that you give him the same generous support
you gave us, and we know the boy will make good.

The boy is giving up a good trade to continue the old name
in Roslyn, it is a matter of filial pride with him, and we are
proud of him, and, we know he is going to win out; the
Pickering stock never goes under.

For the time being our main Antique and Rare Book
business will be conducted as usual at our East Broadway
store, and until Fall there will be a 25% reduction on our
present prices as our entire stock must be disposed of.

Mrs. Pickering and I take this opportunity to thank the
people of this community for their many acts of kindness
and sympathy in our affliction. We knew we had many
friends, but, never realized until now that the whole
community were our friends.

That is something to be proud of and we are deeply grateful
for it.

Sincerely yours
Mr. and Mrs. Wm. Pickering

(Dated by hand July 15, 1929)

"The boy" who the notice referred to had already turned 30, married, had two sons, and
that "good trade" he was giving up was a struggling business in a second hand store
sharpening saws on the side. This was the same "boy" whose sister Emma remembered
being one side of a family argument in which their father had threatened him with a
knife. Jack and his wife Nelly and their sons moved into the apartment above the new
store on the main street.

Might be the last photo of William Pickering. Summer 1929.
Couple on left are and Tommy and Mary Manion Hayes with her arm around Tom Pickering Jr., Tommy holding George Pickering, Emma behind her father leaning on Helen Conklin, Helen Nelavaiko Pickering and son Jack Jr. on right.

Throughout July, and August Billy's condition grew worse. So did the family finances, which had never been very good in any case. They discovered, however, just how rich in friends they really were. As Billy said in the notice turning over the business to son Jack, he and Emma had a "whole community" of friends.

On September 14 *The New York Times* took note of how their friends came to their aid. The headline read:

Proprietor of Old Curiosity Shope Stricken, so his Customers Plan Auction

After describing the shop and its variety of items inside and overflowing to the curb the reporter comes to the event and its cause.

Mr. Pickering, 63 years old, who started this shop long ago, after having been a gardener on the estates of Judge Townsend Scudder and Clarence Mackay, is mortal ill of cancer. His only assistants in the sickness have been his wife and children. The business has been peculiarly individual. He alone has a clear idea of what he paid for many of the thousand and one items or what they ought to bring.

A changing trade is the antique business, when it is remembered that the early American furniture which Long Island housewives used to be glad to get rid of now out sells mahogany in Madison Ave.

It is necessary that the business be promptly liquidated. Mr. Pickering, now at the Hospital for Incurables in New York City, cannot do much about it, and the stock cannot be sold rapidly by ordinary means. So a group of Mr. Pickering's old customers from the countryside all the way from Westbury to Syosset and his friends and fellow townsmen in Roslyn have decided to conduct an auction at the Roslyn War Memorial next Friday from 10 AM to 6 PM. The stock will be on display on the preceding Tuesday, Wednesday and Thursday.

The Roslyn war Memorial Hall, just across the road, has been loaned for the occasion, the trustees deeming Mr. Pickering such a worthy citizen that the sale of his wares is a public occasion. Members of the American Legion are going to move the stock across the road, and S. A. Chapman of the Anderson Gallery in New York, has volunteered his services as auctioneer.

The Anderson Gallery on Park Avenue had been one of America's most prestigious art auction houses. Some of his possessions were sold privately before the auction began on Friday morning, September 20. Katherine Mackay helped Emma to find buyers for the most expensive and rare items. Both *The New York Times* and the *New York Herald Tribune* carried articles about the auction. The *Times* headlined the story:

HOARDED ANTIQUES
SOLD TO AID ILL MAN

Roslyn Friends of William
Pickering Throng to Buy
His Treasures of Years

$2071 TOTAL FOR FIRST DAY.

The writer repeated some details from the story the week before, but added these paragraphs:

He was rich -- rich in lore and the potential value of the overflowing stock he possessed.

But funds were needed immediately. Realizing this, his friends in Roslyn, rich and poor, who bought his treasures or even merely admired and coveted them, turned out yesterday.

The town donated the war Memorial Hall, just across the street. In auctioneer came from the Anderson galleries in Manhattan. The proceeds of the first days sell amounted to $2,071. In equal amounts had already been acquired through private sale. The auction will continue tomorrow.

The Tribune's staff correspondent, Beverly Smith, also described Billy as a once "penniless" immigrant and emphasized the broad demonstration of support for the dying man across the social spectrum. Smith appears to make up some of her facts. For instance, she has Billy and Emma arriving from England already married with two children. But she agrees with the *Times* writer on the community support. She probably invented the quote in the following passage as a way of summarizing numerous comments:

> Today, the most prominent citizens of Roslyn joined to do Mr. Pickering honor. And, incidentally, to help him in a financial way. These neighbors would not give their names. They merely said: "William Pickering has been a good neighbor. Good neighbors are scarce. Besides that he is a character, a lovable character. We want to show a little appreciation."

"They" seldom speak in this kind of choral unison except in ancient Greek dramas. Her article ends with a sample list of items and an echo of the September 20 New *York Times* article's note that the antiquarian who knew about all these things was missing.

> There were chandeliers and "garendos" [illegible word] 50 years ago, that went for a two dollar gold, silver, copper, and gold luster. All bureaus and tables and weatherbeaten wooden cradles with hoods, relics of the days when the sunlight was supposed to be baneful. There were Pennsylvania and our chests and powder horns; ship lanterns, probably dating from the time of kid; fine old carriage lanterns, of no earthly use today, which Roslyn matrons balked because they "remind me of the lights on papa's old carriage." Funniest of all, for the youngsters, with a splendid and lethal ancient weapons -- to handle swords, blunderbuss is, .72 board dueling pistols, "chastisers," 8 pound spiked iron balls, suspended by a

chain to a hickory stick, used to crack skulls and pierced chests in olden times.

All these precious items sold, at prices from $2-$82 apiece, what a sensual thing was lacking: the advice and knowledge of the elderly man, who knows the detailed story, the romance, back of all these outwardly simple things; the man who knows how this cradle, or that dueling pistol, played its part in the history of Long Island. William Pickering, well these joys of his life were sold, was playing his slow game of pain and death on his cot in a New York hospital.

Among the items sold at auction was the French spinet piano on which Emma had played for five years. With the piano went the bench and every sheet of Emma's music. The package added $400 to the auction proceeds.

The "hospital for incurables" that both writers mention was, in fact, St. Rose's home at 71 Jackson St. in Brooklyn. The home with thirty-five beds operated like a hospice, giving free care to patients dying of cancer. The owners and staff were the Dominican Sisters of Hawthorne. Billy, a devotee of literature, may have known that the founder of the home was Rose Hawthorne, daughter of New England novelist Nathaniel Hawthorne who is still famous for his novel *The Scarlet Letter*. (The home did not close for good until March 31, 2009.) As a nun, Rose was known as Mother Mary Alphonsa. She had died in the home three years before Billy arrived. Billy's daughter Dorothy had become a Catholic for her first marriage, and she later claimed that she had converted her father on his deathbed in St. Rose's.

Billy suffered on for three weeks after the auction, dying on October 11. Billy had known before entering the hospital that he would die this time. He probably gave each of the children a parting gift or memento. His daughter Emma's piano had gone at auction, but she kept and cherished through life several small antiques. One was an ivory shoe horn, another a Japanese box of sandalwood that held inside four smaller boxes, all still retaining the sweet smell of spicy wood.

Jack had already taken over the new store on Willow Street, and Bill had purchased a strategically located small store by the railroad station in Glen Head. "Buster" received his father's gold pocket watch. The words inscribed on the back cover read, "Presented By The LI Newsdealers Assn. June 20, 1915." The association had given it to him as a token of appreciation for his activist service as President. But who conceived the inscription for inside the back cover and when was it done? It read:

To My Son Wallace
Oct. 11, 1929

Did he guess the day of his death, instruct Emma or one of the boys to have it put there, or did one of them decide on the date?

A newspaper notice of funeral services described the store as "a gathering place for writers, artists, book lovers, and students of the arts." The funeral service was held in Roslyn's Trinity Episcopal Church. Emma wrote in her birthday book, "Pop died in St. Rose's Home New York 9:15 am Buried 14th 1929."

The money that his friends raised by auctioning his possessions had to include bids that were higher than the actual value of many items. True or not, the fact that people from every walk of Roslyn life participated to give a poor man a dignified death is almost a mirror image of an event in 1875 when Billy was ten. That year his own father, then a storekeeper, died of a digestive tract ailment and his gravestone and funeral were paid for by "public subscription" and his funeral attended by children, the poor and the local lords and ladies.

THE OLD ROSLYN ANTIQUE SHOP
East Broadway

WILLIAM PICKERING
Phone 177

The mecca for all lovers of antiques, rare books and prints. Always cozy and warm. Unique in every way.

**Wallace and Emma Pickering
after William's funeral. 1929**

CHAPTER 17. THE BLACK SHEEP'S CHOICE

While Billy's life and humor faded in the last months of his life, he wrote from the Burke convalescent hospital that his son Buster had gotten past the nurses and paid a surprise visit. Buster's ease with hospital routines he had learned in the profession he took up in 1919 when masses of returning veterans closed him out of his job at the dye works and even out of "pearl diving" in café kitchens.

Once again his ability to make and keep loyal friends had come to his rescue. A Providence friend took him to see the owner of an employment bureau and talked the woman into taking his case. She sent him for an interview at Butler Hospital where they badly needed lower level help. To locals Butler was simply "The Asylum" because it treated the mentally ill.   He had his doubts whether he wanted to be an orderly in the disorder of the mental wards, but "A friend had told me what to expect of work there. I would have nothing to do except to amuse the inmates, take them for a walk, and in return receive maintenance and $500.00 per month." The nickel and two pennies that he had left in his pocket bought him a one way fare to Butler. He packed his few clothes in a hand bag he had borrowed for the trip and the rest he tied up in a paper package. "I had dressed in a gray suit which I had purchased on the installment plan known as 'dollar down and catch me when you can.'" His friend, older and more sophisticated, boarded the trolley with him, and together they disembarked opposite the imposing gates.

As a new residence, Buster sized up the sprawling campus as they walked to the main building along the winding three quarter mile drive. Large lawns rolled away on both sides, then half way down they passed through wooded grottos. Finally, the landscape opened up and the three story, old, ivy covered, brick buildings lay ahead of them. He then committed his first faux pas—entering through the front doors, a privilege reserved for the medical staff alone.

The cordial but efficient receptionist showed them into the office of the supervisor of the male patients, Bertram C. Kemp. Buster's friend sat to one side and Mr. Kemp laid before the humble 18 year old, former dishwasher an application. Buster looked at the title: "Application for Admission to the Butler Hospital Training School For Nurses." He had never heard of a male nurse, but he filled out the application since he desperately needed any job available. When the supervisor examined his information, he said he had serious doubts about someone so young taking on the responsibilities Butler required. Besides, said the man, with all the discharged veterans looking for work, they could be particular. Buster's friend stood up and asked if he could talk to the supervisor. What he said, we don't know, but Buster started work on a bitter cold February 26.

The reason Mr. Kemp had given Buster a nursing student's application was almost certainly because, contrary to what he told Buster, the hospital was having difficulties finding staff—not orderlies but nurses. In Butler Hospital's annual report for 1920 Physician-in-Chief and Superintendent, Dr. G. Alder Blumer, wrote to the Board of Trustees, ". . . our first and urgent need is for student nurses. Notwithstanding liberal advertisement in the United States and Canada, as well as personal appeals to various organizations of young people in Providence and its vicinity, desirable applicants have been very few." Between June 1920 and the end of the year, the hospital had had only 40 inquiries for positions, and most were ineligible. Students at other hospitals were not asking for training at Butler because their home institutions had eight hour shifts while Butler required 12 hours on duty. Most of the time the hospital had only one male medical officer to deal with an average of 142 resident patients, about half of them men.

About Mr. Kemp, whom Buster would "become fond of", Blumer wrote that he had "conceptions of duty suggesting 'the antique world,' and [has been] one who has coped valiantly and imperturbably with administrative difficulties that might well have driven a weaker spirit to despair." [26]

Blumer was then 63 years old, a native of northern England, graduate of Edinburgh University medical school, and, according to medical historian Ian Dowbiggin, "There were few other asylum physicians in the US around the turn of the century who were held in higher esteem." [27] Blumer and Kemp were passionately committed to working with even the most hopeless patients. Their attitude would soon resonate on a deep chord in the new student whose priority in life until then had been seeking his own liberty and pursuit of happiness. Blumer sums up the hospital's commitment in the same annual report:

Looked at in cold blood, it seems like an almost shameful sacrifice of time and money and professional attainments to keep alive and tenderly care for, for perhaps a quarter of a century, a man or woman who can never hope to comprehend a word which is said to them, but in many cases it must be done, even at the sacrifice of our worthy ambition for the early attainment of leadership among the hospitals of the land in the study of the causes and prevention of mental disease.

When Buster started his training Butler had just retained a new superintendent of nurses, Miss Margaret S. Belyea, a woman in her early 40s and already an experienced administrator. During the war she had served in the U.S. military hospital in Brest as supervisor of the psychiatric department. Her most recent post before Butler had been assistant superintendent of Nassau Hospital in Mineola where Buster's father would later be operated on for stomach cancer. The new head of instruction was also a new face. Dowbiggin says that "treatment at Butler in the early twentieth century was based mainly on the nineteenth-century notion that early diagnosis and prolonged exposure to the hospital's "moral" environment improved the patient's chances for recovery. Blumer and his assistants spent most of their time attempting to enlist the patient's co-operation in a morally rehabilitative process designed to restore nervous energy."

While Buster had found his way to Butler by accident, the fact that he chose to stay there and the passionate interest he developed in psychiatric nursing and the nature of mental illness may have been at least partially nourished by being raised in a family ruled by a dictatorial father and succored by a sometimes depressed and almost reclusive mother. It was also a family whose undercurrents would soon begin to surface in troubled marriages, divorces, alcoholism, three suicides and suicidal depression, not to mention a variety of notable eccentricities.

Butler hospital's shortage of nursing students meant extra work for the ones they did have. Buster's first job in the frigid first week of his work at Butler was washing the old diamond shaped windows. "There was not more than a hundred of these windows, yet it seemed to me as though there were thousands of them." The next day he began work with patients and was surprised at what he found.

"I had heard much about these people from the 'well informed public.' I do not know where the public gets its information. I think each time a tale is told a bit is added to it, and after a few tellings it becomes a monstrous fabrication. This is not the first time I have found the public to be wrong. . . . The Inmates of this ward, which resembled a house in every respect, were sitting in the main living room, smoking, some discussing current events, some performing idiotic actions and a couple were talking to themselves. I did not, either then or since, encounter the proverbial

'Napoleon' who is imagined to live in all insane institutions. One of these patients was permitted the privilege of using the pantry for the purpose of making bonbons, Johnny Cakes, etc. I soon learned that to eat these Johnny cakes was to do a gross injustice to my stomach. This same patient also used the hospital grounds to engage in farming on a small scale. He raised some fine vegetables and flowers.

Buster was fortunate to start psychiatric nursing in a hospital with a small population, an administration committed to individualized treatment and a budget more or less able to carry out that approach. Director Blumer had left the state hospital in Utica, NY for Butler because Utica had become a holding facility for a large number of patients who were all treated with more or less the same regime. About half of Butler's patients came from affluent families able to pay their entire bill. Despite the humane approach to its patients and its funding, Butler did not have the funds for the staff it wanted. Buster consequently "learned the art of housekeeping. . . . . I pushed a carpet sweeper, dust mop, and dust cloth. I waxed floors, washed windows and polished brass. When the house work was completed we took patients out for a walk or did odd jobs around the grounds with them. In the winter we attended the gym three mornings each week. Other days we cut wood, shoveled snow if there was any, or worked around the grotto where we erected benches, bridges and once built an attractive spring."

He also had to learn the art of self defense and physical control of violent patients. He found that while they almost never attacked each other, attacks on the staff were not uncommon. Buster was in good shape but a small, wiry young man with no experience in fighting except an occasional scrap with a brother. He was soon tested. "I was not at Butler long before I was attacked by a six foot tall inmate. My rescuer was another inmate." Butler had no straight jackets, no big enforcers. "When we were confronted with an unruly patient we would put him on the floor and hold him there until he quieted down. If this failed he was put in an ice pack or a continuous cold bath. These measures were never used unless prescribed by a physician, and physicians were always reluctant to order any means of restraint."

Although no one in his family had yet exhibited suicidal tendencies, Buster devotes a long portion of his notes on patients to suicide. He begins, "I have heard people state that not one of us have not at some time in our lives at least thought of committing suicide. Many apparently normal people execute this act in more than one way; also insane people do. Whether one must be insane to commit suicide is still a question for debate." (Each attempt at suicide in his own family would take a different form.)

In detail he relates several cases of suicide and attempted suicide among Butler's patients and muses on whether the survivors really meant to kill themselves and on why people commit suicide. His only specific conclusion: "No doubt many people sincerely believe that they will be conscious after death. They have a feeling that they will be able to see and hear all that transpires during death and the funeral services and think it will be nice to be laid out in a coffin and see all their former friends and just curious people reviewing their remains."

Buster kept careful notes of every patient he attended. Those notes have not survived, but his short memoir records several cases in addition to the suicides. He also praises the staff from top to bottom, including his instructors. Can we attribute his patience and his effort to understand even the most difficult people to growing up with eight brothers and sisters and an eccentric father? Or should his mother's example as an understanding peace maker get most of the credit? After all, despite the many personal troubles that would plague her children, not one of them had a mean streak. This writer remembers looking forward to their attention when he was small, and a child's instincts have more weight than the child.

Buster had the sunniest disposition of all the Pickerings and was just starting on a long and almost always sunny life. He took to the rigors of nurse's training with good will and curiosity. As a "prob" (probationary student for 3 months) the hospital assigned him to "exceptionally comfortable" quarters with meals and any necessary medical service. He received his uniform, but until he had completed probation he would be marked as a greenhorn by having no nurse's cap or bib. Work and study went on from 7 a.m. to 7 p.m. with three hours break time. Night shifts allowed two hours off. Students worked through the morning and took classes in the afternoons and often attended lectures by surgeons at night.

Almost all the men in nurses training failed the first examination. Kemp investigated their activities and study habits, then called them together. After a fatherly talk, "he extracted a promise from us to keep abreast of the 'other side' (this is the female school)." At the end of his group's three years only Buster and one other male passed, and only Buster took the state board exam to win his certification.

During those three years his views on both the mentally ill and on nursing had changed. Since he devotes a piece of his memoir to "enlighten" the public, and since the public never had the chance to read it, the main points are summarized or quoted now.

Hospitals did not require a high school diploma for admission into their nurse training programs, although they preferred it when they could be choosey. During the war and in 1919, as the Butler reports confirm, they had little to choose from. Each ran its own 'college' so to speak. Since many hospitals did not provide training and experience in all areas, the hospitals traded students. Butler received trainees from many other hospitals since most did not treat mental illness. Butler's mentally ill, however, were frequently physically ill and its students could spend their entire training in one place, as Buster did.

The preliminary requirements he listed emphasized, "A sound physical condition; above the average in intellect and of undeniably good character. If any of these requirements are lacking this defect is soon discovered to the disappointment of the applicant." The pay was low, the hours of work and study consumed almost every hour not spent eating or sleeping.

Buster lists the subjects in the standard training courses:
Anatomy & Physiology.'
Practical nursing;
Medical, surgical, contagious & pediatric nursing:.
Materia Medica
Drugs & solutions
Dietetics Psychiatry
Hygeine & sanitation
Operating room technique
Laboratory technique
Obstetrics
Bacteriology
Chemistry
The history of nursing
X-Ray technique
Social service
Community nursing
Hydrotherapy
Massage
Occupational therapy

He clearly took considerable pride in being admitted without a high school diploma and at an unusually young age. In his conclusion he speaks of nurses in general, but he is describing his own qualities and success when he writes, "If one is willing, loyal and progressive, advancement is rapid as soon as their training qualifies them." His passage from pearl diver to registered nurse was not all Goody-Two Shoes. In the middle of his note about the rigors of training he writes, "Breaking rules was a joy--if not caught." He does not say, however, if the authorities caught him. Looking back a few years later, he wrote, "In view of the hard work and small compensation, I consider my three years spent in training the happiest days of my life. Seeing sick people returned to a state of good health is the greatest pleasure I have derived from life. Trained nurses are the best qualified wives and mothers of the present generation." The irony of that last sentence being written by a man without wife or children did not occur to him. He did practice what he wrote since he would soon marry a nurse.

His opinion of Butler and the other nurses was also tested in his own experience when he came down with a bad case of flu. (This was only a year or two after the great flu epidemic of 1918 had killed hundreds of thousands of Americans.) Doctors at that time often recommended the removal of a sufferer's tonsils to reduce infection. Buster recalled, "I walked into the operating room; viewed another boy's tonsils which were reposing in a basin. I then laid out on the table; took a few drags of ether under the Influence of which my own tonsils and adenoids were removed." His bout of flu must have been serious enough to raise the possibility he might die as so many others had done. "I owe an everlasting debt to those who cared for me; no king received better treatment. That I am alive today bears me out in this statement."

Buster, however, was too much his own man to get along with everyone on the Butler staff. In the summer of 1920 when he had finished his first 18 months of training, a supervisor with whom he had often clashed had him assigned to a Boston hospital for training in medical and surgical nursing. Br'er Rabbit was thrown in the proverbial briar patch. "This course lasted one year. A class mate accompanied me to this institution. . . . If this year could be classed as a penalty, I certainly have no objections to being penalized for the remainder of my life. "

He began his Boston year in a ward for alcoholics where once again he met one of nursing's heroines, a woman who was very strict, and whose reputation had preceded her, transforming her into a tyrant. Buster, however, had months ago decided to "find out for myself," and what he found was a thoroughly professional nurse from whom he learned a great deal. "A lazy nurse was like vermin to her; if one worked hard and conscientiously, a splendid report went to "center" (the superintendant's office)." In the end, he concluded, she was also "the patient's best friend." He left her ward reluctantly for surgical training. There he met the medical challenges and patients who continued his education in urban life. His patients included all races and religions, men and women, victims of street violence, domestic fights, construction and factory injuries. One day several men who had been crushed and partially buried when laying a sewer line in a ditch were brought in. One had $3,000 cash sewn into his jacket. He claimed he did not trust banks.

In Boston Buster's pay had increased to $8.75 a week. When he returned to Butler in September 1921 he received the jacket of a "senior" with its emblematic black cuffs and enjoyed $45 a month. He was now thoroughly acclimated to nursing and everything it required. After one of his patients had died, he attended the autopsy along with a group of 'probs'. When the examiner held up the corpse's liver and asked the 'probs' to identify it, which they easily did, Buster announced his patient's liver would be served in the morning for breakfast. "Sure enough, we were served liver as I predicted. Indeed, it was not the liver I had reference to. However, I learned that the chef commenced an investigation to determine the cause for the return of 'all the liver he dispatched to the two nurses' dining rooms for breakfast'. Those probs were brave girls; not one fainted and all proved to be good listeners."

To Buster's surprise, one of his supervisors called him in during the year to give him a special assignment—the care of a man whose wife "had an affinity for young men." Buster was given this man's case because his supervisor informed him, "I know you will not get mixed up with this woman for you don't care for women." At Boston and at Butler Buster had always enjoyed the nights on which dates were allowed, as well as many on which they were not allowed. Of this assignment he wrote only that he had passed through this trial "without any scandal."

He went on to pass his State Board Examination. "With reluctance, we were now a graduating class. We were all dressed, in new and specially laundered uniforms for the graduating exercises. In these we marched up the center aisle of the hall. Behind were the old "grads" then followed the female and male pupils. My knees actually shook when I arrived at the designated row of seats for the graduating class. It seemed to me that I was leaving a life I would never live again; no futures of life would equal that."

Buster had become the first person in the Pickering family to receive a diploma for completing his education. None of his brothers and sisters had yet or would ever graduate from high school. He had received an even higher degree and his disbelief is credible. "It took days to make me realize that I was now a full fledged member of the second greatest profession in the world."

He was not only a full member, but his standing at Butler earned him a promotion immediately after graduation to assistant supervisor, age 22. He had just begun to feel comfortable with his executive duties when, "Restlessness returned to me; hence I re signed from my office with the intention of making much money and seeing the world."

Buster with mother and sisters Annie and Emma about 1922

He saw the world from slums to palaces as a freelance nurse in several eastern cities. His modus operandi was to select a city, list his name with a registry of nurses looking for work, then wait for a call. Sometimes he would wait for more than a month as his savings slowly disappeared. "My days were spent in doing anything I could devise to pass the time. To be out of hearing distance of the phone jeopardized my chance of securing work. . . . One hundred and eighty days employment in a year is a good record for the private duty nurse."

The slums his work took him to were immigrant slums where every person or family had to fend for itself. He describes a typical area as he searches for a new assignment.

> After walking more than a couple of city blocks I located the number of the house as was given to me by my registry. This street was littered with rubbish of all kinds; dirty soft drink stands and dark dingy stores emitted foul odors. Children who had probably not been bathed since birth, dressed in shabby clothes, played upon the street. They built fires and played ball irrespective of the honking autos and cursing teamsters. I entered thru a dark hallway which had only a flickering gas light for illumination. Sawdust was freely scattered upon the stairs and landings. Reeking odors were rampant. The stairs emitted loud groans when trod upon; the banister assumed the form of rubber when I grasped it. At last I arrived at my destination and knocked (door bells were absent) which brought a request from the inside as to my errand. I replied satisfactorily for instantly a lock responded; another and another. I thought I was entering the U. S. Treasury as a result the action entailed in admitting me. . . . The patient was found in a double bed in a room not large enough for me to turn around in. It turned out to be "winter quarters for the trained flea circus". Bed- bugs were rampant; the roaches were large enough to utilize in place of expensive draft horses. It is not unusual for nurses to transport these creatures to their own homes. Many a nurse has deemed it advisable to have their effects fumigated. It is just one of the embarrassing and inconvenient incidents of our profession.

The wealthy families he worked for almost all required a psychiatric nurse. The interesting details of the cases are not the homes but the patients.

After a few years the periods between jobs became too much for him. He accepted a friend's proposal to form a business partnership, although he does not say what the business was. It soon failed. "I think God blessed nurses with "hopes"; otherwise the suicide rate among them would be appalling."

He returned to nursing in a doctor's office. To his great satisfaction the doctor was both a great and generous humanitarian who never turned away a patient. "Whether a patient could afford the doctor's fee or not, he was treated until cured, if a cure were possible." The doctor who Buster never names he calls "a born humanitarian and philosopher as well as being an expert teacher." In his office the young nurse "made everlasting friendships and acquired information that I had never dreamed of attaining."

"Everlasting" is either an exaggeration for a man in his twenties or exhibit the gift of prophecy. Nevertheless by the late 1920s Buster seemed to have his choice of jobs and entre to very rich clients.

In 1927 or 1928 Frank Doubleday, president of the famous Doubleday Publishing empire engaged Buster as his nurse. It's possible that Buster made the connection with Doubleday through his father or his father's friends since Doubleday lived not far from Roslyn on his Oyster Bay estate. Or Christopher Morley, a friend of Doubleday's and a frequent visitor to the Pickering store in Roslyn may have recommended Buster. Doubleday was about 68 when he engaged Buster to accompany him and his wife on several voyages and cruises. Buster was then 27, a dapper young man with a ready smile, a good wit, the latest clothes, and an eagerness for travel. Buster had also been well seasoned in every kind of nursing from the infectious diseases and traumas of city ghettoes to all kinds of nervous and psychiatric disorders. Doubleday always booked Buster in a first class cabin and soon began to call him "Doc."

Frank N. Doubleday and his nurse, Wallace George Pickering

Doubleday may have identified a lot of himself in the restless young nurse. Doubleday had been born in Brooklyn, the son of a struggling hatter whose business failed when Doubleday was a teenager. He bought a printing press and began printing advertisements, then rose quickly in the publishing world to create his own company and become the first publisher to see book selling as a business. He was also a populist supporter of Teddy Roosevelt and unafraid to publish the very controversial exposes on the meatpacking and other industries by Upton Sinclair. He became good friends with many of his authors, including Rudyard Kipling who gave him the nickname Effendi in the late 1800s. Until Doubleday's death, friends like Helen Keller, T.E. Lawrence, and partner Walter Page called him Effendi and he named his Oyster Bay estate Effendi Hill.

Exactly what services Buster provided for Doubleday he never recorded, but the publisher has some notoriety as a man who suffered from "flatulence" and would tolerate no aspersions or jokes about farting in books he published. Coronary disease for this high living man is also a possibility since a heart attack would kill him in 1934. Doubleday referred to the problem as "my weakness" but whatever it was, he did not want to travel without professional medical assistance at hand, and Buster agreed to accompany him to England.

Buster's father Billy had entered Mineola hospital on May 11 and the operation for his stomach cancer took place May 21. He remained in good humor before and after the operation, and Buster can hardly be faulted for not abandoning his employer and his first trip abroad. Buster received his first passport on May 17, 1929. He lists his height at 5 feet 6 ½ inches, brown hair, hazel eyes. His address is 535 W. 110 St, New York City. On the line for "IN CASE OF DEATH OR ACCIDENT" he requests notice be sent to his mother.

On May 25, 1929 Buster boarded the grand steamer U.S.S. Leviathan with Mr. and Mrs. Doubleday for the six day voyage to England. With them was the young and beautiful Mrs. RhondaTanner Doubleday who had been the second wife of the Doubleday's adopted son Felix. When Felix had divorced his first wife after only 2 years of marriage, he quickly settled on the beauty, Rhonda Tanner. Rhonda would meet her next fiancé, the wealthy Chicago brother of Cyrus McCormick, in Paris, only to sue him in 1933 for $1.5 million for breaching his promise to marry her. (The judge awarded her $65,000 and soon she sued Major Max Fleischmann, chairman of Standard Brands' finance committee for $100,000 when she overheard him on a golf course refer to her as a "blackmailing tart.") During their brief stay Frank Doubleday, with Buster at his side met with his friends T.E. Lawrence and Rudyard Kipling.

Among Buster's souvenirs was the menu for the 10 course Decoration Day (Memorial Day later) dinner. After two weeks in England Buster and the Doubledays boarded the British steamer Berengaria for the voyage home without Rhonda. They steamed into New York harbor on June 21st. That day Billy Pickering went to Westchester's Burke Foundation for two weeks of rehabilitation. As soon as Buster had settled in again, he went up to visit his father. He remained in New York working for Doubleday as his father's life faded and reached its end. The family records and memory, however, leaves blank how any of the children or Emma dealt with Billy's departure. They saved a few clippings about the sale of his possessions and the notice of the funeral service, but nothing else survives.

Buster made new plans to travel again with Frank Doubleday. He had become more than the publisher's nurse. A letter Doubleday sent to him in December makes an allusion to Buster's participation in late night festivities.

"Dear Doc:

I am sending you a check which I hope you will use to buy new tonsils. I am sure that if you have them re-inserted in your throat, your midnight songs will be more appreciated by me.

If you do not want these tonsils, spend the money for something else. At all events, I want you to realize that I appreciate the great care and good nature which you have shown for my weakness.

As always,

Sincerely yours,
FN Doubleday

In January 1930 Buster again joined Frank N. Doubleday and his wife for a cruise, this one a more leisurely trip to Nassau in the Bahamas on January 30. Doubleday had hoped to see his friends Rudyard and Carrie Kipling but they had to stay in Bermuda when Carrie suffered a burst appendix. Buster and the Doubledays returned to New York on April 9. They prepared for another voyage to England in May or June. Buster went to the British consulate in New York and received another visa on May 13. Kipling wrote to Doubleday from Bermuda that he was glad to hear they would meet again in England in June. Doubleday's health, however, began to fail rapidly and the trip was cancelled. Doubleday went into the hospital in September for an operation.

Doubleday was soon back at work although not traveling. In New York with medical care available day and night on short notice, he no longer needed a personal nurse. No records of Buster's career for the rest of the 1930s survive. He seems to have returned to using nursing as a way to satisfy his travel lust in the United States. His travels would end when he began work in Belmont, Massachusetts' famous McLean Hospital for the mentally ill. Whether he might have met the wife of F. Scott Fitzgerald there, one of many famous patients during the 1930s, we don't know, but in the late 1930s, he did meet a 25 year old nurse from New Hampshire named Beulah Whitaker. She was a cheerful farmer's daughter from the little village of Plainfield. Her fondness for Buster's jokes, her generosity, her professionalism, and the "peaches and cream" complexion one of her girlfriends recalled ended Buster's roaming bachelor life. With no regrets he followed her back to the family home after their marriage in 1940 and they lived there for almost half a century.

They worked together as nurses for more than 30 years at Cone Blanchard Machine Tool Company in nearby Windsor, Vermont. Buster, who became known locally as "Pick," soon engaged in village politics in the same dogged populist fashion he had learned from his father in Roslyn. A friend who described him could have been describing his father as well. The way Buster took on community improvement projects like the long battle for the village water system had all the toughness and community loyalty that had made his father loved in Roslyn. "The quality I remember most about him, really," his friend Steve Taylor said, "was his tenacity. Everybody else said, 'Pickering, you haven't got a chance,' but he just worked on it till he did it, because he was that kind of guy."

Pick and Beulah, 1946

If Beulah had many of the qualities of his mother, so did Buster. He was the peaceful center of life around him. People in trouble turned to him and found a ready listener and genuine sympathy. Above all he loved children though he and Beulah had none. Their home became a refuge and a haven of consolation and happiness for Buster's brothers and sisters, and for nieces and nephews. Their home, their friends, the good cheer of their married life renewed adults and inspired kids.

After 45 years of marriage, when Alzheimer's overtook Beulah, Buster became her constant nurse, staying on duty in the long months when she no longer knew him. His friend, state legislator Peter Burling, said, "There are only a few people who are as faithful as Pick was to Beulah and his community." Beulah's care had almost exhausted their life's savings. On his death his possessions were auctioned to pay his medical bills just as his father's had been. But Peter Burling had helped him write a will in case any money remained. The last $18,000 of his estate he left to the town of Plainfield in her memory, and with a provision that would keep her memory alive. That provision was not a plaque or monument, but the command that for 100 years the town should leave the money untouched and invested. Toward the end of the 21st century it will have grown to several million dollars and be known as "The Beulah Whitaker Pickering Trust." In her name it will be used for "the assistance that people need when their house is destroyed by fire or other calamity, the assistance that a young person needs to get an education when he has not the wherewithal to pay for the same."

Buster and Beulah's marriage was the longest and continuously happy marriage in the Pickering family. It endured through sickness and health till death did them part.

Left, 1934 with Eleanor Buck, Emma, Anne Clair Buck -   Right: 1944 with Art, Buster, Bill Kaufman

CHAPTER 18. LOCKED UP AND LIBERATED

By 1929 when Billy died Emma had been working fifty-five years, had borne 10 children, had raised 8 to independence, and faced her final worry—what to do about a spunky, attractive, and love-struck 17 year old daughter who had dropped out of school to help during her father's long dying. Young Emma, like her two sisters, had never received the warm, sympathetic love from a father that steadies many young women and provides them a confidence to wait and perhaps the ability to judge the young men who hunger for a woman who might fulfill their dreams of being a real man and captain of a family. She also ached for what her brothers and sisters now had—independence. Her mother and at least her closest brothers understood. She worried them. Their father no longer ruled with his strong will, but what if he had? Emma might run away as her sisters did.

Emma Pickering, 17 yrs old, 1928

Her mother and her brothers had seen Dorothy run away from home, marry, have a baby, and divorce. Annie too had run away to marry. Young Emma had had "crushes, puppy loves--Duncan Leckie and Fred Erickson--but I hadn't been in love." Without school and without her father, and with the business in her brother Jack's hands, she had time to herself. Like her sisters, she wanted romance. She had eyes that were seeking, often sad, but a rewarding smile full of warmth and gratitude.

Mary Manion and Emma Pickering, 1929

Charlie Smith (no date)

Her first love, marked in her notes for the summer of 1927 as "16th birthday, first love" she managed to keep secret with the help of her sister Annie and her friends Mary Manion and Bess McCue. Charlie, a Roman Catholic, lived in an unnamed "neighboring town." Emma wrote, "Like my sister Annie before me, I was not allowed to date. Strange to say, her boyfriend was a brother of my boyfriend Charlie [Smith]. Some days after school he would meet me and take me for short rides. Only on Sunday afternoons could I meet Charlie secretly. Together we would drive to Mary Mannion's home, and the three of us would drive to Bar Beach. On other occasions, Bess McCue and I would be allowed to go to the local movie house. Charlie would meet me there. Bess McCue also had to meet her boyfriend secretly."

Emma Pickering with George Lemine Olsen, 1930

Her infatuation with Charlie lasted a few months, but other suitors were easy to find. Once out of school she would have to choose a future, and single men contemplated choosing her. The three Klammer boys who lived a short distance out of the village on Northern Boulevard were always eager to see her. Same for Rich Haughwout in Roslyn. She was also very fond of George Olsen (later Olsen became Lemine) whose family both her parents liked. The first real love of her new life, however, sailed into Roslyn Harbor on a yacht belonging to financier Henry D. Walbridge who in 1921 had been part of a consortium planning to build a pontoon bridge from Yonkers to New Jersey. In 1929 after the Roslyn Harbor channel had been dredged deeper, Walbridge built a boathouse for his 200 acre estate and four story mansion on the West Shore Road of Hempstead Harbor.

Like many of the American nouveau riche, Walbridge created the air of established wealth by hiring English servants. For Emma all things English were from the Golden Age. In that age her own mother had been a beautiful and happy young English woman who took strolls along a colonnaded walk of The Pantiles; who ate rich steaming dishes like "toad-in-the-hole" and "roly poly," Yorkshire pudding, and plum pudding. Her mother had gone to London to watch the grand carriages at Picadilly Circus. The Walbridge yacht now brought to young Emma from that English world a lanky young steward in his creased slacks and high necked black sweater. The English language rolled sweetly from his tongue like the unpolluted springs of a river.

Wilfred Hill took an instant liking to the flirtatious young American. He and Emma began taking long slow walks along the streets of Roslyn Village. What Wilfred's intentions were, we don't know, but to Emma he was exotic and attached to the motherland and to the romance of the world of yachts and mansions that only four years earlier F. Scott Fitzgerald had celebrated in his smash hit novel, *The Great Gatsby*. The Walbridge yacht and its boathouse at the north end of Roslyn Village were part of Gatsby's world and his estate a couple of miles up the harbor. Emma didn't know much about the world or romance because she had grown up in a photographer's darkroom and among the small merchants of the village. Her parents were strict Victorian Anglicans. Both environments can weaken the eyes of romance.

Emma and her Englishman in his creased white slacks walked around the millpond and through the park across East Broadway from her house. Her brothers Art, Bill, and Jack, however, were young men with a sense of right and wrong, at least for baby sister. Curly haired, hot tempered Jack had worked as a carpenter in a shop near Roslyn Harbor, and he knew sailors and yachtsmen. Nothing about Englishmen enchanted him. Jack was running the Pickering store in its new location across from the harbor. That was his lookout and listening post. Jack and Art followed the lovers like a pair of hired detectives. On one occasion Bill was dispatched to snatch Emma away from a party on the boat and bring her home. They permitted Emma no privacy until Wilfred sailed away.

But Never Forgotten: *Emma would never forget the disappointment. Romance is hope while love is a sacrament whose severance is as painful as the severing of Siamese twins without anesthesia. She carried the hope of meeting Wilfred through fifty-seven years. When she turned 75 my brothers and I treated her to her one and only foreign journey—a trip to see the England of her mother's stories. Since she was afraid to travel alone or even on a tour, and since my brothers had steady jobs and I was my own boss, in spring I became her tour guide. For two weeks she suffered my driving and thrift and I suffered her complaints about the weather and the food and the cramped hotel rooms. We visited a few welcoming distant relatives and scoured a few graveyards in vain for her mother's kin.*

In our last two days in England she let go of the family search and turned to the one condition that surely banishes depression--love. Love is nothing if it is not hope and optimism and joy, or at least the expectation. I was not surprised that at 75 my mother still had that hope.

Fifty-seven years after her "proper Englishman" Wilfred sailed out of Roslyn Harbor, my mother and I sat in a tiny hotel room in London thumbing the telephone directory. We found the name Wilfred Hill. In our stuffy little room, unashamed to have me listening, my mother dialed. She introduced herself to the woman who answered, and said, "I am looking for a Wilfred Hill who visited America in 1929." At the other end of the line a very cautious voice said, "Yes, Wilfred Hill is my father, and he did go to the United States in 1929." She did not remember, however, that he had ever said he worked on a yacht, and maybe it was Boston he had visited, not New York.

My mother smiled, one of her few smiles during our trip. "I would like to talk to him," she said in her usual direct way.

"He's here, but I'm afraid he is not very well," the woman said in her indirect British way. He could not come to the phone and "his memory is very bad now anyway, you see."

Was she saving herself the trouble of chaperoning aged lovers, or was she telling the truth? Did she have any idea what she might be doing to my mother's last hope or illusion? My mother said meekly, "I understand." My mother left her name and address. Wilfred Hill's daughter promised to talk to her father when he was "up to it." He never was. My mother would never again try to find the loves she had lost. She remembered them often.

Bill Smith, Emma Pickering, Helen Reibel, Richie
1930

Helen Reibel and Emma Pickering, 1931

In school Emma had been an earnest student, solidly in the middle of her class. She knew what she wanted to be--a secretary, typing and taking shorthand. She had always been the best speller in the family. She would work for somebody important, and she would get his words down on paper just like he said them. As a secretary she could show her stuff, impress someone important. Her last term in school she had a 90 in English and 100 in math.

Her romances, however, troubled her mother and her brothers. And shortly after her father's death, the stock market crash of October 1929 signalled the beginning of the Great Depression. Her favorite brother Buster conferred with her mother, and together they planned for Emma's future. They thought it best to get her out of town and under the supervision and discipline of nurse's training. Buster was already making a fine

living as a nurse and he knew nursing would also give his sister a lifetime profession. He knew all about nurse's training, but of course, he failed to reason from his own evasions of rules and supervision that Emma might do the same and that maybe New York City was not the best place for a young woman to evade curfews or even to be alone when the rules permitted.

Very reluctantly, trailing a 73 in high school biology and without ever having studied chemistry, Emma packed the few things she would need and enrolled in the nursing program at New York Homeopathic Medical College at Flower Hospital. (Colleges and universities left nurses training to hospitals in that era.) Flower Hill Hospital was privately owned but included two wards for city patients. No matter which ward a patient entered, the medicine practiced and learned by nurses and M.D. students was homeopathic. (Homeopathy treats illness with a variety of highly diluted compounds of materials that cause similar symptoms in healthy people. Homeopathy has never been supported by rigorous scientific testing and scientists generally consider it a form of quack medicine.)

Emma's mother may have influenced the choice of that hospital. Throughout the 19th century homeopathic medicine had been popular with the English upper class and aristocracy, including members of the royal family. Homeopathic practitioners operated one of England's notable hospitals in the resort and spa town of Tunbridge Wells where Emma's mother had last worked as a servant and possibly a low level nurse. (Despite homeopathy's lack of scientific support, the British National Health Service funded the Tunbridge hospital until 2009.)

Emma and the 26 other members of her class lived at the Nurse's Home on 64th St. She became fast friends with the good natured Helen Shelton who shared her room for two years. They also shared each other's lives and misfortunes.

"We were two country girls getting a taste of city life. Our first months of school were interrupted by Helen's operation and the collapse of my left knee about the same time." They had to drop out to recover, and Helen became a frequent and well liked visitor to Roslyn. Both re-entered nursing school in September of 1930. For the first four months of training they wore their blue and white striped dresses with the broad white aprons and bibs. "We felt pretty big in our 'proby' uniforms." After five months they were "capped," and as junior students their on-the-job learning meant twelve hour shifts on the wards—sometimes at night, sometimes the day shift. No matter what shift they worked, they also attended classes. They fell asleep over their notebooks, and even when their eyes were open, their notes were illegibly scrawled. Neither Helen nor Emma knew the first thing about chemistry. Their heads swam with the names and formulae. Together they struggled to understand how certain combinations worked and others would not. Together they despaired. Among the many things about chemistry they never understood, Emma said, was how they passed the course. They did have free time and that meant dates. Emma and Helen went out with other students and Emma with a young doctor LaMonica.

Helen and Emma were still together in 1931 when they went to the famous New York Foundling Hospital to train in pediatric nursing. When they graduated as Registered Nurses in January 1933, Emma's mother, her brother Bill, her married sister Annie and her Roslyn girlhood friends Helen Conklin and Mary Mannion attended the ceremonies at City Hall and the reception in the dorm. Then, or within a few days, Emma revealed a secret she had kept from them since July. She was married.

The plans of her mother and brother Buster had achieved the results they were meant to avoid. Neither the close supervision of the hospital or its dorm had kept Emma from looking for romance. In fact the regime and its isolation from the familiar may have made her lonelier. Removing her from her Roslyn boyfriends may have reinforced her determination. Some of her brothers were dismayed and even outraged that the young man she met and married, while not Catholic, was Jewish. Emma had sent him her nurse's graduation picture, signed on the front, "Love to Artie." He signed a photo of himself on the back, "To Emma, Love Artie."

Emma's nursing school yearbook presented the list of typical "superlatives"—members who had been chosen most typical of a certain quality of character. Emma was not most intelligent, most successful, or most beautiful. She was voted "most aloof." She was not looking for society and social life. She was looking for love.

How did Emma and Artie meet? Years later when my brothers or I would ask that inevitable question—how did you meet Pop?—she recited a famous verse from the song "While Strolling in the Park."

While strolling through the park one day
In the merry merry month of May
I was taken by surprise

> By a pair of roguish eyes
> In a moment my poor heart was stole away.
> (Ed Haley, 1884)

We used to sing the lilting lines in our childish voices as if they described a naughty event. By the customs of the Pickering household, marriage into the Kaufman household was worse than naughty.

Emma's father, who had forbid her to go out with any boys, was not alive to protest as he certainly would have. To her older brother Bill, the sailor who had spent World War I on a battleship chasing German boats in the stormy Baltic, the marriage was a shipwreck and surrender. He refused to set foot in any apartment or house where Artie and Emma lived for the rest of his life. Eventually he would come to respect Artie's devotion to his sister and his hard work, but not his origins. Except for Bill, each brother and sister at his or her own pace came to accept and befriend my father, especially when children arrived.

Emma probably never realized that her marriage was the working class parallel of the marriage that had roiled the great Mackay Family on its Harbor Hill Estate on the bluff above the store. Episcopal Ellin Mackay had eloped with her Jewish lover in 1926. The Berlin-Mackay marriage had behind it the same social changes that made Emma and Artie's marriage more likely. Since 1910 class, religious, and ethnic divisions in American had been eroding more rapidly than ever before. The reasons are many but included the redefinition of the American girl who no longer wore long skirts and stockings, but who often became the flapper in bare legs and short slinky dresses. Business required secretaries, and secretaries were almost always women. In business itself many of the richest businessmen in America, especially those on the cutting edge of technology and production methods and those transforming Vaudeville into radio and movies were first and second generation immigrants who remembered poverty. And all successful businesses found they could compete best by hiring the most talented instead of the best connected or socially acceptable. In the literary world the famous Alqonquin Round Table combined writers and wits from America's oldest WASP families with immigrant Jews, not to mention liberated women like Dorothy Parker and the beautiful poet Edna St. Vincent Millay.

In 1922 when "Abie's Irish Rose" opened on the Broadway stage. The story told how a young Jewish man marries a Catholic girl and tries to convince his parents she is Jewish. The play by Ann Nichols, received many bad reviews but went on to a record 2,327 performances before it closed in 1927. The next year a former car mechanic turned

film director, Victor Fleming, showed America his film version. (Fleming would go on to direct "The Wizard of Oz" and "Gone With The Wind.")

Despite the general blurring of social and religious boundaries in America, in 1933 no one in Emma Pickering's family could be relied on to celebrate her marriage or her discovery of love with her—except one, her brother Buster, also a nurse. When she told him of her marriage in February of 1933, Buster wrote a letter to their mother. He was keenly aware of his mother's misfortune--that she had never attended the marriage of any of her children. Each except bachelor Bill had eloped or married secretly. Buster had been briefly married, according to several family members whose story cannot be documented. It's said that he had married a Margaret Sanger but had sent her away when she became pregnant with a baby that he swore was not his. Young Emma said she remembered her mother receiving a picture of the baby, named Robert. Buster would not marry again until 1940 and never had children in that happy marriage. When Annie's daughter Eleanor once brought to her mother's attention a Margaret Pickering living in Washington, DC, her mother told her never to mention that name ever. Buster's letter about Emma's wedding gave his mother the gift of a grand and elegant marriage worthy of the Mackay's who lived on the grand Harbor Hill estate above Roslyn Village and the Pickering home.

Wallace, G. Pickering.
Apartment 52A
225 W. 69th St.
New York City
New York

Saturday, February 18, 1933

Mrs. Emma H. Pickering.
The Original harbor. Hill.
Roslyn, Long Island,
New York

SUBJECT

THE WEDDING OF MISS EMMA H. PICKERING.
TO
MR. ARTHUR KAUFMAN

Dear Madame:-

In compliance with your commission of January 1, 1933, I am here with enclosing my report of the wedding of your daughter, a dame known as Ms. Emma H Pickering, to a young buck known as Mr. Arthur Kaufman. I have written it as it was seen through the eyes of the thousands of watchers.

The chauffeur, smart looking with a mustache, under his long nose and bordering upon his upper lip, clad in military cut, nicely fitting brown uniform removed one arm from the wheel and handled the gear shift of a new, shiny Rolls-Royce town car, with a footman clad as the chauffeur and sitting beside him on the box. The dazzling rays of the car's polished metal made bystanders blink as the car came to a slow halt, like a private ambulance at the entrance to a hospital, at the main portal of the Rt. Reverend Bishop William T. Manning's edifice on Cathedral Hill, the Cathedral of St. John the Divine, atAmsterdam Avenue and 110th St., New York City, New York. I looked at my watch, it was exactly ten fifty-six.

From early morning thousands of people continued to gather around the Cathedral to witness the event of the year; the marriage of Ms. Emma H Pickering, the popular debutante and daughter of Mr. William H Pickering, of the Original Harbor Hill, her luxurious estate on Long Island, to Mr. Arthur Kaufman, the son of Mr. and Mrs. Kaufman, 233 E. 89th St., and Sag Harbor, Long Island, the youngest member to ever hold a seat on the New York Stock Exchange, and one of the most promising financiers of this generation, at eleven a.m. Saturday, February 18, 1933.

This great event had been heralded for months; the crowd, members of society who had not been invited, friends and neighbors and townspeople from the village of Roslyn, whence the bride came, and likewise from the groom's neighborhood, and thousands of plain curious, awaited with anticipation the arrival of the bride.

The approach of the Rolls-Royce, owned by the bride's elder brother, William H Pickering, a bachelor and prosperous real estate operator of Long Island, and accompanying her to the Cathedral, was a signal for the thousands to invade cordon of police, mounted and on foot, firemen and Boy Scouts, who were endeavoring to maintain order, and assure the security of the bride and handsome groom as well as the wedding guests. They made rapid progress toward the display of automobile engineers.

Brass buttons and blue coats, nightsticks and pikes were being ground to threads and splinters at the feet of the curious, who were not going to be done out of the opportunity of seeing a real picture book bride once in their lives.

The bride, wearing a forget me not studded veil, a ladies, silk, tight fitting gown, with no wrinkles showing, on its surfaces, and carrying a bouquet of American Beauty roses, her favorite flower, became the heroine of the day, and her own rescuer. Her beauty stunned the surging, frantically fighting in frenzy, bruised and cut mob, into insensibility. They stood still in their paths of progress.

The groom, a much sought after young man by the eligible members of society, had arrived thirty minutes before, and was admitted to the Cathedral through the side entrance. He was accompanied by his brother and best man, 'Snooks" Kaufman, better known as "The Vacation Artist," by his friends. They, with their parents, Mr. and Mrs. Reginald Kaufman, and sisters Sandy and Celia, were awaiting the bride and her family and entourage within the main entrance.

Her emergence from the car was followed by that of her brother. He quickly donned his topper, proffered her his strong arm and escorted her into the church with his customary military execution of moves, which he learned while serving his country in the Navy during the last war.

Miss Rita Witte, a former Sunday school teacher of the bride, and her many brothers and sisters, too numerous to mention here, struck up the chords of Mendelssohn's Wedding March on the organ. Slowly, the bride and her brother, who gave her away in marriage, led the procession down the endless. aisle to the Chancel.

The ring bearer, six-year-old Anne Claire Buck, a niece of the bride, apparently had not been properly trained in the duties of the position. As she reached the altar, she appropriated the sacred plush cushion to her own use and comfort, as well as steps of the chancel, where she assumed a horizontal position, with a pillow under her head, and entered upon a journey to dreamland. Apparently, the Angels, painted upon the Windows, had affected her thus. To mess up the works completely, she, the ring bearer, swallowed the wedding ring, without removing any of the diamonds, just as her stalwart father reached for it!

(Excuse, lady, but here I could taste the castor oil that her mother, Nancy Buck, would give her immediately she gained possession of a bottle of same. I'm glad I do not have to include that report in this paper.)

Bill Smith, a gentleman farmer of Roslyn, L.I., and a mourner, came to their rescue with a well-worn wedding ring; one that he has carried for the past 10 years, and one that has burned many holes in his trousers.

Good old Bill!

The brown Rolls-Royce, escorted by a cordon of police, was now being shifted from its dangerous position to one at the rear of the edifice, away from souvenir hunters, and the nails of kids shoes, we were told during the ceremony.

Bishop William T Manning, assisted by the right Rev. Patrick McCauley, James Joseph Murphy and Michael O'Leary, performed the ceremony efficiently and with all of the grace and reverence of his office without any interference. Other than the continual rat tat tat of ironworkers' trip hammers, the lack of electric lights, which were discontinued just as the bride and groom knelt before him, due to a short circuit, a little bird told us in the press box.

They dispersed the crowd by sending the choir out to sing to them. Then the bridal party entered cars, and with screeching police sirens spend to the groom's parents' palatial home on E. 89th St., one of the few remaining show places in the city.

Here a luncheon and reception were accorded to the party.

Scores of detectives were on hand to keep out the curious and sorehead uninvited guests of society. But that was not their sole duty. They were there to guard the costly wedding gifts.

Twelve of them, with heavy flat feet to keep them on the floor, and protruding fronts usually found on these men were guarding the five strand necklace with a ten carat diamond pendant. This, we were advised from the card adhered to the same, was from the Hon. Ralph Dirby, owner of the estate and adjoining the Original Harbor Hill, and a lifelong friend of the bride's family. It was whispered around that even Lloyds refrained from taking out insurance on it; its value is too great a risk for them.

The stunning and stately, Miss Helen Riebel, a classmate of the bride at the Flower University, was bride's maid of honor. She, it is said, will soon take to the same altar in equally modest room as did the bride.

Other classmates of the Bride's were in attendance. They all wore large picture hats of peach color, and dresses of the same color with corsages of orchids (in these hard times).

The newlyweds, the happiest lovebirds seen in many a day, and the writer has seen many days, only a few having passed by him, and many lovebirds, so feels justified in making this declaration, were last seen waving goodbye from the deck of the Europa to friends on the pier as she pulled out at midnight, Europe bound. They will spend six months on the continent, then return to occupy an apartment at 265 Park Ave., New York. ------------

Excuse me, lady, I see I have reported the wrong wedding to you. Don't pay any attention to it. I do that once in a while.

Your daughter was married by the dapper Mayor O'Brien in the City Hall chapel on Saturday at 11 AM.

I attended a reception at their home Saturday night. Indeed, Gram, they certainly appear to be happy, if I am any judge of happiness. The Kaufman family have taken them in as one of their own.

Say, tell Nancy not to give Anne Claire that castor oil!

And Bill Smith still has his ring, the one he thought he would at last dispose of. Poor Bill! Hoping that you are all well, I close.

Affectionately,

Bus

Buster's letter was not only an ironic gift to his mother, but it reflects his father's populism. The simple home they grew up in across from the swamps, becomes the "Original Harbor Hill," since it predates the Mackay mansion on top of the bluff by 75 years. Bishop William Manning, didn't preside at the wedding, but he had become identified with calls for religious tolerance. Buster probably knew that on March 27, 1933 Manning would speak beside rabbis and other religious leaders to a massive Madison Square Garden rally to protest Nazi persecution of Jews and call for a boycott of Germany. (The new Roosevelt administration refused to move.) The "Ralph Dirby" he mentions is a thinly disguised Ralph Kirby, one of the owners of Roslyn's Kirby's Corner who sold Billy Pickering his house and land in 1902.

When Emma and Helen Reibel went for that fateful walk in Central Park in May 1932, the Great Depression had America in a tight grip, but no one could imagine how deep the country would sink and how long the misery would last. Besides hope and change had appeared on the political horizon offering an attractive alternative to the failing measures of the engineer president from Iowa, Herbert Hoover. The upbeat, affable, Harvard educated, Franklin Delano Roosevelt who had grown up in a bubble of great wealth and luxury, represented what Americans could be, and he also believed it was his Christian duty to lift up the poor. Although he had been careful in the campaign to say very little about his plans, he convinced Americans he could lift them back onto the path to prosperity. Whether Artie and Emma paid much attention, they were convinced their life together would be happy.

Besides, romance is not an economic condition, and the hormones of young men and women are subject to only the most dire effects of poverty. The young man Emma met, Arthur Kaufman, lived a few blocks east of the Park in Manhattan's "Little Germantown," also known as Yorkville. On that balmy afternoon in May he and several friends had wandered west down 86th Street, "German Boulevard," to take in the action in Central Park. That day's action came along in the forms of two attractive young women in nurse's caps and capes, white shoes and white stockings. What words or what gestures or looks caused Helen Reibel and Emma Pickering to stop and assay the charms of the young men or listen to them no one recorded. Who thinks of posterity when romance strikes? Artie was never clever with words, so the charm may have been turned on by his more articulate friend Freddie Jenzen. Emma remained friends with Freddie throughout life and always remembered him fondly.

Artie may have appealed to Emma because he was easy to get along with and maybe easy to charm. One of his nieces who was old enough to remember him before marriage and throughout the 30s and 40s, told me years later, "Your father had no balls. He was very complacent, compliant, never said anything. Your mother never let her guard down. They truly were not made for each other." If that

Bill Hughes   Freddie Jenzen   Artie Kaufman   Joe Nixon

were true neither Artie nor Emma knew it. Artie's sister Fannie doted on him. Her son says Fannie thought of her brother as "A man's man, the cat's meow." Compared to his softer and non-athletic brother Harold, Artie was more manly.

He and Emma didn't hesitate long over any doubt, though they were an unlikely pair. Artie's two oldest sisters had already married and for several years the remaining older sister had been hoping to marry her steady man. He was next in line. Although Artie was Jewish, his older sister Fannie had been engaged to an Irish Catholic immigrant, and then, on the rebound, had secretly married a Catholic and become a Catholic. Jennie thought this Benny Clemente something of a ruffian and a rogue but she tolerated him. The middle sister Marion had married a non-practicing Jew. Artie's engaged sister, Celi, had a Catholic fiancé. Artie was ready for his turn, and religion would not stand in his way.

Artie Kaufman, like many Jews, came with no middle name. His father hadn't needed one, and he didn't get one either. Artie and his friend Freddie lived a block apart and had gone to school together. At the end of his sophomore year in 1928, Artie dropped out of school and took a job as a runner on Wall Street, carrying documents about stock transfers for Seligsberg & Co. He earned a little more than $1 a day. His younger brother Harold had also begun to work as a runner and called his $12 a week "big money." On weekends and holidays Artie would use his big money to go to Coney Island or stroll around Central Park and its amusements with friends. He had thick black wavy hair, dark brows, and dark eyes and a quiet smile. As an outstanding student in elementary school, he had qualified for Stuyvesant High School, a five story structure devoted to the "manual arts." Although a vocational school, Stuyvesant was already exercising the selectivity that would continue until in the 1930s when it became the city's leading math and science school. In those few months before the stock market crash of October 1929 Artie and many boys like him saw more opportunity in work than in education.

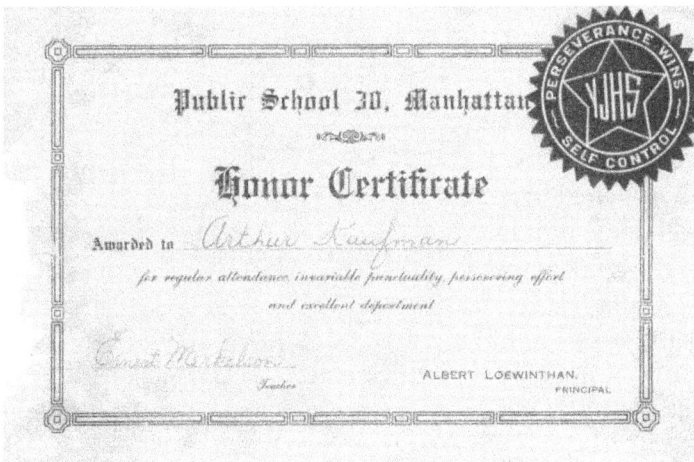

Public School 30, Manhattan

Honor Certificate

Awarded to *Arthur Kaufman*

for regular attendance, invariable punctuality, persevering effort and excellent deportment

Ernest Markelson
Teacher

ALBERT LOEWINTHAN,
PRINCIPAL

Artie had dropped out of Stuyvesant to make a living, but felt he had a future and that this pretty nurse should be part of it. In Artie's Public School 30 his outstanding attendance certificate has a seal that declares: "Perseverance Wins— Self Control." We do not know how long Artie had to persevere, but on July 16, 1932 he and Emma appeared in City Hall before the magistrate who married them. Then came self-control until Emma's graduation. On that event she would be released from dorm life and from the secrecy of their marriage.

Shortly after Emma's graduation Franklin Roosevelt gave his first inaugural address and told Americans how desperate their condition had become. Having campaigned on hope and change and fellowship, he now announced, "This is preeminently the time to speak the truth, the whole truth, frankly and boldly." 1933 was the darkest year of the Depression so far. Roosevelt summed up in the first minute of his speech, "Values have shrunken to fantastic levels; taxes have risen; our ability to pay has fallen; government of all kinds is faced by serious curtailment of income; the means of exchange are frozen in the currents of trade; the withered leaves of industrial enterprise lie on every side; farmers find no markets for their produce; the savings of many years in thousands of families are gone." Nevertheless, with the assurance and naiveté that only a man secure in great inherited wealth could muster, he assured Americans who were losing their homes, cars, education, and even their food, that he shared "our common difficulties" and that, "They concern, thank God, only material things."

Romance, of course, can make people equally as daft and blind as wealth, maybe more so since the first blush of romance seems to be the best kind of wealth, the kind that makes material things irrelevant. Emma and Artie may not have thought about politics very much, but they did believe in Roosevelt, and in each other. They would have agreed with Roosevelt's most famous statement in his inaugural address: "The only thing we have to fear is fear itself—nameless, unreasoning, unjustified terror which paralyzes needed efforts to convert retreat into advance."

As soon as Emma graduated, she went to live with the Kaufman's in their second floor apartment. From the kitchen one could step into the main bedroom. Beyond that was another bedroom, then the parlor. Two of Artie's three older sisters, Fannie and Marion, had moved out with their new husbands, but the apartment was not large and had no privacy for newlyweds. Still at home were Cecelia or "Celi" and Artie's pudgy younger brother Harold. Harold's friend Harry Merrims probably lived there also. When he had been orphaned or abandoned as a small boy, Jennie had taken him in with her own five children and brought him up.

Celi had had the same young Catholic fiancé, Frank Mathis, for several years, but he could not decide on marriage. His future son, Edward, said he thought his father "was not the marrying kind."

Harry Merrims, abt 1930
Taken in and raised by Jennie Kaufman

The apartment was also graced by the loud and sometimes vicious Polly the big, gray-green parrot. She may have been accompanied by a flock of canaries that the Kaufmans had been proud to raise. At floor level two black and white spotted mongrels, Peggy and Whitey, carried on their affairs. Those affairs often led to litters of puppies. If no one was inclined to walk the dogs, the kitchen window opened onto the small flat roof of an adjoining store. While customers came and went below, Peggy and Whitey "went" above. Marion's daughter Elise remembers the apartment as a "do what you want" place.

Artie's father Emmett took the crowd and the noise for granted. He was an easy going, jovial man. He was also a practical joker. One evening his daughter Fannie brought her boyfriend Benny Clemente to the apartment for a card game. Although Benny was a construction laborer, he was a bit squeamish. When he got up to leave and put on his jacket and he pulled out his keys. He also pulled out a dead canary that Emmett had been saving in the refrigerator.

Emmett's tiny wife Jennie shared his sense of humor, his outgoing nature, and his tolerance for noise and disorder. Instead of the German accent of their immigrant origins, the Kaufmans spoke "Noo Yawk" English with its "th" turned into "d" for dis and dat and dose and dem and "ong" and "ing" they pronounced as in LongKiland and and singk me a songk. Emma, of course, had grown up in a crowded household, but beyond that similarity, the Kaufman household was everything the Pickering household was not. Emma and Artie together were very much a part of America becoming more American.

Emma and Artie: An Album

Above: Artie and Emma about 1933;   below: 1933 and 1940s

Artie and Emma Kaufman, 1933

Artie and Emma Kaufman, Emma P, Bess McCue and
Ralph Kinne's Wedding, 1935

Artie and Emma Kaufman

Orange, Connecticut, 1936

Arthur Kaufman,
1932

CHAPTER 19 HOW THE OTHER HALF LIVED: THE KAUFMANS

Billy and Emma Pickering had come to America from the village and small town culture of England, and fit easily into the small town, largely Protestant culture of Long Island's north shore. Artie's parents, Emmett and Jennie Kaufman were the children of Bohemians, but not the kind that affect high culture and avant-garde tastes. The most common meaning of Bohemian, the one referring to nomadic artists and writers often living on invisible means, originated in the early 19th century when the French applied the term for gypsies to wandering artists. Those gypsies often had their origins in the region of the modern Czech Republic then called Bohemia. Their families were probably part of the large Jewish population of Prague. Samuel Kaufman and Theresa Hesky, Artie's grandparents, left Bohemia for America in their early twenties.

That was the early 1870s just after the Hungarians defeated Austria in war and refused to create a tri-partite country: Austria-Hungary-Bohemia. Constitutions and governments came and went like visitors passing through a train station. With their coming and going the legal status of Jews changed too. After centuries of being welcomed in, then kicked out of all the European countries, Jewish antenna were sensitive to both changing moods and the promises of safe havens. The "*Auf nach Amerika*" (On to America) movement in Bohemia grew. Both Theresa Hesky and Samuel Kaufman, still in their early 20s, became part of it. To America they brought with them all the culture of poor Jews who had wandered from city to city in Europe, learning portable trades and how to adapt to the ebb and flow of persecution.

Jennie Lauber

Samuel and Theresa made their first home in Washington, DC. Samuel appears in several city directories as a tailor. They had six children in close succession, four boys and two girls. Their lives left little imprint on America's records, but what survives indicates that the children quickly became more American than Jewish. Only Emmett, born Emmanuel, bore a distinctly Jewish first name. The others were Cecilia, Harold, Edward, Max, and Sarah.

An old family story says that at least some Kaufmans went west in a prairie schooner, but if they did, no record says who they were, when they began their journey, or why. Emmett and his brother Max went north by train. In New York City they met the Lauber sisters, Jennie and Carrie. Their parents were second generation American Jews. Jennie and Carrie's grandfather Isaac and grandmother Karoline had emigrated to America from Switzerland before the Civil War. Max married Carrie. Emmett married the small, birdlike Jennie. Neither the Laubers nor the Kaufmans would have been happy if their children had married a goy (gentile).

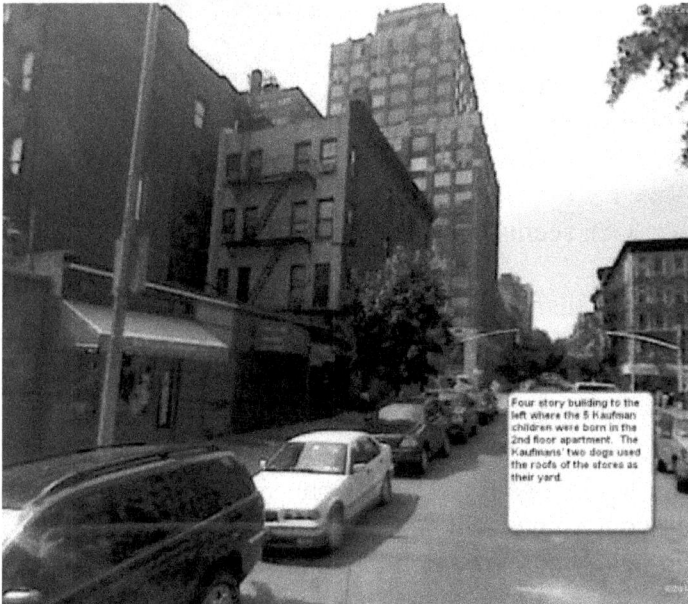

Four story building to the left where the 5 Kaufman children were born in the 2nd floor apartment. The Kaufmans' two dogs used the roofs of the stores as their yard.

Jennie and Emmett settled in a second floor apartment in a five story walk up at 410 E. 82nd St. just two blocks from the East River. The 80s along 1st and 2nd Avenues was a predominantly German but not a very Jewish neighborhood. Emmett and Jennie negotiated a discount in rent for service as janitors. Their apartment was "railroad" style—each floor of the building with a central corridor and an apartment on both sides. The kitchen overlooked the street in front and on one side the tarred roof of a ground level store. The bedrooms and parlor were in back. The kitchen coal stove served for cooking, heating, and firing the bathwater that was poured into big tin tubs. A moveable partition in the kitchen's soapstone sink could also turn that basin into a small tub. A single hall toilet served both families. The water tank hung high on the wall above the toilet bowl, and the yank of a pull chain released a loud rush of water into the bowl and down the drain.

In this apartment aided by the ever ready Dr. Shane, Jennie delivered her five children, one every other year from 1905 to 1913. For many Americans, especially the poor, hospitals were not places for birth but for death. When Jennie felt her time was near, someone would fetch Dr. Shane. As she labored, the good doctor would lie in the bed beside her to rest. "When you're ready tap me on the shoulder," he told her. Any children in the apartment were ordered out to sit on the steps until sister or brother had arrived. The three girls came first—Fannie, Marion, and Cecelia. Shane made only one serious mistake—he forgot to register Harold's birth. This was not a problem until Harold volunteered for the Army and they asked to see his birth certificate.

Fannie turned into a quiet, inward looking girl and an avid reader. From the crowded and often chaotic apartment, a book could take her away as surely as a time machine. When she was an early teenager a fire broke out in the building. Everyone evacuated, except Fannie who had traveled far away in her current book. Firemen and trucks arrived. Firemen rushed up the stairwell, broke down walls and extinguished the fire. Fannie's son Emmett says that when Jennie came back into the building and found Fannie reading, "Grandmother was so upset that the kid didn't get out of the house that she beat the hell out of her." Marion was more outgoing, more romantic. She would set her mind on something—like the man she wanted to marry—and she would not give up. Celi seems to be the most taciturn of the three sisters.

Fannie Kaufman 1932

Outside the apartment where city transportation was evolving from horses and wagons to cars and trucks, the streets were quiet enough for the boys to play stickball, ring-a-leevio, tag and whatever they invented.   After elementary school Artie, then Harold, attended Public School 30, Yorkville Junior High on 88th Street, a school for boys with a heavy emphasis on vocational skills. In Principal Albert Loewinthan's January message to parents, he wrote, "Our slogans are 'Self-Control'; 'Listen and Obey,' and these slogans carried into your homes will help you a great deal in the tremendously difficult task of raising our children properly." In that same school magazine, *The Eaglet*, a student writer said the school's slogan was "A Better School for Better Boys." A two page centerfold spread in the magazine shows half a dozen students mounted as medieval knights carrying banners that say, CLEANLINESS, PUNCUALITY, EFFORT, COURTESY, SELF-CONTROL AND PERSEVERANCE.

"LEAD ON, LEAD YORKVILLE"

At the Kaufman apartment all five children did the nightly homework, and when they finished, they often played cards. A card game might bring together the whole family. When the girls brought their boyfriends home, they often settled in for intense and long evenings of pinochle and talk. They played for money, but no one could afford high stakes.

Fannie, Celi, Marion, Arthur, Harold, and Jennie Kaufman, about 1914

As Artie and Harold grew older, for a nickel they rode 20 blocks uptown to the Hecksher House. The trolley everyone called the "banana line" because the cars came in bunches any time they were held up by a problem on the line. At the Hecksher House for $2.50 a month they could swim once a week. They took swimming lessons, but neither of them learned more than a clumsy crawl. If they attended a synagogue, no one remembers. At 13 both Harold and Artie had a *bah mitzvah*, but that initiation left no trace in their behavior except a gold watch kept by Harold. They were much more interested in the world beyond their religion and Yorkville. At the public library they checked out armloads of books. Among Artie's favorites were Zane Grey's westerns. Grey, an Ohio dentist and baseball player, built his often violent and sometimes racy novels on the people and places he knew from his western travels. Artie, like many Americans in the East, loved the bullets, blood and romance of the best seller, *Riders of the Purple Sage*.

272

Arthur Kaufman: Above from about 1925 and 1927. Below with niece Elise Ullman (left) and friend Freddie Jenzen (right)

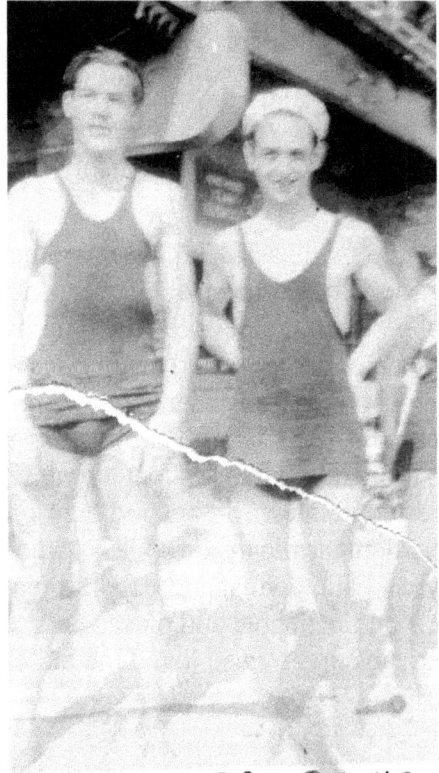

Artie's father Emmanuel, known to family and friends as Emmettt worked for a shrewd investor Solomon Waldheim who specialized in serving the poor and those facing financial hardship. He had invested in cheap real estate--apartment buildings in Harlem, and he owned a pawn shop. Emmett wore cheap three piece suits, chewed his cigars, smoked his pipe, and collected weekly rents in Harlem for Waldheim. Literature is full of mean, demanding rent collectors, but Emmett's success was his genial personality. He had accepted his place as one of the human cogs in the machinery of the big city, and he understood people who had to accept their own burdens. The little man with the kind eyes shared life's jokes with them, sympathized with their troubles, and wished them well. As much as a man could, he considered everyone his brothers and sisters in life's struggle.

Emmett also worked in the boss's pawn shop. In that little side of his life that was left for personal time, he sold musical instruments, cameras and razor blades. He sold them but he didn't buy them. Artie's brother Harold explained: "He [father] was a kleptomaniac. We had cameras galore. He'd make up a bundle and put it out the backdoor of the pawn shop, and a lady from upstairs would come pick it up. I was the schlepping boy." Harold remembers, "We had banjos and violins all over the place. Nobody could play them."

Sister Marion had also helped her father steal. Her daughter Elise believed her mother may have "been in love with one of the Waldheims." Solomon Waldheim (possibly the boss's son), "was crazy about my sister Marion," Harold remembered. Solomon in his wisdom would look the other way while Marion examined the wares. "Marion would put her finger in the ring tree and would come out with rings you wouldn't believe."

The razor blades Emmett sold came from a woman friend who would steal the razor blades by the thousands from a factory she worked in. Harold said, "She had a sack in her dress that she'd put them in. One for the company, one for me. Everybody would sit at home at nights, even my sisters' boyfriends, and we would wrap them up in packages of ten and sell them." Nevertheless, money was always tight. Harold says, "My parents didn't know how to save." But they had things—stolen things. His mother would often go to the butcher's and say, "Put the meat on our bill." The butcher might ask, "Jennie, do you have a camera we could have?"

Emmett Kaufman's brothers Max and Harry had both settled in the city. Max worked in the import-export business. Harold says, "He stole everything too. We were all kleptomaniacs." (Like my father, in middle age Harold went to work for Grumman aircraft and stayed on. His last week there before retirement, March 8, 1983, he called me in North Carolina and announced he would leave Grumman in a week. "Listen, I am going to retire next month. Do you need any rivets or tape, metal screws . . . Give me a call back and let me know. I'll see what I can get." Family tradition lived on.)

Harry Kaufman (later Merchant)

"Harry was crazy," Harold said. But he was wily enough to change his name to Harry Charles Merchant. (Kaufman, 'man who buys,' translates to salesman or merchant.) Charles Merchant disguised Harry's Jewish identity and allowed him to bid more successfully for work in a world controlled largely by WASPS (white, Anglo-Saxon Protestants). Harry Charles Merchant then found work on merchant ships. He was also the first Kaufman to marry a gentile. He married Mary Ann Campbell whose Scottish Presbyterian ancestors had emigrated to America in the early 1700s and whose grandfather had fought in the Revolution. Harry, however, had a lot of Kaufman in him. "He was always in the brig—theft," Harold said.

Harry told his nephews Harold and Artie, "You should add another F or N to your name and it could be German." (Kaufman with one f and one n is almost exclusively Jewish, at least in origin.) Neither Harold nor Artie changed their names, but Harold, like his three sisters, would marry a Catholic, and Artie would choose an Anglican.

By the mid 30s Emmett Kaufman's diabetes had become uncontrollable so that at times while making his rounds, he fell down and lost consciousness. He might be carrying hundreds of dollars, but he was never robbed. His granddaughter Elise Hiller says that when he would collapse in the street, the people of those tough neighborhoods, instead of robbing him, would pick him up, tend to him, and hail a cab to get him home. She remembers him very warmly. "He was very sweet gentle man."

Elise visited the apartment often when she was a girl in the 1930s. She says, "His love was fishing and listening to baseball." When he wasn't working he often sat at a small table by a window and listened to the ball games. On Saturday or Sunday if the weather

was good, he would take his box of fishing gear, walk three blocks east to Carl Shurz Park and sit for hours by the East River trying to catch whatever swam in the dark waters that carried all the wastes that ran off city streets and out of illicit discharge pipes.

For this man who paid little attention to matters of religion, one of his few moments of anger came when his daughter Fannie named her first born son Emmett after him. He protested that Jews do not name children after living relatives. (This was a strong tradition among the Ashkenazi Jews of Europe and Eastern Europe but not among the Shepardic Jews of the Mediterranean basin.) For Jews of European origin, naming a child after a living person could mean cursing th[Emmett and Jennie]t was already suffering serious diabetes and near his death.

Emmett Kaufman defied the general rule that second generation immigrants do better than their parents. He had been born in Washington, DC to immigrant parents from Prague, but while he struggled to support his five children, Jennie's widowed sister Bella enjoyed an apartment on Lexington and 95th. There Harold remembers they ascended to their apartment in a hand pulled elevator, and in the apartment Bella's son Bernard had "toys as big as real animals but on wheels—and no one was allowed to touch them."

As the Depression took hold and Emmett's health declined, Harold and his friend Lou Galade decided they would object to the company now paying them three weeks' wages for a month's work. They sent the boss a letter threatening to sue. The boss called the lawyer and said, if they went ahead with the law suit, Arthur would be fired. They dropped it. As times got worse the runners had to put up with "Scotch weeks"—one week for pay, one week without.

For Emma and Artie, life in the crowded and noisy Kaufman apartment was cheap, but it was no nest of love. Emmett was easy going, kindly, and jovial, but only he showed any great affection for Emma. Emma enjoyed the good humor of her father-in-law but she was not remembered as someone who fit in comfortably. The nurse voted most aloof in her graduating class, also remained aloof from most of her new family. Jennie was probably not unhappy that Emma and Artie had begun a desperate search for any place where they could afford to start what they considered real marriage. With both working, they had a chance. They didn't start on the ground floor, but in the cellar--a two room basement apartment on 33rd Street. With the speed of Cupid's arrow they moved in with a few kitchen utensils and no furniture. Friends and family gave them a studio couch, blankets, sheets and other necessities. The next piece of furniture was a cheap bedroom set that they bought on time. "When we could afford to pay it off," Emma said, "I had Dad take the money out of the bank. On his way home from work on the subway, someone picked his pocket of $86. He cried!"

Their life was not all work and tears. Like so many New Yorkers they spent New Year's Eve 1934 at Times Square with Emma's Roslyn friend Bess McCue and her boyfriend Ralph Kinne. After midnight they went to Astoria with Emma's sister Dot was working in a bar. The goal was to loosen up Ralph enough that he would propose to Bess. At 6 in the morning, back at Emma and Artie's apartment Ralph had not yet proposed.

Jennie may have become increasingly preoccupied with Emmett's failing health and her own increasing troubles with asthma and emphysema. She had always been entirely dependent on Emmett's income. She saw his end coming but no end to the Great Depression. Of her children, only Marion had any prospects of extra income, and that was from her husband's business. Marion, on the rebound from the failure of her romance with Solomon Waldheim, had become secretary to Louis Ullman, a self-taught tradesman, inventor and entrepreneur. Lou's father, Elias, had been a maker of fine shoes who claimed to have made shoes for Buffalo Bill Cody. He was a man of grand schemes that failed, and he was married to a woman who could not speak English. They had arrived from Riga, Latvia with their menorah, several feather filled quilts, and a samovar.

Nevertheless, the shoemaker's wife insisted her boys go to the trade school for immigrants founded by Baron DeHirsch. While their father, pursuing another dream, went to South Africa, the boys all became successful tradesmen and businessmen.

As a young man in the early 1900s Lou had built a car from a kit. He and his brother Israel became two of the first electricians licensed in NY. Louis told his brother that if he used his real name, Israel, "They'll kill us." They were in an Irish neighborhood of Manhattan. Lou began to call his brother Joe and it stuck for life.

Louis' family was Jewish, and he had stayed obedient to the tradition that the older son does not marry until his older sisters have husbands. He had saved money to go to South Africa to join his boot-maker father, but when a man finally agreed to marry his last single sister, a homely woman, the man insisted on some kind of dowry. Lou's savings went into that dowry and became the funds for his new brother-in-law to open a large hardware store on Broadway in Yonkers.

Lou had to make do with a small shop, one big long room on a side street, 10 Lawrence St. There he made keys, fixed and sharpened lawn mowers, tinkered with new inventions, and filed successfully for several patents on devices like a new kind of grease gun and springs for baby carriages. Elise says that he sold his patents because he had no money to develop them. He turned down a lucrative offer to bring his talents to Yale Locks and he formed his own company. For a while he had at least three small factories producing his inventions. He was working on the viscosity of oil when he died.

When Marion came to work for him he was 41 and tired of waiting for his sisters to marry. Elise says, "My mother was looking for somebody older. She was on the rebound. My father was older and had money and he was a good catch. . . . When my mother wanted something she went after it." Marion's success and Celi's frustration with her own fiancé's indecision and her life's suspension caused a small explosion in the Kaufman apartment. When Marion announced her engagement in 1928 and opened the box containing her new ring, Celi seized it and threw it across the room. It did not help that her fiancé was an employee of Lou's.

Lou and Marion married in June and their married life ran into trouble soon afterward. She immediately became pregnant. Old Dr. Shane who had delivered her mother at the Kaufman home in Yorkville told her that because she had RH positive blood and Lou had RH negative Marion needed the very best obstetrician, and he was there at Columbia Presbyterian, the man who had written "the Bible of obstetrics." Marion thought he was too old and cold, so he assigned her his understudy, a younger but equally talented obstetrician, Dr. William Studdiford. She gave birth without trouble to her daughter Elise on March 16. The special care cost Lou $1,000. (The equivalent of almost $50,000 in wages for a skilled worker in 2011.) Despite Lou's success as an inventor and owning several workshops, his daughter says he had a bad head for business, and money was always scarce. Both Lou and Marion were stunned by the hospital costs. However, when she became pregnant again and miscarried twins, the same doctor sent them a bill for $5.

The year after Elise's birth Lou's legs suddenly became paralyzed. Doctors at Columbia Presbyterian Hospital found that the cause was pressure on the sciatic nerve. After treatment Lou was back on his feet, but never entirely well. When he lost his last production shop he and Marion had $5,000, and he took her to look at houses in White Plains and Yonkers. Marion thought rural White Plains "was like the North Pole." They chose southern Yonkers near his shop. That shop was as close as Lou would come to Paradise, and in some ways it was not far from it. Elise says, "He knew where everything was but it looked like a jungle to anyone working in. Largest key board [key blanks and models] for miles and miles around. He loved every dirty rag and piece of machinery. Maestro Toscanini's Italian helpers would bring in lawnmowers from the famous conductor's big Riverdale estate. The Ullmans called them "the Luigis." The Luigis would plead for Lou to "make them quiet so the maestro won't be disturbed." Lou sharpened and adjusted the rollers, wheels and blades so finely that they mowed in near total silence.

The Great Depression ground on year after year defying predictions from the White House that this or that new program or policy was going to ease the suffering and that the nation was about to rise again. It was a hard time to be young and starting out. It was a sad time to be old and needy.

Louis Ullman and bros. Car made from kit

CHAPTER 20. DEATH AND BIRTH

Emma Pickering, mother of ten children and a widow, turned 67 in 1939 when her daughter entered nursing school, and that same year she went to the doctor with chronic stomach problems. The diagnosis—stomach cancer. She consulted with her two nurses—Buster and Emma, and they decided the recommended operation was too dangerous. Emma had already lived beyond the life expectancy of 63 years for women, and she was growing weaker all the time. They might also have decided the diagnosis could have been wrong. They were almost certainly right. Nevertheless, her complaints continued. Two years later as Artie and Emma were settling into their underground apartment. She wrote in her day book for July 5, "My Last visit for x Rays at Hempstead/33".

She had lived through almost 40 years of strife between her own children and their father, and she had seen all but Bill run away from home. She had watched helplessly as her husband turned a modestly profitable business into an unprofitable collection of books, artifacts, and antiques.

As soon as each of her children had married, she had begun to see the trouble in their own families. Dorothy had married Leonard Clarkson in 1921. The following year they had a baby named Gloria whose life lasted only eight months. Dorothy was soon divorced and by 1926 remarried to George Nolan, another Catholic, with whom she had a chestnut haired daughter named Jean. Dorothy and George were soon divorced. Emma's 8th child, the dapper, curly-haired Arthur, showed signs of becoming a heavy drinker.

Then in the summer of 1934 the troubles led to the first death. On Friday June 15 Ted's twelve-year old son Bruce came home from school as usual. When he climbed the stairs to the attic looking for something, the first thing he saw was his father, hanging from a rope. For the rest of his life that scene haunted his dreams.

Emma had been confined to the house feeling ill that week. She wrote in her day book, "Ted Passed out 19/34. Aged 41 yrs. 27 of this month" (meaning she thought of his birthday

coming on the 27th. Why she wrote '19/34 instead of 15/34 is unexplained'). She remained too sick to attend the funeral, but she gave her daughter Emma a birthday card for Ted and said, "Put this in his coffin." Had she already written it, or did she write it after his death? What she wrote, no one knew.

Throughout her life she had made constant use of her little prayer book by Charlotte Murray, *For The Master's Sake*. In the birthday card she might have written one of two verses marked in that book as a favorite.

TWENTY FIFTH
DAY.

(hrist is all, and in all. *Col. III.11.*

For the weariest day
May Christ be thy stay!
For the darkest night
May Christ be thy light!
For the weakest hour
May Christ be Thy power
For each moment's fall
May Christ be thy all.

On Monday, June 18 Ted was buried with his birthday card and his mother's last good-bye inside. Ted and Bill were both members of the American Legion, though Bill was far more active and becoming a leader. Bill made sure that Ted received full military honors at his funeral. *The Roslyn News* for the next week recorded the funeral, the blunt facts, and a mini-family history.

Legion Gives Military Funeral for E.H. Pickering

Edward H. Pickering, 41 years old, lifelong resident of Roslyn and a carpenter and builder, was found dead early on Friday morning hanging from a rafter in the attic of his home on Mott Street, Roslyn Village. His son, Bruce, discovered the body.

Dr. Aaron Borton of Main Street, Roslyn, was called and pronounced him dead by strangulation. The police said that despondency had caused his suicide.

Mr. Pickering was born on what now is the Childs Frick Estate, the son of Mr. and Mrs. William Pickering. He received his education in the Roslyn Schools and in April, 1918, enlisted in the 89th Division, 314th Ammunition Train, at Mineola. After action in many battles he returned to this country and was discharged from the army on June 3, 1919, at Camp Upton, Yaphank, L.I.

Funeral services were conducted by the Rev. Harry Lee Rice, rector of Trinity Church, at 2 p.m. on Sunday, with burial at the Roslyn Cemetery. He had a full military funeral with color bearers, firing squad and American Legion funeral services at the grave.

Mr. Pickering is survived by his wife, the former Miss Hazel Tilley of Roslyn; five sons, Edward, Bruce, Frederick, Earl and Robert; his mother, Mrs. Emma Pickering; five brothers, William, Thomas, John, Wallace and Arthur; three sisters, Mrs. Anne Buck, Mrs. Emma Kaufman and Mrs. Dorothy Nolan.

Funeral arrangements were in charge of Henry J. Hutchings of Roslyn.

Mr. Pickering was a member of one of Roslyn's oldest families. His father, for many years active in all civic enterprises in Roslyn, conducted the old antique and stationery shop on East Broadway that was the stopping place for several generations of school children.

This historic structure recently has been razed to make way for a new building.

Mr. Pickering was well known and popular in Roslyn and his passing is lamented by virtually everyone who knew him. Scores of his friends mourn his death.
from Microfilm, Bryant Library, June 23, 2000

The Pickerings were hardly "one of Roslyn's oldest families" after 34 years, but the description testifies to either the youth of the writer or how deeply the Pickerings had woven themselves into the community.

Suicide always raises the question, Why? The answer that became the accepted story reached back to Ted's time in the infantry in World War I. His sister Annie and young Emma both passed on the bare details—he had fallen in the German mustard gas attacks that had become more frequent toward the end of the war. Someone even noted the date Ted was supposed to have been gassed—the St. Mihiel offensive on Sept. 28, 1918. Mustard gas was one of several gases used by both sides. It was not the most deadly gas, but it was the most troublesome since the oily gas could stick to skin and clothing and strip the mucous membranes in the throat and lungs causing severe pain. Where it touched the skin, large mustard colored blisters formed.

Ted's own notes and letters make no mention of being gassed. The official records in the 89th Division histories and the lists of wounded do not provide any evidence that Ted was gassed. His one mention of being wounded was his letter to a Roslyn friend in late October 1918 where he describes a harrowing ride through No Man's Land between the lines and being "unable to move" because of a "bad leg." Many years later his sister Emma's notes about her brothers say, "Ted's depression was from being shell-shocked in WWI. After discharge, he worked on WPA relief program. He worked on a rock pile and that upset him (noise of war?)" Other reports from family members recall someone saying that he had become depressed when he learned that his children might go blind. This story must have had a specific origin, but the seed of the story long ago disappeared, and none of his children lost their sight. More likely the struggle to feed five young boys weighed on him.

In the 1930s suicide often fell on a family like the shame of a moral lapse. No one understood or even imagined the genetic influences or the chemistry and physiology of depression. When family members blamed the war, maybe they were picking a convenient reason beyond the family itself. It could also be the accurate naming of a contributing factor. In Ted's case, 16 years after the war, putting the entire blame on distant experiences, if in fact they occurred at all, only delayed and discouraged thinking about other influences.

As the 1930s and the Great Depression wore on, Emma's children had been bringing more and more grandchildren to visit. To those grandchildren she recited the English nursery rhymes of her own childhood as they sat at her feet or on her lap. Through her flowed centuries-old Mother Goose and Little Tommy Thumb verses that she had learned as a girl living with her great aunt at the mill in Hornchurch east of London. Her own children told their children stories of growing up in Roslyn Village, of home life, and work in the store. The old life, however, and the places that it had been lived were rapidly coming to an end. Emma certainly saw her own life coming to an end also as she grew frail and lost most of her teeth. She still did her own cleaning and sometimes scrubbing her clothes by hand on a washboard as she always had since she was a small girl. She did agree to have Dyckman laundry pick up the sheets and towels.

Early in 1934 Emma's son Bill, now the only bachelor still living nearby, decided he should build a modern house for his mother's last years. During the months before Ted's death she had watched as Bill tore down the old store where she and the children had labored for so many years and where she had spent so many of her daytime hours.

With the store gone, Bill ordered fill dirt to bury the foundations and build the lot up level with the front porch of the old house. Where the front of the old store once stood he raised a 6 foot high stone retaining wall. To place and spread the dirt he hired a man with a shallow steel pan called a mule scoop and a big white work horse to pull it. The horse sometimes had to do double duty giving rides to his nieces Eleanor and Anne Claire.

Work stopped only briefly for Ted's death. As the house continued to rise during the summer of '34, Emma noted on July 7, "33 years in the old House." On November 10 she wrote, "moved into new house." She might as well have written, 33 years in the old life, moved into a new life. Implicit in her two notes is the recognition that her time of taking care of her family had ended. She was now the one being cared for. She contentedly fit into that life shared by all grandparents—waiting for the end while watching new beginnings.

Bill, a carpenter before and during his Navy service, built much of the new house himself. Above ground it fit the standard for the day with three bedrooms and a bathroom upstairs, a comfortable living room and fireplace, modern kitchen and dining room downstairs. His part of the house was below. Between the old and new homes Bill built a garage that connected to the basement of the new house through a short tunnel. Off the tunnel he made a small den for with a stained glass door. Inside on the wall he hung "Esquire Girls," the shapely but well covered forerunners of *Playboy* centerfolds. On shelves and between the pictures he displayed his souvenirs, keepsakes, and banners. This was the part of the house that was all Bill. Like his personal secrets, it was underground.

I remember only two things about that house from my own visits. One was that underground tunnel and Uncle Bill's den which we saw only in glimpses as we passed down the tunnel from my aunt's car to the stairs that led up to the kitchen. Second, I remember a clock with a loud tick tock. Tick . . . . . . tock . . . . tick . . . . . tock it said loudly as my brothers and I sat on the floor enduring what seemed to be endless adult conversation that seemed to be about nothing. Sometimes the clock said "Too bad, too bad, too bad . . ."

In the 1930s Emma and Artie confronted the burdens of the Great Depression by working as much as they could, saving here and there and being sure not to have children. Hospitals paid nurses not much more than janitors. Their work, in fact, was largely cleaning up – rooms, beds, patients themselves, then the bedpans and dishes the patients used. But Emma found the work was steady. Artie continued to collect and deliver documents in the financial district. In 1937 they moved to an upstairs apartment in a row of simple brick buildings on Link Court in the part of the Burrough of Queens called Maspeth. They paid $25 a month rent and had a few dollars left for food. Between pay days they often had less than a dollar in cash. A month after they had moved in Artie came home from work and told Emma his pay had been cut by five dollars a month. Emma recalled a day when the old couple who lived downstairs with their disabled son knocked on her door and asked if she could spare any money at all. They were starving. She invited them in and emptied her purse in her hand—nothing but coins. She counted out the twenty-six Indian head pennies and gave them to the old lady.

Artie had been promoted from runner to clerk at Seligsberg's, and in the summer of 1937 he was making $19 a week when Emma told him she was sure she was pregnant. On February 23, 1938 at 2 a.m. Emma woke up and told Artie her water had broken and she was in labor. They had expected a March birth and had not yet prepared anything. They had no phone in the house. Artie dressed quickly and went out to find the nearest working telephone. He called the little jovial Italian Doc Fierro whom my mother revered. At 7 a.m. Fierro drove up outside their apartment in his old car and took them to the hospital. Emma tells the rest of the story:

> Thus followed 14 hours of terrific pain, nausea, and misery. About every two hours some nurse or doctor would poke, probe, and examine, and consult, and question. They let me labor until my heart was going bad then had to act. They hoped the child would turn. Also by that time I guess they suspected twins. Arthur was a breech presentation. The doctor had to reach up to his elbows to bring Bill down. These premature infants (8 months) were placed in incubators. It was touch and go for Bill for several weeks.

When the doctor came out of the delivery room and told Artie he had twins, Artie shot back, "You're a damned liar." They could not afford twins.

Emma's mother noted in her birthday book:
"Emma's twins born"

Having two children, Emma and Artie could honor both sides of the family with names. The first twin out they named Arthur Emmett, the second William John. What Artie's father and mother thought about having yet another grandchild named for a living relative we don't know. By the tradition of east European Jews the naming of a child for a living relative could be a fatal act, but by this time Emmett was probably confined to the apartment. With his own near death certain, maybe he did not object to a new grandchild with his name.

After the birth Emma spent several days in the hospital recovering. She described the aftermath of the twins' delivery:

> Mom, well, she could not void for five days and had to be catheterized all that time. And the misery of 14 stitches! (in a tender spot) Those days they kept mothers in bed. I didn't even set eyes on Bill until 14 days later when they let me out of bed. Then about all I could see was ears. He was still in the incubator. He remained in the hospital for a month. I did have the pleasure of attempting breast feeding with Arthur, not very successfully. But at least I had the pleasure of holding my firstborn.

One of her first baby presents was a wide carriage from her mother.

Before the twins were born, the old couple in the downstairs apartment had moved out, and Artie's sister Fannie and her husband Benny had taken the vacant apartment. Benny was one of the lucky unemployed who had found work with the new government organization, the Works Project Administration. His job was to distribute food to the poor, and he counted Artie and Emma and the twins among the poor, supplying them with butter and eggs. Cribs and high chairs they bought from the Salvation Army. Emma's sisters Annie and Dot who had had their own children also pitched in.

When the great hurricane of 1938 swept across Long Island on September 21, Artie and Emma were in no danger on its western edge, but it scared Emma's mother and her neighbors in Roslyn where 14 to 16 foot high tides swept into Hempstead Harbor and 100 mile an hour winds blew down trees, blacked out the village, and tore off roofs. In the neighboring village of Sea Cliff it also put the coup de grace to the once popular boardwalk. That completed the once trendy summer tourist town's descent into a forgotten square mile of decaying and very affordable Victorian houses and cheap summer cottages where Artie and Emma would buy their first home nine years later. Shortly before or after the storm, Emma told Artie she was pregnant again and due in April. Maybe because she had been unable to breast feed the twins, she had conceived when she didn't expect to be ready.

After the village had cleaned up from the storm, the older Emma was delighted by fall weather that brought out the flowers she noted in her "birthday book."

Nov. 13. Had Salvias blooming 1938. Away into this month.
Nov. 24. Had Chry blooming till the snow storm came to night

That Christmas Annie drove her mother into Queens to visit Emma, Artie and the twins and deliver a few gifts. Her mother noted, "Dec. 25. Beautiful Day no snow/38 Visit to the twins." By that time the younger Emma had become a noticeably pregnant woman pushing a wide carriage with infant twins. Neighbors and strangers offered sympathy.

Her third child, 71 years after his birth, is now writing this sentence. Since the incident of his birth brings the writer himself into this story's events, I'll change to the "I" of the first person.

Emma was ready when her time and my time came in April. She refused anesthetic or anything for the pain until the last moments. Twenty-seven years later when I told her I was expecting the birth of my own child, she would write a description of my birth.

If your rush to enter this world was any indication, I might have known what a determined person you would be. Your birth was almost a natural childbirth. That is, until the very end, I had no medication. It was a wonderful experience to feel you rebelling against the walls of my uterus causing strong and painful contractions. A three hour labor. You were born about 10:25 a.m. on a Monday.

Did you ever try to force a baseball through the eye of a needle? Anyway that is some idea of natural childbirth. I would recommend it for any healthy woman as it is an experience never to be forgotten. Also it has a meaning I cannot express,

The baseball metaphor was gentle compared to the watermelon comparison used by a friend's mother. My mother's delivery doctor did not know she was conscious. She heard him say, "Another boy, and she wanted a girl. I wonder what she'll do now."

She croaked "I guess I'm going to have a baseball team."

The evidence that she had wanted and even expected a girl exists in the silk padded "Baby Book" album like the ones she had bought for Art and Bill. Theirs were blue, the new one pink.

April was an important month for my grandmother. On the 6th her son Buster married a young nurse from New Hampshire, leaving only her son Bill unmarried. Bill, of course, was also living in the new house with her and providing what she needed.

On the 10th my grandmother wrote in her birthday book: "Emma's 3rd boy, born 10:30 am April 10th/39, Wallace Vickers Pickering." The next day's entry was "fell down outside and hurt my Ribs."

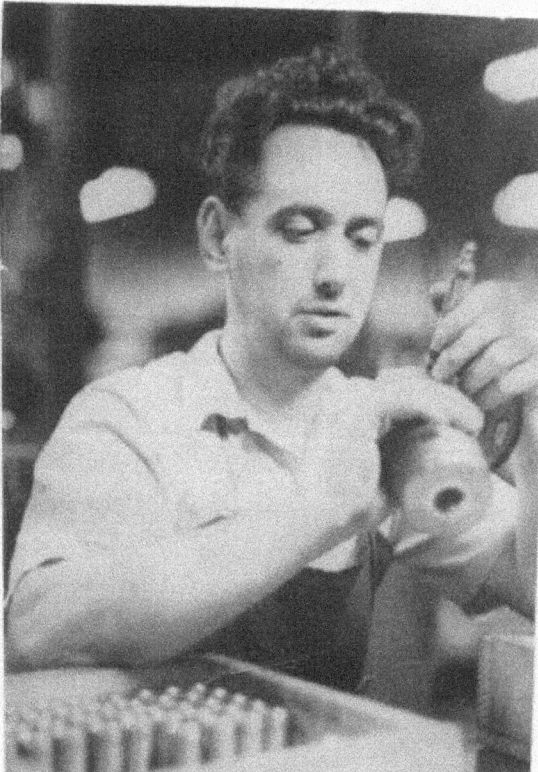

A week after my birth Seligsburg cut my father's salary by $5 to $14 a week. Annie often brought her mother to visit, and their charity may be my first durable memory. I can still see my mother, my aunt and my grandmother seated at the kitchen table in our apartment. I watch from my crib as they place a jar of jam and other gifts on the table under the yellow light of a single hanging bulb.

From aunts and uncles with older children we received hand-me-down clothes. We were also lived partly on the thieves' culture that had been nourished in the Kaufman family. My uncle Harold asked a friend in the garment district to bring him heavy wool fabric. From this my mother sewed winter coats. She also sewed diapers, nightgowns, and shorts, and she gave us our first dolls—long socks stuffed with rags and buttons sewn on for eyes and noses. (I note that today you can buy a sock doll kit complete with buttons, produced and packaged in China. No one's father or brother has worn the sock.)

With three children to feed and the embarrassment of living on the charity of their families, Artie and Emma decided he should attend Delahanty Institute and learn to be a machinist. When he was home, Emma would work part time as a nurse. When they both had to be away, my uncles, aunts and cousins would baby-sit. Meanwhile they moved from Link Court to another, possibly cheaper, apartment at 33rd St. in Astoria.

Artie's niece Elise remembers coming to visit Artie and Emma and their three boys one Christmas around 1940. "I remember going there for Christmas and we came with food and presents, and I can only remember this face of utter exhaustion. They couldn't even smile. My mother brought your father a pair of pajamas. I remember him with these frayed collars.

Artie and Emma's plan, however, paid off in 1940 when Artie became an inspector at Delcraft Manufacturing on 118th Street in Manhattan. He may have chosen a career as a machinist because of some training in his two years at Stuyvesant High. He loved the work. Its precise and definite measuring and the production of useful and technically perfect objects gave him a pride that delivering and tallying stocks never had. With three children and a little more money we moved again, but only to 41st Street in Astoria.

Emma took her infants regularly to the Maspeth Health Station for routine exams, and as soon as possible she had them vaccinated against small pox. Small pox was then largely conquered, but faces ravaged by the pustules were still common among adults. As a nurse, Emma made sure her boys were clean, well fed, and warm and that they slept well. She could not protect them, however, from the most common killer of infants. In mid January 1940 Billy, a healthy toddler approaching his second birthday, developed a cold, then began to cough and have trouble breathing. Sometimes he could not take a breath until he stopped coughing violently. Even before his struggles to take a breath developed the ominous whooping sound, Emma knew he had whooping cough. Soon a thick gluey mucus would clog his windpipe and prevent him from eating. As soon as she recognized the symptoms, she knew her other boys would almost certain catch it. The disease had a 90% infection rate among children exposed to siblings. Arthur also started whooping, vomiting and stopped eating. Billy had not been a strong baby when he was born, so she rushed him to the Kingston Avenue Hospital on January 24. The next day she took Arthur. Four days later she took me. One in twenty-five children died from the disease or the pneumonia that often followed as the bacteria moved from the throat to the lungs. Emma and Artie began an anxious vigil.

Art and I responded to treatment and returned home within a week, but no one was sure Billy would survive. He fought on and in mid February began to eat better and gain strength. On February 25th, two days after his second birthday, Emma and Artie brought him home, but continued to nurse him through a severe bout of asthma. All three boys would continue coughing for more than a month, the typical course of a disease sometimes called "the 100 Day Cough."

Billy never regained his full strength, and in November he developed a high pitched cough and began to struggle to breathe. Emma moved Art into a bed with me, a pairing that would continue into our teens. She brought a vaporizer into Billy's room to create a warm mist that helped him breathe easier and sleep better, but his condition grew worse. The diagnosis was "obstructive laryngitis." A bacterial infection was quickly causing the tissues of his larynx to swell and cut off the air passing from his nose and mouth through his trachea to his lungs. In December doctors at Wykoff Heights Hospital cut into his trachea just below the jaw bone and inserted a tube through which he could breathe.

For Emma and Artie the troubles they had had during the Depression and after the birth of the twins had not seemed unusual for any young couple of their rank in life. Now, faced with medical bills they could not pay, they faced what Emma called "the first serious crisis of our married life." Her family and its standing in Roslyn Village saved them. Her brother Jack gave her money and the war bonds he had bought with his savings. Volunteer firemen from Roslyn came to the hospital to donate blood for Billy. Although Emma and Artie lived in a borough of New York City, it could now be said that the life-giving blood of Roslyn flowed in the blood of their son named for her father, a man who had dedicated much of his life to the village.

The hospitalization for whooping cough my mother recorded in spare detail along with the other abbreviated essentials in the pink padded "Baby's Book" that I still have, the reminder that I was supposed to be a girl. Under Health record, along with my small pox and diphtheria inoculations, she records that she breast fed me supplemented by "Grade A milk 11 oz water 10 oz DM 2 T" and that she began to give me orange juice at two weeks.

On the page labeled "Development of Character" she records the following:
Is Baby Sensitive? "Slightly."
Responds to praise "very early."
"   Punishment "Dec. '39" (I was 8 months old. What had I done?)
Other Notes: "pleasing personality – cunning."

Some of her comments are addressed directly to me: "5 mths of age. Very active – trying to sit up, roll from place to place and crawl. (You are an extraordinary baby)" At other times she writes in my voice, "6 mths: Sit up by myself" and "12 mths old – 7 teeth climbing on tables and chairs. Do most everything my brothers do."

The gifts for my birth and first birthday testify that no one made any pretense about the family's situation. In fact, my mother records only three gifts for my birth. My grandmother and my Uncle Jack, who already had a family of his own to provide for gave "cash," and a Mrs. Taulman gave a blanket. That first Christmas we had Christmas Eve dinner in Roslyn with my grandmother. On Christmas day a big gathering for dinner in the apartment. My aunt Marion brought her mother and her 10 year old daughter Elise. My Aunt Dot brought her 12 year old daughter Jean, a graceful, chestnut haired beauty. The gift list was simple: "cash, soft doll, rubber cat, bathrobe, 2 suits, socks." For my first birthday the list is "cake, cash gifts."

Jean Nolan

As soon as I was a year old my mother went back to nursing at nearby Doctor's Hospital in Astoria, Queens. My Aunt Dot who had once been a baby nurse took care of us when both my mother and father worked. Her own daughter had already achieved a measure of self-sufficiency at age 14. At that time sociologists had probably not minted the phrase *extended family*, but we were the happy beneficiaries not only of Aunt Dot's care, but of the attention and minding of several aunts, uncles, and cousins—all with their own troubles and sorrows which never distorted the warm and generous attention they lavished on us.

For Memorial Day a month and a half after my birth, my Aunt Annie came in to Queens and drove all of us to Roslyn for my first visit to Grandmother's. Our grandmother would become more permanently and clearly engraved on the few memories of my first two years than either my mother or my father—as clear as the Teddy Bear jump suit I came to love for the bear picture on the chest. She was so much a part of Roslyn village that we called her 'Gramma Roslyn.' Our other grandmother was simply Gramma Kaufman.

That May we also met for the first time my mother's brother and my namesake—Uncle Buster. He and Beaulah came to visit Gramma Roslyn on their "delayed honeymoon," as he called it. When they had finished their honeymoon travels in early June he sent his mother a letter describing Washington, the Civil War battlefields, the Blue Ridge Parkway, and the Shenandoah Valley. Except for visits to New York City, Gramma Roslyn had never left Long Island, and he knew she had no time or strength left to do it now. He was a good story teller in person or in letters, and a year or two later he would rise to first place in our pantheon of uncles uncle after we visited him at his new home in New Hampshire on the farm where his wife Beaulah had grown up.

In 1940 and '41 we visited "Gramma Roslyn" often, and she visited us when she felt up to the drive and my Aunt could bring her in. My Uncle Bill made a habit of leaving his car keys where his sister Annie could find them. Annie who had chauffeured her father as a teenager, now became her mother's chauffeur, taking her and Eleanor and Anne Claire to visit almost twenty grandchildren. They also took her to visit the Pickering plot at the Roslyn Cemetery that would soon hold more of the family than the Village itself.

For my brothers and me Gra'ma Roslyn was a very wrinkled old lady, unsteady on her legs, her hair turned to grey wool, but for children before the age of 4 or 5 tenderness, safety, comfort, and attention outweigh all else. Their sense of "normal" and "weird" is diaphanous at best. Gra'ma Roslyn was like the "little old lady" in so many children's story books. Besides, she lived in a house with a green lawn in front, big trees on the slope behind it, and a string of "duck ponds" across the road. At an age when mothers are much more important than fathers, we had a mother and a grandmother who were part of Roslyn.

My brothers and I were only the last three of her many grandchildren, but of course, we were too young to know that. As far as we were concerned, she was very much *our* grandmother. None of the cousins were small enough to sit on her lap and listen to her rhymes and stories. But she was ours for only two years.

We did not know that one reason we remembered her as a woman always sitting down was because she could no longer walk more than a few yards. She had finally been slowed to a painful shuffle by the legacy of her impoverished years of growing up. My Aunt Annie's daughter Anne Claire who was 14 in 1941 spent many happy hours with Gra'ma Roslyn, and she says, "We never took walks together because she had very bad feet. Her black shoes , they were always black, had leather patches in the side and toe area because she had bunions. Gram's feet were ruined by shoes that were handed down from child to child." Her mother and my mother both went to great trouble and extra expense to be sure we had shoes that fit well—a legacy of care from our grandmother.

Her health was failing rapidly in 1941, but if she worried about it, no one remembers. Anne Claire said that she did worry more and more about the fact that her boys and her grandchildren might have to join the war that was already threatening to deliver her homeland into the hands of the Nazis.

In November 1941, a month before Pearl Harbor, she began the irreversible decline toward death. She wanted to be sure to get her Christmas cards written. Her son Bill said, "Ma, what are you doing writing the cards now?" Others asked her too. Her answer was, "Well, I just want to get ready." And she was. My mother and my Aunt Annie were with her on the afternoon of December 3rd when the doctor advised they give her brandy. This woman who had once lived in a Baptist tabernacle had never touched a drop of liquor, and her daughters didn't believe she would do it on her death bed. She did. A short while later she asked for more. Before she closed her eyes, she spoke her last words, "It's raining."

The skies were clear, the temperature in the 40s, an ordinary early December day on Long Island. During the night she suffered a massive coronary attack. She was dead. She had not lived long enough to know that her worry about her grandchildren going to war was well founded.

My mother and my Aunt Annie prepared her and with my Uncle Bill they had her laid out in the parlor. My cousin Eleanor remembers that Wednesday morning. Her family was living in an apartment in adjoining Roslyn Heights but had no phone. About dawn Uncle Bill had called the landlady who wakened Eleanor's mother. "Dad drove her down [to her mother's] with the two of us and then he took us to Pat's Diner in the village for breakfast before school. He let us order whatever we wanted, which was strange. I got to school and started crying, and the teacher finally called Mother to come get me." Her mother was annoyed but dropped her off with the family's old friends the Conklins across the street from her grandmother's. "I was finally allowed to go into the house to see Granny and got crying like mad again, so that was the last I was allowed in the house until church, which I was not allowed to go to either."

The day after her children buried her they awoke to the news that the Japanese had bombed Pearl Harbor. Shortly after Pearl Harbor her grandsons, Jack and George Pickering, Arthur Pickering, Tommy Pickering and her granddaughter Hazel would all enlist or be drafted. Her son Bill at age 46 re-enlisted in the Navy.

Emma Susan Hazell Pickering had spent her life almost entirely at home and in the store. She had joined other women in making clothes and bandages for the troops in World War I, and she had attended Trinity Church regularly. Otherwise few people in Roslyn knew her except from the store and as a mother. My mother suspected that she suffered from depression, and in the scale of generations, even her endurance and kindness failed to save them from that plague. Her oldest son Ted's suicide would be followed by three more (one the slow suicide by alcohol and drugs). My mother who bore her name made two attempts but like her mother, she survived.

Roslyn took little note of her death beyond a couple of short and ordinary obituaries. The only other notice of her death that survives is a sheet of paper with a few lines written by her friend Mrs. Penson and read aloud to the St. Martha's Guild at its regular December meeting. The words are not lofty or very original, but they reveal that her friends understood her.

"She was as sweet as sweet could be" is certainly the woman who sheltered nine children from a tyrannical father who loved his children but failed to convey that love in any warm or convincing way. The writer tells Emma's friends, they must "carry on as she would wish and give a helping hand." Just so—Emma wished little attention, and had spent her life helping others to carry on. "She will be surely missed by all who really knew her well." Few people did know her very well, and it's probably true that even her own children knew well only that part of her that had comforted them during their growing up.

Emma Pickering, 1940

CHAPTER 21. OUR MOTHER'S KEEPERS

Emma and Artie's stay in the Kaufman apartment on 86th Street had been short, and after their departure, the apartment began to empty of animals and people until by the late 1930s three people remained—Artie's younger brother Harold, his father and his mother. In 1935 Emmett had been diagnosed with diabetes mellitus. With his failing health, Jennie began to wither both physically and emotionally. When Emmett became unable to work the family's income stopped. Jennie took work as a cleaning lady, but her own health had also started to fail. She was tired. After a little exertion she was out of breath. She had little time and little energy to take much interest in her latest grandchildren.

In January of 1938 Emmett developed gangrene in his right foot. Doctors believed the infection might have come from his poor teeth. They pulled them all. The first week in June he was rushed to the hospital. Doctors amputated his right leg above the knee on June 7, but gas gangrene had set in. Before dawn on the 9th of June he died. As he had wished, his body was cremated. Artie and his two brothers-in-law, Benny and Frank carried his ashes through Carl Shurz and Park to the bank of the East River where Emmett loved to fish. They threw his ashes over the waters.

His death left Jennie at home with her youngest son Harold, and he was working full time. Jennie's sister Bellah had lost her husband. So had sisters Carrie and Lily who both moved in with Bellah. Jennie wanted to join them, but they had no room for her. With Emmett gone, and Jennie unable to act as janitor in the apartment, they no longer received a discount on rent. She and Harold had to move.

Marion and Lou, the only ones with space and any money to spare took her in, but their spare money had shrunk to a trickle. They were living in the upstairs apartment of a two family house in Yonkers. They gave Jennie and Harold the enclosed sun porch. Harold and Jennie shared the fold-out couch-bed. Lou was also sick and only a few years younger than Jennie. "He just didn't want anybody living in his house," his daughter Elise says. Marion was mad that no one else would help. Elise was eight or nine but remembers her grandmother as a "lost soul. Nobody would support her. She couldn't cope after Grandpa died." With a child's eye for details, especially frightening or odd details, Elise recalls, "She had Bell's palsy, and she'd wake up and her mouth or her eye was sagging. She was still talking but the teeth [dentures] were hopping out of her mouth." She also remembered her grandmother's heavy stockings and how they kept getting twisted and falling down. Emphysema and asthma had also begun to cause a constant coughing and gasping for breath. Nevertheless, Jennie helped when she could, and Elise loved her kohlrabi in sauce.

During the war as Artie and Benny and Frank began to earn a little more their families helped with Jennie, each taking her for a few months, then passing her on to the next one. Harold had married but had been drafted. He sent regular payments from his $35 a month pay. Jennie had grandchildren in each house, but none remember her fondly, because she expressed little or no fondness for them although she was not mean either. For children she was a frail, shriveled little woman with a quick temper and a sour disposition. Whatever fondness she felt she could not show in a way that mattered to children. She often took out on her sons-in-law and even her own children her disappointment with life.

Clementes: Ralph, Emmett, Fannie, Ben
at Baw Beach

When Benny and Fannie had enough to move from the projects, they bought a narrow little house in Astoria. Elise recalls that her cousin Ralph slept behind a curtain in the kitchen. But they found room for Jennie when it was their turn. Benny developed a way of coping with a mother-in-law who had never been fond of him and who now had begun calling him "you bald headed bastard" or sometimes "you Guinea bastard." Benny thought a good shot of whiskey would be ease her asthma. In the years before modern cough suppressants and asthma medicines, the relaxing effect of alcohol, or at least its numbing and pain relieving powers were the best poor people could do. Jennie apparently agreed with Benny's prescription. Each morning before he went to work he would pour her a drink. During the day she would often help herself to more and replace what she drank with water. One New Year's Eve Benny followed his usual custom and invited some of the gang of fellow subway workers to his house to salute the new year. At midnight he poured each a shot and they toasted. Then they chided Frank on such weak drink. After that when Benny poured Jennie her morning drink, he would take out a pencil and show her that he was making a line on the bottle.

Although his wife, Fannie, had converted to Catholicism before their marriage, they still respected Jennie's traditional taboos, but they didn't like it. On more than one occasion she appeared on a holiday when Fannie had just boiled a ham. Jennie came in at the front door, the ham went out the kitchen window.

Marion's husband Lou also medicated her asthmatic cough with whiskey, and he too found he had to make a line on the bottle to control her drinking.

My own family had no room for her until we moved in 1944 to a row house in Roslyn Heights. There, and later in a rented apartment in nearby Sea Cliff she would occupy a bed used by my brothers or me. In 1946 my brothers and I were glad to be in a new apartment in Sea Cliff where we could walk down the street to the harbor and where we soon had a lot of friends nearby. We rented the top two floors of an old Victorian house with another family in the main floor and basement level. We had a bannister to slide down, and above the bedrooms a tiny "widow's watch" room. From that room we could glimpse the harbor and all its promise and mystery.

Into this new life in the spring of 1946 came our little wheezing grandmother with her croaking voice, her hair curled tight on her little head like a helmet of gray tangled wires. My mother moved me out of my narrow room and installed her there. She seldom came out. Occasionally Dr. Marsden came on a house call and went in to see her. One morning we woke and my mother immediately herded us downstairs to the kitchen and told us to stay there. Grandma had died. Men came. We were not allowed to see her carried out. With all the self-centered egotism of childhood, my greatest concern was that she had died in my bed. For months afterward my room and my bed were a place of nightmares. I often woke up in the middle of the night thinking she had returned and was lying beside me.

Her daughter Marion and her husband Lou paid for Jennie's burial in the Ullman family plot in New Jersey. After Marion's death her daughter Elise paid for perpetual maintenance.

Only after she was gone did we get any pleasure from her. My father, her oldest son, followed only one Jewish tradition. Each year on the day his mother died he would bring home a large straight glass tube filled with a white candle. He would light it and put it on top of the refrigerator. We had never seen a

candle that could burn more than a few hours. My brothers and I would make bets on when it would go out.

Carrie and Jennie, sisters, 1930s

EPILOGUE: MY MOTHER'S QUESTION

I began recording these stories because when my mother knew her independent life was over, she left a question taped to her desk for me to find when I cleaned up her townhouse—WHY? I admit that I have come to this end and I don't know if I have answered the question. In fact, I am still not sure I understand the question—why *what?* So I have recorded everything that I think could answer a version of that question, from the very specific to the broad and mysterious. Why the dark history of depression and suicide in her family? Why did her life have to end in an assisted living facility? Why didn't her dreams come true? Why did she marry my father and why did that marriage become so troubled? Why is life so confusing? Why do families fall apart? Why are we here at all?

Sometimes we can answer a question best by showing that it cannot be answered simply, if at all. Most attempts to answer questions about human life and behavior end up not as answers but as signposts on a journey. Some of us are near the end of our personal journeys, and dozens of much younger people who are descendants of the people in this book are just beginning. I hope some of these signposts will be useful or at least entertaining. But before I end, I should tie up the loose ends, record the endings of those lives in the generation before mine—the children of Emma and William Pickering and of Jennie and Emmett Kaufman.

In a family tree the most prominent data is "b" for born and "d" for died followed by dates. Much more important is what happened between those dates. I have tried to fill in the detail that has been long forgotten and was liable to be lost forever. More information exists somewhere—in public records in England, Scotland, Austria, the Czech Republic, and the United States. The pursuit of these records and their preservation and publication continues for scholars, genealogical researchers, and librarians although they are not mining for Pickerings, Vickers, Kaufmans and relatives. The information on these families will appear as incidental material in their pursuits. Any future reader of this book can add to the story as history becomes accessible and as family members live it.

The story I've told ends with the death of Emma Susan Hazell and her husband William Henry Pickering on my maternal side and with Jennie Lauber and her husband Emmanuel "Emmett" Kaufman on my paternal side.. They passed on to their 15 children many names that had been in the family for centuries. In the stories I've recorded we see both the culture they bore through centuries and the character coded in our unseen genes. Science indicates that about 50% of our character can be determined by genes. Much of our appearance and our physical strengths and weaknesses also come with our genes. In a very real sense, we are who the people in this book once were.

Because of the arbitrary stopping point of this narrative, I provide below brief summaries of the lives of the children of Emma and William Pickering and of Jennie and Emmett Kaufman. Each of the 14 lives of the 15 children who became adults is the beginning of a sequel to this book. Each story can be more fully documented from modern sources and family records, and written by better writers. Here are notes for those stories.

Edwin "Ted" Pickering, 1893-1934.

Emma Pickering and first born, Ted, 1893

Ted's life and death are encompassed earlier in this book. He married Hazel Tilley whose family had long roots in Roslyn and nearby Sea Cliff. He and Hazel had five children and were still married when he took his own life in 1934.

Ted with Hazel, 1919

Ted with (probably) Bruce, Earl, Edwin

William Hasell Pickering, 1895-1991

"Uncle Bill" remained a single man throughout his long life. He was angry that his father did not leave the store to him or sell him part of the newspaper delivery territory. After working briefly for Curtis Aircraft after WWI, he bought a small store at Glen Head railroad station and opened his own business. Like his father, he also acted as a real estate broker. The store became known as "Bill's". After his mother died a few days before Pearl Harbor, Bill re-enlisted in the Navy and served in the Pacific. An accident with a landing net in Australia in early 1944 sent him to the hospital and required a painful recovery of almost 6 months. The Navy sent him back on duty with only 50% use of his right arm and shoulder, his back and knee still painful. Through all of that his letters remained optimistic and his greatest worry was his sister Annie and her two girls. When Annie went into the hospital for exploratory surgery in March of '45, he wrote to Emma, "Very much upset to hear of Ann's trouble. Spare no expense and attention for her. I am powerless to help way. . . Tell her not to worry about the business. Her and the girls come first." He returned to his home in Roslyn and shared it with his divorced sister, Annie Buck, and her daughters Eleanor Jane and Anne Claire.

He was a popular uncle to his many nieces and nephews. He was never jovial, but he was always ready to help. He had strong opinions on all social and political issues, and his active participation in the Legion as well as his strong and bluntly voiced opinions mirrored his father's commitment to public service. For at least the first 12 years of my life, I remember that on every birthday my brothers and I had, he gave us brand new one dollar bills equal to our age. And at Christmas each of us received another one dollar bill.

Throughout his life he was active in the American Legion, served as an officer in the local post and attended many conventions. In retirement he traveled often and lived near his close friends the Fyfields in Florida. In the last decade of his life he became a non-stop talker whose mind leapt suddenly and without warning from one topic to another. At age 87 he had returned to Long Island from Florida and wrote to my mother, "Didn't want people to see that I died in Fla."

He returned to New York and spent his last years in a veterans home in St. Albans, Queens. In his 90th year he wrote to his niece Eleanor, "Many a night I dream of the war days and the rough nights we experienced. I think that's what's keeping me alive." When asked what he remembered of his visits to relatives in England during the first World War, he recalled a number of facts but concluded, "All I remember was a cousin by the name of Nell." She was the married cousin who had written intimate letters to him while her own husband was in France.

His niece Eleanor who lived with him with her sister Anne Claire and her mother for many years, now traveled frequently to the home to visit and be sure he had everything he needed. Three years before his death he sent my mother and his sister Annie large checks. My mother's diary for September 14, 1988: "Big surprise today!

Check for $4,368.64 from brother Bill." At age 93 he was still pushing other veterans wheel chairs although he was in considerable pain himself. "How I'm sticking it out I don't know," he wrote to his sister Emma. He had already given his sister Annie instructions for his funeral. He died at age 94 in 1991.

Bill Pickering on his front steps
World War II

Thomas Vickers Pickering, 1896-1954

Tom was the first of the Pickering children to marry, and his marriage probably kept him out of WWI. In 1916 at age 20 he married 18 year old Anna Kemmerer. They lived in a house on a small lot in Roslyn Heights and Ann, whom we called "Nanny", operated a small café across from the Roslyn railroad station.

He and Nanny had three children—Thomas Vickers, Jr, Hazel, and Elizabeth. During WWII Thomas Jr. flew as a crewman on planes making the dangerous journey over the Himalayas to supply the besieged government of China. Hazel also joined the service.

When my brothers and I were very small and we still lived in New York City, we looked forward to every visit to Uncle Tom and Nanny and their solid little black Scots terrier. After we moved to a row house in Roslyn

Emma Pickering and son Tom, about 1913

Heights in 1945, Nanny often fed us at the café. Uncle Tom, then an Oldsmobile salesman, taught us the catch company song—"down the road of life we'll steal, in our merry Oldsmobile." At that age, he was our favorite uncle. Every year just before Christmas our phone would ring and Santa Claus would talk to us. When I was 6 I realized Santa Claus was Uncle Tom.

Tom loved kids and as a former Boy Scout from the early days of Scouting, Tom became an Assistant Scout Master for Roslyn Blue Troop, No. 1.Although always upbeat and jovial with other people, his marriage was troubled and he had a period of heavy drinking. In 1945 Nanny left him for the man who delivered bread to her café. Tom went to live with his sister Annie and her girls on East Broadway and kept himself busy painting and doing repairs, especially after a hurricane. Annie wrote to Bill in the Pacific, "it keeps his mind off of Anna which means a lot. He only has breakfast & supper here, he pays me $10 a week. . . . He and Emma are having a garden up near Emma's [on a vacant lot in Roslyn Heights]."

Tom and Anna divorced and he remarried Olga Sherbety.

During one of my mother's episodes of depression Uncle Tom drove her to Long Island's Hillside Hospital where she was advised to have "therapeutic abortion" and sterilization. Tom told her, "The Pickerings can take it."

In 1954 he took his own life by closing himself in his garage with the exhaust from his Oldsmobile. My mother was in the psychiatric ward at Meadowbrook Hospital after taking an overdose of pills. She was reading the obituaries and saw the announcement of her brother's death. She knew what had happened. His body was brought to the Meadowbrook morgue. In her first attempt to understand the family depression she asked the doctors to perform an autopsy, as if they might see an explanation inside. She remembered their exact answer, "It is functional."

Jack Bill and Tom Pickering about 1942

Dorothy Nolan, 1897-1972

Emma Pickering and daughter Dorothy, about 1901

I do not remember a single visit to Aunt Dot's home although she lived in Queens all her life and she was always a playful and welcome aunt when she visited or baby sat for my brothers and I. Her favorite phrase when we got out of line, was that if we didn't behave ourselves "there'll be nothing left of you but a greasespot." I remember my first interest in wild animals catching fire from a picture book about a gray squirrel that she gave us one Christmas before I could read. Other books in the series followed and fanned the flame.

We were just as fond of her daughter Jean (1927-1967) who lived with her mother throughout her life. She was a chestnut haired, classic American beauty who could dance and liked to ride horseback, who had several "boyfriends" we loved to tease her about. Jean was a heavy smoker. One night she suffered a serious asthma attack. Her mother did not hear her suffering. She died at age 40. Her mother had also been a beautiful young woman. When she ran away from home for New York City before WWI, she became a "baby nurse." She was married early, twice. Both men were gone before I was born. Divorce was uncommon and often made a woman something of an outcast or of suspect character, but no one mentioned her divorce, at least not within earshot of children.

In her later years she had a morbid fascination with death, her own and Jean's and she would send pictures of her proposed grave plot. An ardent Catholic convert, she claimed to have converted her father on his deathbed. She died at age 75 of cancer.

306

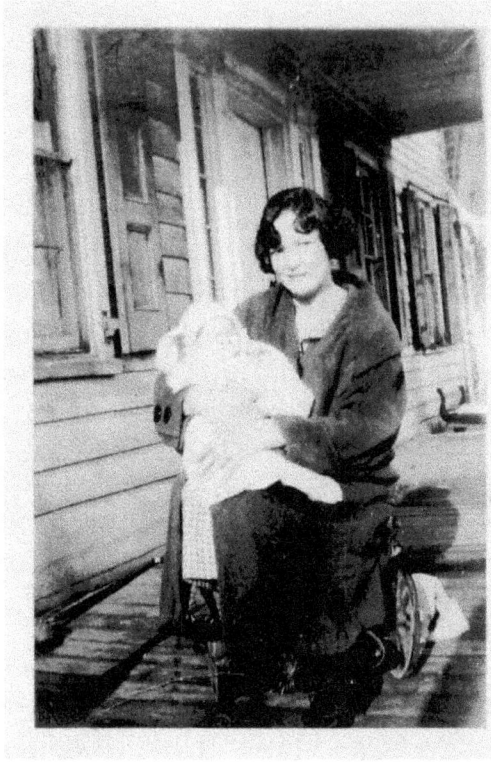
Dorothy and Gloria Clarkson (1922-3)

Dorothy and Jean Nolan, 1950s

Dot, about 1911

John "Jack" Howard Pickering, 1898-1944

A few months before Billy Pickering died he signed over his new store and paper business to Jack. Jack had been running the store for several years, and he and his wife Helen had moved into the apartment above the store on Roslyn's main street. In 1923 their first child, John Jr. was born while they lived there. That was the same year Jack and Nellie bought a 50 ft by 100 ft lot at 112 Burnham Ave. in Roslyn Heights for $100. Jack was a good carpenter and began building a house on that lot. Their son George was born in 1925, and in 1936 their daughter Catherine.

Jack Jr. and sister Catherine Pickering

Helen and Jack's marriage soon became stormy. The boys were often sent to their grandmother's to ride out the storms. In the spring of 1941 Jack and Helen separated, and he took a room in the St. Regis Hotel on Northern Blvd. Catherine turned to her older brother Jack for comfort and protection, and they remained very close throughout his life.

Jack Jr. joined the army and George joined the Navy to serve on a submarine chaser. Their father had sold the store to Jim Kehoe and for a while tried to make a living from his own carpentry shop in Roslyn. That was followed by a variety of jobs, the last being with Roslyn Iron Works. He lost that job in September 1943.

He was then suffering from serious depression. He was in a nasty fight with Helen over support payments and he had a large back income tax bill he could not pay. She was threatening him with dire consequences in a bitter battle for child support. Jack was alone with his problems. His sisters Annie and Emma worried about him and about the pressure Helen was putting on him. On January 11, 1944 he started his car and killed himself breathing its exhaust. His sister Emma's notes say, "Before my brother Jack committed suicide, he had crying spells and was deeply depressed. He would not see a doctor. So sad that my sister Annie and brother Tom felt helpless, try as we did to persuade him to seek help. He disposed of personal items which made us very suspicious."

Emma had to tell her brother Bill in a "V-Mail," government letter form used during the War. "We do miss Jack coming in and I can still see him bringing his fishing tackle and his tools. He certainly had it on his mind for a long time and planned a lot. He even brought light fixtures and door knobs with the screws and even light switch plates and radiator pipe plates from the house. I guess he cleaned up for her. I don't know how he held on so long. He certainly was tortured mentally. His boys being away did not help. He said he thought he was tough but he missed them. . . Even though we miss Jack, we will always have pleasant memories of him and know she can't annoy him longer."

Jack Jr. was on his way home for leave when his father committed suicide but the Red Cross was unable to find him. When he arrived in Roslyn he went to the diner by the station run by his Uncle Tom's wife Anna. He asked her if she knew where his father was. When Jack Jr. grew older he also suffered from serious depression.

At the funeral Helen received mourners in one room, her angry sister-in-law Annie in another room. Jack had left letters for both sons and had given them to Annie to deliver. Jack probably received his at the funeral but Annie held on to George's until he would ask for it. When he didn't, she eventually told him she had it but it was not until her death 61 years later that Annie's daughter Anne Claire found the letter and gave it to George. The letter was dated New Year's Eve, 1944. He was bitter about his burdens and Helen. He asked his son for forgiveness if he had done any wrong.

Helen went to work in 1943 at the Dade Brothers aircraft factory in Mineola, sending her daughter Catherine to live with her grandmother in Glen Cove. After the war she went into partnership to open the Station Laundry at Railroad Plaza in Roslyn Heights. When she sold the business, she went to work in the laundry at St. Francis Hospital from March, 1948 to 1959 when she retired at age 65.

In the 1990s her daughter Catherine began to work with her Aunt Emma on the family history. Catherine's diligent work in the U.S. and England produced the first hard facts about the Pickering family origins in northern England. She and Emma shared the belief that unpleasant facts that others had tried to ignore or hide had to be part of an honest record.

Jack Pickering 1943

Jack Pickering in his store, 1930s

Wallace George "Buster" "Pick" Pickering, 1901-1990

How we went from the gritty sweltering row houses of Queens to the cool and sweet summer air of rural New Hampshire when I was three years old, I don't know, but I found myself there with a magical uncle and aunt who had a barn full of hay, a huge shotgun, a field full of berries, and a house full of delicious homemade food. When they put the light on at night in the attic bedroom where my brothers and I slept, suddenly the rafters were alive with beige moths casting huge shadows as they flew under the single light. In the morning mists we awoke to the sound of cowbells and looked out the window to see Mr. Jordan walking behind his brown and white Ayrshires as they went down the main road of Plainfield, NH to the milking barn. Uncle Bus and Aunt Beulah were as strangely wonderful as Plainfield. From then until we graduated from high school my brother Art and I wanted to be farmers and live in the country.

"Pick," as he was known to locals and to adults in the family, gave up a well paying career as a free lance male nurse to marry Beulah when he was almost 40. They both worked in Windsor, Vermont's Cone Automatic Machine Co. as nurses. He wrote well and we always looked forward to his letters and the stories of hunting and local characters. He and Beulah were surrogate parents to a local boy who began to disappoint them as teenager and continued on into adulthood. Beulah and Pick had no children. Family stories say he had a wife just after WWI but disowned her when she became pregnant and he was sure the baby was not his. Why he was sure or if the story is factually correct no one can say.

He and Beulah had the only fully happy marriage of all the Pickering children. When Alzheimer's struck her in the early 1980s he was with her every day even when she was in a nursing home and no longer knew who he was or she was. My mother visited them in 1986. "My brother wants and tries to get her dressed as she was normally, even to shoes with heels. She no longer walks. She has to be fed. She is incontinent." Only when a stroke in April of 1987 left him partly paralyzed and unable to talk was his vigil ended.

He was my mother's favorite brother, the gentlest, the happiest, the closest to her in age. She wrote in her diary April 6, "I too am paralyzed, feeling so helpless. He is so far away. I long to hold his hand & be there. . . . Cold I bear up seeing my fun loving brother so helpless & failing day by day? Better I remember him as he was on my 75th birthday. Then he was laughing and happy to be with so many family. Now he cannot talk. Anne [Claire, niece who lived nearby] says he does manage to get out a few cuss words "

He recovered enough by July that my brother took my mother to visit and took him out to lunch. "Mentally he is alert. He still dresses well and even wore his red bow tie as I jokingly requested." She said good-bye to him on July 7 after they shared his birthday cake.

Freelance nurse, man of the world

New Hampshire, with Art, Wallace, Bill
Kaufman, 1942

1922

1987

Arthur Charles Pickering, 1903-1952

Art was the curly haired, last boy in Billy and Emma's family, arriving a year after two year old Robin died of pneumonia. Even before he left home he began to feel the world was rigged against him, starting with the work his father demanded of him. His drinking problems forced even his mother to prohibit him from coming home because of his aggressive character. My mother's note about him says, "A bad alcoholic. I saw police club him outside our home one evening as he was causing a disturbance about my sister Annie and her boyfriend. When involved with AA he had long sober months and peace. It lasted only about two years. His children thought he was also on drugs which they found in his apartment.

He married Helen Biggers of Sea Cliff in 1923 and soon had a daughter, Virginia, then a son named Arthur Charles. He and Helen were soon divorced, and in 1931 he married Edith "Edna" Quigan. Their daughter Joan was born in December of that same year.

After WWII he came to live with us briefly in the row house we rented in Roslyn Heights, sharing a closet and a couple of drawers in the dresser that my brother and I used. Most of the time he lived in Brooklyn.

In the last years of his life he tried several times to stop drinking, but in the end the slow suicide of alcoholism worked its way. Drunk one night, he killed himself when he tripped and fell down a flight of stairs.

With daughter Ginnie and sister Emma
Roslyn Hts. 1945

1930s

Annie Pickering, 1906-2005

Annie playing dress up and mother

She had no middle name. When she asked her mother why not, her mother said, "You're my Annie Laurie."

As early as I can remember my Aunt Annie lived with her daughters Eleanor and Anne Claire who were old enough to baby sit my brothers and I and who in many ways were our big sisters. Her husband Bill Buck seemed present mainly as the ticket taker in the Roslyn movie theater who let us in free when Eleanor brought us there. Even before WWII he and Annie began to have trouble. Her mother wrote in her will that Annie's brother Bill should take care of her and the girls. They never divorced, Annie saying that if he wanted a divorce "He can go get it and pay for it." He didn't. She valued her independence too highly to marry again.

She seemed to be ever present in our lives, especially as a chauffeur since my mother never drove and my father learned only when I was in high school. Our rides began in the rumble seat of her brother Bill's car which she used, and later in one of the first mini-cars to become popular in America, the British Austin, which she called "my puddle jumper."

She remained close to my mother and her brother Bill whose house she and the girls shared for several years. During WWII she also ran his paper store in Glen Head. She never remarried but had an active life with many friends and participation in the American Legion's affiliate, Eastern Star.

In 1945 doctors sent her to the hospital for exploratory surgery, suspecting a tumor in her womb, but she came back strong and worked as a practical nurse until 65 and after that took occasional duty and volunteered in the hospital until age 94.

She guarded zealously family secrets, papers and photographs, especially in her later years. Some of the secrets and thus family history died with her.

314

Annie left with Emma, 1920

Annie 1980s

Emma Hazel Pickering, 1911-2001

Emma Pickering and mother, about 1914

My mother often referred to herself as "the baby of the family", the last of her parents ten children. That position had a meaning for her that I have not fully understood. Looking back I see that my cousin Elise on the Kaufman side is right when she says my mother dominated my father. However, that was not necessarily bad. She wanted to move the family to Roslyn, and they did. She wanted us to be brought up in the Episcopal Church and we were, my father even attending confirmation classes and converting, then becoming a church vestryman. She cooked English and nothing German or Jewish. When we moved to Roslyn from the city, we seldom saw any of my father's relatives.

She says her depression began with early menopause in the late 1940s. She would record in her family notes on depression and suicide that she was committed four times. The first may have been after an accidental pregnancy during early menopause. The details were kept secret by the adults who knew. The treatment recommended and accepted was a "therapeutic abortion" and hysterectomy. Not long afterward my parents began to have loud arguments after my brothers and I had gone to bed. In 1949 they separated for a few months. She tried suicide twice in those years and was committed to a psychiatric hospital where she voluntarily had electric shock treatment. She said it erased many bad memories that plagued her but also blamed it for wiping out and weakening memory in general.

When her brother Tom took his own life she said, "That was a turning point for me. I realized I had an inherent tendency of depression. Once you admit to yourself you have a problem, it is easier to cope with." Yet, in the diary I gave her for her 70th birthday on the first page she wrote, "I was advised by psychiatrists to continue therapy. I never did & so do not overcome my antisocial complex. . . . (My mother also antisocial)"

When my father died in a car crash on the way home from work in the summer of 1957, with my brothers and I out of the house, she moved to Florida to be near her childhood friend Helen Conklin. She lived in a trailer park near the Gulf shores, spent her days writing and beach combing for shells, and more for companionship than love, she married Stewart Wert, an older man who was caretaker for the park. They were married for almost 18 years before he died.

My mother moved to Pittsboro, NC near my home in the mid 1970s. In '86 she was diagnosed with a small lung tumor. In her diary for August 11: "I stopped smokiong on 11th!!! This time so far no problem. I'm scared and determined." My two brothers arrived and we accompanied her right to the operating room door. After removal of a third of one lung, she had no relapse. In 1999 she moved to an assisted living facility in Lee, MA where my brother Art, a UCC pastor, could visit and help out. From the early 1950s until her death she took anti-depressants and at least one glass of wine daily.

Pittsboro, NC 1997

Buckingham Palace, 1987

Frances "Fannie" Kaufman, 1905-1968

Eggbeaters brought together Fannie, the oldest of the five Kaufman children with Benjamin Clemente one of several children in the family of an Italian stone mason. The mason's first wife and three children had died in an epidemic that swept the Naples area. Fannie and Benny were both working in the factory owned by Louis Ullman, Fannie's future brother-in-law. The factory produced an egg beater that Lou had designed. When Benny and Fanny met, she had recently been engaged to an Irish immigrant who ended their romance suddenly.

When the Depression and Lou's dubious business talents forced him to close the factory, Benny found himself unemployed. Then one day that he found out that the subway system was hiring men. The line of applicants was hundreds of men long but he found a way to get to the head of the line. He began his life's work for the transit system as a track walker underground. He and Fannie and the boys started out living in "the projects" as public housing was then called. As the economy and their circumstances improved, they bought a two family house in Queens where they would live most of their lives.

In 1936 their first son, Ralph was born, followed by Emmett in 1938. Fannie stayed home to bring up the boys and do the housework. She remained an avid reader and believed education was the only way her boys would get out of the projects and find careers. She had dreams for them. Benny believed in education—if it were practical. "Learn, that's great, but get a job with it," was his approach.

When Emmett was ready for college, to pay his expenses, Fannie took work with the city. Several family members recalled the work was cleaning bathrooms or serving as bathroom attendant in public buildings. Emmett thinks she may have become a secretary. Emmett justified her sacrifice by going to St. Johns for undergraduate and graduate work, then becoming a pharmacist. Eventually he founded his own successful pharmaceutical company, producing pediatric medicines.

Ralph loved agriculture much like his cousin, my brother Arthur. Two years before Arthur he began to study at Farmingdale Agricultural College. And like Arthur he dropped out and enlisted for military service. After a medical discharge for bad knees, Ralph became a postal carrier until he retired 37 years later. Like his father, his brother Harold, and his sister Fannie, he suffered from diabetes. However, after retirement he developed acute myelocytic leukemia (AML). His brother Emmett was often with him for the next three years until he died around 2006. A year later Ralph's son John learned he had the same leukemia.

Fannie's niece Elise remembers her as "a sweet lady. She was a reader and would rather have a book to read than to do housework." Fannie, like her father and her brother Harold and probably her brother Artie, had diabetes. Her case was severe and she did not follow a diet carefully. However, a rare cancer of the biliary duct finally brought her down. When the diagnosis was made, her sister Marion moved in to look after her. She died in 1968.

Fannie and Marion about 1909

Fannie with Ralph and Emmett, 1938

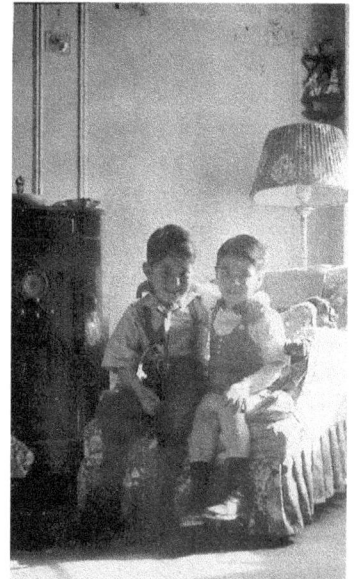

Ralph and Emmett, 1942

Miriam "Marion" Kaufman, 1907-1974

Marion was "on the rebound" from her romance with the son of her father's employer, and Louis Ullman, a successful inventor and entrepreneur, was fed up waiting for the last of his sisters to get married. Marion was his bright, competent and attractive secretary. He was 40, she was 21 when they married in 1928. The next year their only child, Elise, was born.

Looking back on her parents' lives, Elise says, "She should never have gotten married. She would have been one who would have worked in an office with possibilities. She would have risen to the top." The only business she commanded, however, was Lou's shop. She worked with him from 8 a.m. to 6 p.m. Monday through Saturday. On Sundays "they were fanatics with cleanliness" as they cleaned their home from ceiling to floor. Lou had three serious heart attacks as Elise was growing up, and the treatment in those years was weeks of bed rest and months with no work. Marion took over the shop for six months at a time to keep it open even if she could do little more than make keys.

After Lou lost his shops in the Depression, they used the money from liquidation to move to south Yonkers in a peaceful blue collar neighborhood. Marion's sister Celi, living with her family in a rundown neighborhood said, "You live good." In fact, the Ullmans were renting the second floor of a two family house for $45 a month, a rent that didn't go up for 28 years because Lou could and did fix everything and anything that needed fixing in either unit. When the owner of the bank begged Lou to buy the adjacent 2 family foreclosed house for $2,300, he turned them down. "We didn't have anything," Elise says. "My parents never had anything."

Marion and Lou did have high expectations for their only daughter, but after taking care of the shop and her husband Marion had little patience. Elise says, "I don't know how much of her was left. She really tried, but when you have a husband who is sick and old and you have all this responsibility . . . I don't know if I would have packed it in. She was the kind who made a bargain and stuck with it." Elise grew up a shy girl, perhaps, she says, because her parents had "Very little tactile emotion, because they weren't shown it."

Elise grew up bitter about some things in her life, but on reflecting she said, "You start off being very bitter and you learn there are circumstances that make you that way. When you're trying to make a living the last thing you think about is someone else's feelings."

After Lou's death of a heart attack in 1955, Marion taught herself to type and became a secretary for the Girl Scouts. She died in 1974.

Cecelia Kaufman, 1909-1975

Celi's man, Franz "Frank" Mathis did make up his mind or she made it up for him. Frank's family had come from southern Germany and Frank's father, a strong Catholic with little use for Jews, didn't hesitate to appear at Lou Ullman's store and use him as a translator. Lou could speak Yiddish and understood enough German. Celi had converted to Catholicism when she became engaged to Frank and they married in 1935. The ceremony and costume were befitting a long awaited event

Frank began his working life as a jeweler who was also good at watch repair. He found his lifelong employer when walking around lower Manhattan and hearing about a small company named International Business Machines that was hiring. The firm had less than 20 employees but whoever interviewed Frank felt his ability to fix watches and small mechanisms was a talent they could use. His father had told him he better get out of the house and get a job, so he took IBM's offer.

While he was visiting business offices to service their machines and punch card readers, he met a young punch card machine operator—Cecelia. Frank and Celi set up house at 500 Southern Blvd in the Bronx in a gritty working class neighborhood. Celi's life was taking care of Frank and the two boys, Edward born in 1938 and Arthur born in 1941. Edward went to a Catholic high school, on to Iona College, also Catholic, then to Buffalo for his Ph.D. in economics. Arthur went to public schools.

Celi's only strong personal interest she may have picked up from her father—baseball. She was an ardent Yankees fan, and if the boys were not in school and the Yankees were playing at home in the Bronx, she would often take the boys to the game. Neither she nor Frank had any interest in taking their leisure anywhere but home. Frank, some family members say, was a "functional alcoholic," although his drink was beer—two quarts on a weekday night, four or more on a weekend day. His son Edward the economist once did a rough tally of how many gallons of beer he had drunk during his life—more than 20,000 gallons.

For reasons no one in the family now comprehends, Celi and Frank became estranged from her sister Marion for over 20 years. Celi, like her two sisters, smoked most of her life. She quit in 1966, but she died of emphysema in 1975.

Emmett, Annie Hartz (?) Cecelia, Frank Mathis, Frank's brother

Arthur Kaufman, 1911-1957

One evening in August of 1957 my cousin Eleanor's husband Paul Millwater found me in a little park overlooking Hempstead Harbor. I often went there to read, think, stare over the water, watch the sun go down, or wait for the chance that I might meet a friend. I had never seen Paul there. He came to take me home because my father had been killed when the car taking him and four others home from work had run off the road and hit a power pole. I remembered an evening early in the spring when my father had come to find me in the park excited and beaming. He wasn't a man who got excited. He got worried. Sometimes he got mad. He had come to tell me I had won a four year scholarship that would pay most of my expenses.

Only a few years later I began to understand all the sacrifices he and my mother had made so the three of us might have opportunities. When he had encouraged me to be an aeronautical engineer instead of a poet, I resented the presumption when I should have appreciated the hope and confidence. One of my older cousins reflecting on the young man she knew when she was a girl, said, "he had no balls." I knew him as a man who left for a boring job early in the mornings and often came home late after overtime, fell asleep reading *The Daily News*, and went to bed. Only after his death I came to understand that he had what Russians call "vuiderzhka" which is something like "stick-to-it-iveness".

\   He stuck to it when he had to support a family with three children on $19 a week. He stuck to it and to my mother throughout her difficult depressions. When my mother couldn't work he stuck to it by working as much overtime as he could and by caddying on weekends at the golf course, sitting in the same dark caddy shack with my brother Art and I.

With Buster, 1951

With Arthur, 1939

Wallace, Arthur, Bill with parents, visiting in Roslyn, 1941

Harold Kaufman, 1913-1987

Harold had false teeth as far back as I remember him, and he didn't hesitate to entertain us by poking them part way out of his mouth and making them click. He was also almost blind in his left eye, the result of falling into a plate glass window as a child. He was who he was and he didn't mind. In the late 1930s he married the short, plump and upbeat Josephine Taulman who came from a poverty stricken family of illiterates. Her father worked on the docks as a stevedore loading and unloading boats. He was a quiet and easy going man until he suffered a serious head injury. After that he became erratic and mean. By then Jo had Harold and they became inseparable.

The government ordered Harold to report for Army service on Aug. 29, 1942. Jo followed him wherever he was posted. He did most of his service with the Army Air Corps as an aircraft armaments maintenance instructor at Lowry Field in Colorado. He left the service with the rank of sergeant.

They had no children, but we were ready for them to have us whenever they came to visit. My brother Art visited them often in their later years and visited Harold after Jo died. In Harold's later years he told his niece Elise that he was impotent.

Using the GI Bill benefits, Harold went to Westchester Commercial School for accounting and business administration. Also with help from the GI Bill, Harold and Jo moved out of their apartment on Alexander Ave. in Yonkers and bought a home on Barnyard Lane in America's first mass produced housing development—Levittown. It had sprung up on the treeless potato fields of Hempstead Plains. The 1200 square foot homes (today's average is 2,800) had no basements, garages or porches and except for color they were almost identical. Americans made jokes about coming home at night and not remembering which one was yours. Like tens of thousands of other young Americans who never thought they would own a home, Harold and Jo were proud they did.

Shortly after my father began working in Grumman Aircraft, Harold too found a job there. The week before he retired he called me in North Carolina to see if I needed any nuts, bolts, rivets, or other things he could easily take from the supply room. Like father, like son.

Both Harold and Jo had diabetes, but Harold lived into his eighties. He retired to southern New Jersey after Jo died and found romance with a new wife, Ethylene.

Jo and Harold in the early 1940s

Jo and Harold's wedding
?? bridesmaid, Arthur Kaufman (R)

Late 1930s or early 40s

POSTCRIPT: ROSLYN AGAIN, AND GOOD-BYE

I became the last member of our family to live in Roslyn Village when I returned to the U.S. from graduate school in England. I needed a place to live and learned that a Mr. Emil Rinas owned a decaying three story Victorian on Main Street facing Roslyn Park. For almost a year I lived there and often walked in the park where my uncles Bill and Ted had trapped muskrats for fur and where once the mosquitos lived that had infected my mother and many others in Roslyn with malaria. Next to the upper end of the park the Conklin's house still stood. Across the narrow and now one-way East Broadway my Uncle Bill's house had not changed, but the Kirby house where all the Pickering kids had grown up had already been remodeled and modernized. Change was taking place everywhere in the Village, but to me it had the feeling of a theater stage. A long running play that I knew well had closed. The stage was being reset for the debut of a new play.

Rinas house in 1964

193 E. Broadway: The Pickering family house, about 1910   2008

The Pickering studio/darkroom (low building), store and home, about 1908
East Broadway, Roslyn Village

NOTES:

---

[1] The full obituary, salvaged from an old tattered clipping is as follows:

"IN MEMORIAM"—We have this week to record the death of one well known in the neighbourhood of Silverdale as the "Poet of the Village," viz., Mr. Henry Pickering. For several years the deceased was a schoolmaster in Silverdale, during which he made numerous friends, for he had a kind word for all and,-
,   " Kind words are the gems of earth,
         Flowers on the wide world's way."

All who knew him (and especially the young folks) loved him. He was always to to be found first and foremost in every charitable movement, to render assistance to the utmost of his abilities by pen, tongue or otherwise. But the loved friend and humble Christian is now no more. and the songs of the birds in the village churchyard at Doveridge
        "Ring through the yew-tree's gloomy shade—
        The yew, whose roots strike down among
        The grave where our beloved is laid.

In 1872 the deceased resigned his position as schoolmaster, and became the co-operative store-keeper at Doveridge. He was, however, ever and anon found visiting old friends, and taking parts in concerts and various other meetings, where his good humour and genial nature made him the most welcome contributor to the entertainment. That he was as thoroughly esteemed at Doveridge as he had been before at Silverdale will be apparent from the following paragraph which we clip from the *Uttoexeter New Era* of Wednesday last :

   A sad gloom has this week been cast over the above pretty village (Doveridge) by the sudden death of the worthy store-keeper, Mr. H. Pickering. He was appointed to the above post, upon strong recommendation from his friends at Silverdale, by the committee of the Doveridge Co-operative Society in 1872, but though the time had been thus brlef, his conduct has been so exemplary that he has won the esteem of all with whom he has come in contact. This was strikingly plain at his funeral, when the whole village, from Lord Waterpark and A. W. Lyon, Esq., to the humblest individual, even the children, assembled to do honour to one whom they had learned to love. He was conveyed to his last resting-place by the members of the committee and a few intimate friends preceded by tile Rev. C. J Hamilton, and a number of Good Templars of Doveridge and Uttoxeter, of which body he was an invaluable member; and followed by his bereaved and sorrowing family, by many old and tried friends from Silverdale, and by nearly a hundred of the school children, each bearing a neatly arranged nosegay, the last tribute of affection from loving hearts which had entwined themselves around the deceased through the great and increasing interest he had always taken in everything which had contributed to their happiness. Distinguished ladies of the village alike contributed to the general feeling of respect by making some beautiful wreaths and placing them upon the coffin. The burial service was impressively read by the esteemed Vicar, who afterwards spoke most feelingly of the departed, showing how the most humble individuals may honour God in their daily lives, and thus win the affection of a whole community. The children sang that now well-known hymn, "Safe in the arms of Jesus," and then marched by the grave and threw in their floral offerings, thus literally burying their friend with the flowers he had loved so well. No one could witness the many sorrowful faces, or the numerous instances in which the people strove to show their respect and affection for the departed, without being convinced that he who could in such brief period draw forth such general, deep, and sincere feelings of sorrow, could have been no ordinary person. He was a devoted husband, a fond father, a conscientious servant, a sincere Christian, in fact, he was all things to all men in order that h hmmm do some good to some . . . [rest missing]

[2] Kilburne, Richard. *Survey of Kent*, 1659

[3] From Wallace G. Pickering's Ms. "Life Of A Professional Nurse," p. 2

[4] "Memories of St. Mary's Church," by Peter Elmer Lynch, Bryant Library Collection, http://www.nassaulibrary.org/bryant/Localhist/StMarys.html (accessed 08 June 6)

330

[5] Dubois, Ellen Carol, Harriot Stanton Blatch and the Winning of Woman Suffrage, Yale University Press, 1997, p. 110.

[6] The New York Times, Aug. 2, 1905

[7] Ibid.

[8] New York Times, June 27, 1910

[9] William Hasell Pickering, tape of oral history in the possession of Bryant Library, Roslyn, NY

[10] Wodehouse, "Stanford White and the Mackays: A Case Study in Architect-Client Relationships," Winterthur Portfolio. Vol.11, No. (1976), p. 230. Stable URL: http://www.jstor.org/stable/1180596

[11] NY Times, March 3, 1909

[12] New York Times, March 23, 1907

[13] New York Times, July 2, 1911

[14] http://www.saintc.org/default2.asp Web page of St. Chrysostom's, excerpts from Chapter 2 of its history.

[15] New York Times, April 26, 1909, p. 2

[16] New York Times, Feb. 4, 1909, p. 1

[17] NY Times Nov. 2, 1907

[18] http://www.eyewitnesstohistory.com/lusitania.htm

[19] Lansing, Robert, The War Memoirs of Robert Lansing (1935).

[20] "America Declares War on Germany, 1917," EyeWitness to History, www.eyewitnesstohistory.com (2006).

[21] Willard Family Poems on http://mjgen.com/willard/poems.html

[22] Records of the Great War, Vol. VI, ed. Charles F. Horne, National Alumni 1923

[23] Lieutenant Francis T. Hunter's account of the surrender of the High Seas Fleet is from his memoir BEATTY, JELLICOE, SIMS AND RODMAN, Yankee Gobs and British Tars, as Seen by an 'Anglomaniac' published in 1919 by Doubleday, Page & Company.

[24] New York Times, September 14, 1929

[25] In Emma Hasell Pickering's notes she has a one page sketch of her father and refers to her father traveling with "Mrs. Ledden". In other notes the woman is Mrs. Ludlam.

[26] For this information and the following information on Butler I relied largely on it's annual report for 1920 found at http://www.archive.org/stream/annualreport03hospgoog/annualreport03hospgoog_djvu.txt and consulted last on September 30, 2009.

[27] For this and other descriptions of Blumer's approach to psychiatry at Butler I have relied on http://www.pubmedcentral.nih.gov/picrender.fcgi?artid=1036631&blobtype=pdf Medical History, 1992, 36: 379-402. "AN EXODUS OF ENTHUSIASM": G. ALDER BLUMER, EUGENICS, AND US PSYCHIATRY, 1890-1920, by IAN DOWBIGGIN

www.ingramcontent.com/pod-product-compliance
Lightning Source LLC
Chambersburg PA
CBHW080526090426
42733CB00015B/2501